全国高等学校外语教师丛书

U0587303

Questionnaires in Second Language Research:
Construction, Administration, and Processing
（Second Edition）

第二语言研究中的问卷调查方法
（第二版）

Zoltán Dörnyei （英）
Tatsuya Taguchi （日） 著

外语教学与研究出版社
FOREIGN LANGUAGE TEACHING AND RESEARCH PRESS
北京 BEIJING

京权图字：01-2011-2934

图书在版编目（CIP）数据

第二语言研究中的问卷调查方法 ＝ Questionnaires in Second Language Research: Construction, Administration, and Processing (Second Edition)：第二版：英文、中文／（英）佐尔坦·德尔涅伊，（日）龙谷田口著. —— 北京：外语教学与研究出版社，2011.10（2021.1 重印）

（全国高等学校外语教师丛书. 科研方法系列）
ISBN 978-7-5135-1443-9

Ⅰ. ①第… Ⅱ. ①佐… ②龙… Ⅲ. ①第二语言－问卷法－英文 Ⅳ. ①H003

中国版本图书馆 CIP 数据核字 (2011) 第 216539 号

出 版 人	徐建忠
项目负责	段长城
责任编辑	郑丹妮 刘晓娟
封面设计	覃一彪 华 艺
版式设计	吴德胜
出版发行	外语教学与研究出版社
社　　址	北京市西三环北路 19 号（100089）
网　　址	http://www.fltrp.com
印　　刷	北京九州迅驰传媒文化有限公司
开　　本	650×980　1/16
印　　张	14.5
版　　次	2011 年 10 月第 1 版 2021 年 1 月第 15 次印刷
书　　号	ISBN 978-7-5135-1443-9
定　　价	53.90 元

购书咨询：(010) 88819926　电子邮箱：club@fltrp.com
外研书店：https://waiyants.tmall.com
凡印刷、装订质量问题，请联系我社印制部
联系电话：(010) 61207896　电子邮箱：zhijian@fltrp.com
凡侵权、盗版书籍线索，请联系我社法律事务部
举报电话：(010) 88817519　电子邮箱：banquan@fltrp.com
物料号：214430101

记载人类文明
沟通世界文化
www.fltrp.com

Contents

总　序

　　"全国高等学校外语教师丛书"是外语教学与研究出版社高等英语教育出版分社近期精心策划、隆重推出的系列丛书，包含理论指导、科研方法和教学研究三个子系列。本套丛书既包括学界专家精心挑选的国外引进著作，又有特邀国内学者执笔完成的"命题作文"。作为开放系列，该丛书还将根据外语教学与科研的发展不断增加新的专题，以便教师研修与提高。

　　笔者有幸参与了这套系列丛书的策划工作。在策划过程中，我们分析了高校英语教师面临的困难与挑战，考察了一线教师的需求，最终确立这套丛书选题的指导思想为：想外语教师所想，急外语教师所急，顺应广大教师的发展需求；确立这套丛书的写作特色为：突出科学性、可读性和操作性，做到举重若轻，条理清晰，例证丰富，深入浅出。

　　第一个子系列是"理论指导"。该系列力图为教师提供某学科或某领域的研究概貌，期盼读者能用较短的时间了解某领域的核心知识点与前沿研究课题。以《二语习得重点问题研究》一书为例。该书不求面面俱到，只求抓住二语习得研究领域中的热点、要点和富有争议的问题，动态展开叙述。每一章的写作以不同意见的争辩为出发点，对取向相左的理论、实证研究结果差异进行分析、梳理和评述，最后介绍或者展望国内外的最新发展趋势。全书阐述清晰，深入浅出，易读易懂。再比如《认知语言学与二语教学》一书，全书分为理论篇、教学篇与研究篇三个部分。理论篇阐述认知语言学视角下的语言观、教学观与学习观，以及与二语教学相关的认知语言学中的主要概念与理论；教学篇选用认知语言学领域比较成熟的理论，探讨应用到中国英语教学实践的可能性；

研究篇包括国内外将认知语言学理论应用到教学实践中的研究综述、研究方法介绍以及对未来研究的展望。

第二个子系列是"科研方法"。该系列介绍了多种研究方法，通常是一书介绍一种方法，例如问卷调查、个案研究、行动研究、有声思维、语料库研究、微变化研究和启动研究等。也有一书涉及多种方法，综合描述量化研究或者质化研究，例如《应用语言学中的质性研究与分析》、《应用语言学中的量化研究与分析》和《第二语言研究中的数据收集方法》等。凡入选本系列丛书的著作人，无论是国外著者还是国内著者，均有高度的读者意识，乐于为一线教师开展教学科研服务，力求做到帮助读者"排忧解难"。例如，澳大利亚Anne Burns教授撰写《英语教学中的行动研究方法》一书，从一线教师的视角，讨论行动研究的各个环节，每章均有"反思时刻"、"行动时刻"等新颖形式设计。同时，全书运用了丰富例证来解释理论概念，便于读者理解、思考和消化所读内容。凡是应邀撰写研究方法系列的中国作者均有博士学位，并对自己阐述的研究方法有着丰富的实践经验。他们有的运用了书中的研究方法完成了硕、博士论文，有的是采用书中的研究方法从事过重大科研项目。以秦晓晴教授撰写的《外语教学问卷调查法》一书为例，该书著者将系统性与实用性有机结合，根据实施问卷调查法的流程，系统地介绍了问卷调查研究中问题的提出、问卷项目设计、问卷试测、问卷实施、问卷整理及数据准备、问卷评价以及问卷数据汇总及统计分析方法选择等环节。书中对各个环节的描述都配有易于理解的研究实例。

第三个子系列是"教学研究"。该系列与前两个系列相比，有两点显著不同：第一，本系列侧重同步培养教师的教学能力与教学研究能力；第二，本系列所有著作的撰稿人主要为中国学者。有些著者虽然目前在海外工作和生活，但他们出国前曾在国内高校任教，期间也经常回国参与国内的教学与研究工作。本系列包括《英语教学中的学习策略培训：阅读与写作》、《听力教学与研究》、《写作教学与研究》、《阅读教学与研究》、《口语教学与研究》、《翻译教学与研究》等。以《听力教学与研究》一书为例，著者王艳博士拥有十多年的听力教学经验，同时听力教学研究又是她完成博士论文的选题领域。《听力教学与研究》一书，浓缩了她多年听力教学与听力教学研究的宝贵经验。全书分为两部分：教学篇与研究篇。教学篇中涉及了听力教学的各个重要环节以及学生在听力学习中可能碰到的困难与应对的办法，所选用的案例均来自著者课堂教学的真实活动。研究篇中既有著者的听力教学研究案例，也有著者从国内外文献中筛选出的符合中国国情的听力教学研究案例，综合在一起加以分析阐述。

　　教育大计，教师为本。"全国高等学校外语教师丛书"内容全面，出版及时，必将成为高校教师提升自我教学能力、研究能力与合作能力的良师益友。笔者相信本套丛书的出版对高校外语教师个人专业能力的提高，对教师队伍整体素质的提高，必将起到积极的推动作用。

文秋芳

北京外国语大学中国外语教育研究中心

2011年7月3日

导读——第二语言研究中问卷调查法的特点及应用

　　在第二语言研究领域中，问卷调查方法是使用最多的数据收集方法之一，其使用频率仅次于测试。问卷的特点是易于构建、用途广泛，且能在短时间内收集到大量的数据。问卷设计看起来容易，但要设计出具有良好效度和信度的问卷却很难。正如英国诺丁汉大学心理语言学教授、二语动机研究学者Dörnyei（2003）所注意到的那样，在二语研究领域中不乏提出了很好的研究问题的研究，但是由于其问卷设计得不好而影响了研究质量。究其原因，主要是问卷使用者对于问卷设计和数据处理的理论意识不够，或者说他们并不知道设计问卷需要诸如心理测量学、社会心理学和社会学等方面的知识和实践经验。Dörnyei正是针对这一现状撰写了《第二语言研究中的问卷调查方法》一书。

　　问卷调查方法在国外二语研究领域受到广泛的欢迎，但鲜有这方面的理论或方法论探讨。只有Brown（2001）十年前在介绍语言研究调查方法时对问卷调查方法进行了介绍，直到2003年才出现了关于问卷调查方法的第一部著作，即由Dörnyei撰写的《第二语言研究中的问卷调查方法》（第一版）。时隔七年，Dörnyei于2010年又出版了该书的第二版，更加突出了其实用性，全面地介绍了问卷的设计、实施和处理等阶段所涉及的理念和做法，并详细介绍了如何基于理论开发科学的研究工具，以帮助读者学会如何进行问卷设计、如何进行问卷调查和问卷数据分析，并以亲身研究为例进行了详细的说明。

　　与国外情况类似，中国外语界一方面运用问卷进行研究的文献激增，如笔者以"外语教学"和"问卷"为主题词检索中国期刊全文数据库时发现，从2000年到2010年共有971篇论文，由2002年的19篇论文增长到2010年的174篇，十年间文献量增长了9倍多；另一方面却缺少专门针对外语教学中的问卷调查方法的著述，直至2009年国内才出现了这方面的第一部著作（秦晓晴，2009）。此次外语教学与研究出版社将《第二语言研究中的问卷调查方法》（第二版）引进到国内，可以说在一定程度上弥补了这一缺憾，对了解问卷调查方法的原理、作用和应用具有积极的意义。

一、本书的特点

Dörnyei的《第二语言研究中的问卷调查方法》（第一版）于2003年出版以来，受到各方好评。这是因为：首先，Dörnyei在使用问卷进行研究上具有非常丰富的经验，曾开发并使用过大量的问卷；其次，他作为*Language Learning*期刊的审稿人和编辑，评审过他人大量的问卷研究，看到了很多成功及不成功的案例；此外，他将问卷研究涉及的理论问题通俗化，不是以高高在上的姿态讲述问卷研究的"真理"，而是以谈心的方式与读者分享自己的研究体会和历程（Dewaele, 2005）。

通读全书，不难发现《第二语言研究中的问卷调查方法》（第二版）具有如下特点：

第一，本书突出了问卷研究的理论基础。本书在不同的章节详细介绍了问卷的概念化问题、量表形式、抽样方法、信度和效度检验等理论性强的问题。同时，作者还大量引用了心理测量学、社会心理学、教育学等多个领域在问卷方法上的理念和研究成果。读者阅读本书的前四章后，会如作者所希望的那样大大增强问卷设计和数据处理方面的理论意识。

第二，本书的最大特点是其实用性。国外学者甚至将其比作"烹饪手册"（Schrauf, 2006）。具体说来，其实用性主要体现在以下几个方面：

1) 本书前四章按先后顺序对问卷研究从设计到实施，再到数据处理的每一个阶段娓娓道来，读者可以"依样画葫芦"设计并实施自己的问卷研究。

2) 作者以亲身经历详述了问卷研究过程。读者在了解了问卷方法的理论基础之后，再通读作者的问卷调查研究实践，会对问卷研究方法有更为直观的认识。第二版的第五章是新增的一章，详细介绍了以作者为首的研究团队所使用的"英语学习者问卷"从设计、实施到数据分析的整个过程。而且读者还可从本书附录中找到该问卷的日语和汉语版本。

3) 本书讨论了不同语言的问卷翻译问题，这也是第二版中新增的内容。由于大规模的跨国问卷调查研究日益增多，自然就涉及问卷的不同版本问题，因此第二版辟出专门的章节讨论了问卷的翻译（见2.8节）。

4) 本书新增了关于基于网络的问卷调查方法的内容。网络正日益成为收集问卷数据的重要途径之一，本书介绍了如何通过互联网进行数据收集（见3.2.4）。

第三，本书提供了关于前人使用过的问卷的大量信息，读者可以根据自己的研究兴趣，按图索骥找到相关文献及其问卷。除了正文部分提到的部分问卷文献以外，书中附录还给出了作者所收集到的问卷信息列表。这些问卷信息覆盖了第二语言研究的各个方面，如：学习者方面的文献涉及个人背景、态度、计算机熟悉程度、反馈、集体凝聚力、语言焦虑、学习者信念、学习动机、学习策略、学习方式、语言自信心、需求分析、自我评价、自我身份变化、交际意愿等；教学和教师方面的文献涉及语法教学、课程评价、教学活动倾向性、教师焦虑、教师信念、教师评价、教师动机、教师自我评价等；专门针对第二语言环境的文献涉及移民定居、语言接触等内容。

最后，此次外语教学与研究出版社引进的《第二语言研究中的问卷调查方法》（第二版）还增加了国内学者高一虹等人（2003）的中文问卷研究案例，从该例可以了解高一虹等人关于中国大学生外语学习动机问卷研究的全过程。该研究运用非结构性问卷，同时基于前人的问卷设计出了不同类型的外语学习动因问卷，进行了5次预测，采用分层抽样方法从全国29个省区的30所大学中收集了2,278份有效问卷，最后运用内在一致性的信度检验方法和因子分析的结构效度检验方法，获得了七种动机类型。

二、各章主要内容

第一章　二语研究问卷简介

第一章总体上介绍了问卷的定义和测量内容，问卷的优势和不足，以及问卷在定量和定性研究中的作用。

关于问卷的定义，Dörnyei引用了Brown（2001）对问卷的理解，即"问卷是给受访者呈现一系列问句或陈述句，并要求他们写出答案或从已有的答案中进行选择的书面工具"，是能够获得可靠且有效的数据的测量工具。作者所理解的问卷不包括语法测验和语用学领域广泛使用的以补全话语任务（discourse completion task, DCT）为形式的生产性问卷。

问卷的测量内容主要涉及事实问题、行为问题和态度问题三个方面。其中，态度问题又包括态度、意见、信念、兴趣和价值判断等方面。作者指出，问卷的优势在于节省研究者的时间、精力和资金，但如果问卷设计得不好，所收集的数据会存在信度和效度方面的问题。作者客观地指出了问卷研究存在如下不足：

1) 由于受访者不愿花更多的时间，因此问卷问题需要简洁明了，这样所得的答案自然会存在肤浅和表面化问题；

2) 受访者对问题的理解不一致，甚至会产生误解，因此所得答案可能因人而异，缺少一致性；

3) 受访者还可能对调查热情不高，随便答题；同时，还有漏填现象以及回收率不高的问题；

4) 问卷调查对受访者的文化程度要求较高；

5) 研究者无法检查受访者所提供答案的有效性；

6) 受访者可能有意地提供不真实的答案；

7) 问卷数据的有效性还可能受到自欺倾向、默认倾向、光环效应和疲劳效应等因素的影响。

为避免上述问题，作者建议一方面研究者将问卷法与访谈或其他方法结合起来使用，另一方面设计者设计问卷时需要做到既细致又富有创意，才可能让受访者认真、诚实地回答问题。

第二章　问卷设计

第二章介绍了问卷的总体特征、主要组成部分、问卷内容和多项目量表、封闭性问卷问题的设计、开放性问卷问题的设计、如何撰写高质量的问卷项目、问卷项目的分类和排序、计算机问卷设计程序、问卷试测和项目分析等内容。

虽然问卷调查有其先天不足，但只要注意好各个环节的每一细节，就可以弥补其不足，最终使问卷成为有效的研究工具。好的问卷包括以下几个设计步骤：

1) 确定好问卷的长度、格式和主要组成部分等；
2) 设计并编排好项目；
3) 编写出恰当的答题方法说明和示例；
4) 如果是用外语撰写的问卷，需要将其译为受访者的本族语；
5) 进行试测并进行项目分析。

在问卷的总体特征方面，首先要控制问卷的长度。4至6页长度的问卷一般需要半个小时的填写时间，因此一般应将问卷长度控制在4页以内；如果受访者是小学生，长度则要更短。其次，问卷的外观应该具有吸引力和专业性，如装订成册，文字疏密适中、整齐有序，注意纸张质量，不同部分用不同的颜色进行区分，按照顺序标识等。此外，研究者还要承诺对个人隐私或敏感问题保密等。

问卷主要组成部分包括标题、问卷说明和答题说明、问卷问题、其他信息（包括研究者的联系方式、问卷回收方式、调查结果反馈、访谈邀请）和鸣谢等部分。

问卷内容范围的确定主要通过文献阅读和小型的定性研究等方式。问卷的量表形式有单项目量表和多项目量表。如果是收集个人背景信息等事实问题，使用单项目量表即可；如果测量的是抽象变量（如态度、信念等），则需要使用多项目量表，即测量目标相同但措辞不同的多个项目。

问卷项目包括封闭性问题和开放性问题两种。封闭性问题可采用等级量表（如利克特量表、语义区分量表等）、多项选择题、排序题、数字题和清单列表等形式。开放性问题是指不提供答案选项的问题。总的说来，问卷应以封闭性问题为主，但在问卷末尾可设计少量的开放性问题让受访者提供补充信息，如收集关于受访者具体信息的开放问题、求证问题、补全句子问题和简答题（不是论述题）等。

对于如何撰写高质量的问卷项目，作者建议可以通过对受访者进行访谈或者与其讨论来设计项目，也可以从现有的问卷中借用项目。撰写项目时要遵行的原则是：句子要简短，语言应简单自然，避免歧义或倾向性，避免使用否定结构，避免出现多重含义，避免答案可能千篇一律的问题，同时使用正向题和反向题等。此外，编写敏感问题时不要引起受访者的反感。

在问卷项目的分类和排序方面，不同的项目排序会影响到问题的理解和回答，因为一个问题的意义可能会受到相邻问题的影响。关于项目的排序虽然没有理论定律，但应遵循这样的原则：结构清楚有序（如根据问题的内容、量表类型进行分类），先问受访者感兴趣的问题，后问个人信息和开放性问题。

第二章还介绍了计算机问卷设计程序。目前市面上有三十多种集问卷设计、数据收集和分析为一体的计算机程序。如Sphinx Survey可以帮助研究者轻松地设计出界面美观、具有专业水平的问卷，其功能包括设计各种类型的问卷问题、对问题进行分类、建立问题库等。另外，还有其他数百种基于网络的问卷设计调查工具。

在问卷试测方面，作者强调其作用是收集受访者的反馈以及检查问卷是否能收集到研究者希望得到的数据。试测的作用是检查问卷的内容，如措辞是否含糊不清或难以理解，是否提供了有用的相关信息，开放性问题是否难以编码分类。通过试测还可以了解问卷的可操作性，如实施过程中可能存在的问题以及答案是否可以进行录入、处理等。试测时还可以从受访者那里获得关于问卷形式方面的反馈，如问卷的整体形式、说明的清晰度、封面信的恰当性、完成问卷所需的时长等。试测可分为初试和终试：初试的目的主要是对问卷项目进行精减，有3至4个受试即可，可以是朋友、家人或同事。终试就是接近正式施测，受试者需在各个方面与目标总体相似。如需进行统计检验，受试人数需在50人以上。

问卷项目分析可以在两个阶段进行：第一阶段是在终试以后，其目的是根据项目分析结果对问卷进行微调并形成问卷终稿。第二阶段是在最终问卷调查实施之后，其目的是检验各个项目是否恰当。两次分析的程序相似，需要检查的内容包括漏填情况、答案的变化幅度以及多项目量表的内在一致性。

第三章 问卷实施

第三章讨论了问卷调查实施的程序，包括抽样、调查方式和策略，以及调查者为受试者的回答应承担的保密以及道德责任。

在讨论抽样时，作者先介绍了样本和总体之间的关系，指出抽样的作用是为了节省时间、费用和精力。研究者如果想通过样本了解总体特征，需确保样本具有代表性。所谓代表性就是好的样本与目标总体不仅要在诸如年龄、民族、教育背景、学术能力、社会阶层、经济状况等总的重要特征方面非常相似，而且还要在与问卷项目密切相关的具体特征方面相似，如二语学习背景、二语教学时长和方式等。

要确保样本的代表性，需要选择适当的抽样方法。抽样方法有概率抽样和非概率抽样之分。前者是可以获得真正具有代表性样本的策略，后者往往是研究者运用现有的条件获得相对具有代表性样本的方法。概率抽样似乎更科学、更诱人，但是因为费用高和耗时长等方面的原因不易实施，对于大多数二语研究者来说是不现实或不具可行性的。因此，作者在讨论概率抽样时只涉及了"随机抽样"方法的主要原则，将重点放在了非概率抽样方法上，如便利抽样、滚雪球抽样和配额抽样。不过，通过非概率抽样得到的样本其研究结果在普遍意义上具有局限性，研究者在汇报结果时要指出这一点。此外，第三章还讨论了国外二语研究领域常用的基于自愿原则招募志愿者的取样方法的弊端。

关于究竟需要多大的样本才合适的问题，作者建议：

1）根据问卷调查研究的文献，样本应占总体的1% – 10%之间；

2）从统计学的角度来讲，样本数据要呈正态分布（如人数达到30人以上）。如果达不到这一要求，分析数据时常需使用非参数检验方法；

3）从统计意义的角度讲，抽取的样本应该足够大，才可能使预期的结果达到显著性水平，如人数不能少于50，但对于多变量分析程序来说，需要的人数更多；

4）如果需要进行分组比较，各组人数也要达到上述要求；

5）考虑到可能出现无效问卷或其他不可预测的状况，样本量需要适当加大。

在讨论问卷的调查方式时，作者首先介绍了邮寄调查方法，如所需的封面信、问卷发出一段时间后的跟踪信，以及如何提高问卷回收率等，并重点介绍了一对一调查、群组调查，以及当今日益盛行的电子邮件和基于网站的在线调查。

一对一调查（one-to-one administration）是指把问卷分发给受访者，并约定回收问卷时间的一种调查方法，该方法一般能保证较高的回收率。

群组调查（group administration）是将受访者集中起来答题，集中回收问卷的调查方法，回收率几乎可达到100%。正因为如此，该方法是二语研究者最常用的方法。但使用这种方法需要注意几点，如：不适合10岁以下儿童；受访者为非成年人时需要更多的调查者；防止抄袭、交头接耳等现象发生。

在线调查（online administration）就是通过网络进行调查，尽管目前没有得到广泛应用，但却是未来的发展方向。其优势是容易获得跨地域、多样性的受访者，且更加节省时间和精力。电子邮件调查可以是附件式调查，也可以是嵌入式调查。前者需要受访者下载附件填写后再将问卷以附件的形式发回给发件人，后者则将问卷直接嵌入邮件正文中，受访者只需填完答案后回复给发件人，因此后者的回收率更高，但后者在编排格式上缺少变化。现在比较推崇的电子邮件调查是通过电子邮件向受访者发出调查邀请，并提供链接引导受访者进入调查网站。

基于网站的调查更为有效也更有吸引力，其调查程序与电子邮件调查相似但可用的方式更多，如可在网络讨论群、布告版、聊天室和邮件群上向潜在的受访者发出邀请。在使用网站调查时需要注意以下事项：为了提高回收率，为受访者提供一些物质激励是有必要的，如一张彩票、软件下载服务、购书代金券或者现金等；网站调查用时不要超过20分钟，尤其要设计好问卷的前几页；使用进度条，提示受访者还有多少未完成；以匿名方式进行调查等。[1]

作者认为，问卷的回收率对于成功的调查非常重要，但问题回答的质量也同等重要。如果受访者不合作，随意地回答问题，再高的回收率也没有意义。为此，作者认为要提高回收问卷的数量和质量，需要采取以下措施：

1) 事先通知。在正式调查实施之前，向受访者发送邀请信，介绍问卷调查的目的、内容，还可包含几个样题；

2) 设法取得教师、家长或其他权威人士的支持，如在调查之前与校长联系，提出书面申请并获得书面同意后再与相关的教师联系；

3) 如果调查受某一机构资助，需将该信息告诉受访者，这样有助于获得他们的合作；

4) 问卷实施不能仅仅委托受访者的任课老师来完成，调查者需亲自到场；

5) 调查者还要注意自己的衣着和举止，以获得受访者的信任；

6) 尽管问卷上有调查的介绍，调查者仍需口头介绍调查的目的和意义等；

7) 问卷的格式和排版要专业；

8) 对受访者承诺提供调查结果反馈。

此外，问卷调查过程中需要遵循以下道德原则：

---

1. 关于网站问卷调查的优势，可参见Wilson和Dewaele（2010）的最新研究。但应该看到的是，近年来随着基于网络的调查工具的涌现，问卷设计和实施似乎变得更容易了，但是高质量的问卷研究依然面临着理论和实践上的挑战（Montee, 2011）。

1) 对受访者不能有任何不利的影响；

2) 尊重受访者的个人隐私；

3) 受访者对调查有充分的知情权；

4) 受访者如果是未成年人，还需获得其父母或老师的同意；

5) 向受访者承诺保密既是调查者的道德责任，也是职业责任。

本章最后还讨论了如何处理匿名问题。如果是一次性数据收集可以很容易做到匿名调查，但如果是需要多次收集数据的跟踪调查，则要考虑通过固定座位或由受访者自己编制记号的方式，以便将不同时间收集的数据相匹配。

第四章　数据的处理

数据收集上来以后要做的工作是数据的处理。本章介绍了数据处理的各个环节，包括数据的编码、数据的输入、封闭性问题的处理、开放性问题的内容分析、数据处理的计算机程序、数据的汇总和报告，以及问卷调查结束后的访谈等。

由于大多数计算机程序只能处理数值型的数据，无法处理字符串形式的数据，因此需要对问卷数据进行编码处理，即对受访者的回答进行量化处理。首先是对每份答卷进行编号（以便需要时找到具体的答卷）；其次是对变量、变量标签、变量值、量表类型（定类、定序、定距）进行定义；然后是输入数据，包括创建文件名、通过Excel和SPSS等程序键入数据。

对封闭性问题的处理涉及数据清理、数据管理、数据简化、信度和效度分析，以及数据分析等工作。数据清理的目的是纠正数据中可能存在的错误。数据管理包括缺省值的处理、变量值的重新编码，以及数据的标准化。如果问卷采用的是多项目量表，在数据分析之前还需要进行数据的简化，即根据信度和效度分析的结果，对多项目求平均值后生成新的变量。信度分析包括多项目的内在一致性分析和单项目与全体项目之间的相关分析，分析所得的Cronbach alpha值一般应在.70以上才表明各个项目之间有较好的内在一致性。效度分析可采用因子分析，以达到简化数据的目的。

完成上述工作之后就可以进行正式的数据分析了。数据分析包括描述统计和推断统计。描述统计可用来对数值型变量进行汇总，统计量包括变量的平均值和标准差，但描述统计的结果只限于样本本身而不能推广到样本以外的人群。推断统计的结果如果具有统计意义则可以应用到总体，但达到了统计上的显著性只表明这一结果可能是真实的，并不意味着其具有重要性。

可用于问卷数据处理的计算机程序有很多，其中用于定量数据分析的软件主要有SPSS，用于转写文本的定性分析程序有NVIivo和SPSS Text Analysis for Surveys，还有诸如Sphinx Survey之类的集问卷设计、数据收集和定性定量数据分析于一体的程序（见2.9节）。

本章最后介绍了如何进行结果汇报。汇报结果时需要注意的事项有：

1) 研究结果可以推广到与样本背景情况类似的总体中，但不能概括过度；

2) 定量研究结果易表面化，因此问卷中最好包括一些开放性问题，汇报开放性问题的答案会使结果汇报更生动；

3) 不仅要注重对研究结果的汇报，还要重视对研究方法部分的汇报（包括受访者情况、问卷的设计过程和内容，以及问卷实施过程等），如汇报受访者情况时需要给出人数、年龄、性别、民族、分组变量、二语水平、学习历史等个人背景信息（当然这些信息可以根据与研究的相关性进行取舍）；

4) 数据呈现时要做到界面友好，尽量使用图表进行汇报。

第五章　问卷设计实例

前四章讨论的是问卷设计、实施和数据分析过程中的原则性问题，包括很多理论性问题。为了让这些原则具有更强的可操作性，作者以自己在日本、中国和伊朗等国使用的"英语学习者问卷"为例说明如何运用这些原则。

第五章介绍的研究实例是重复作者等人2006年在匈牙利进行的基于"二语动机自我系统"（L2 Motivational Self System）理论框架的动机研究，该系统由"理想二语自我"、"应该二语自我"和"二语学习经历"三个维度组成（Dörnyei, Csizér & Németh, 2006）。具体的问卷设计过程如下：

第一步是依据文献确定问卷需要涵盖的内容，最终选定了16个变量；

第二步是为每个变量设计3－4个组成项目。除了自己设计的项目外（如 Ought-to L2 self、Instrumentality-prevention），大多数项目来自文献，经修改、翻译而成。问卷项目采用Likert量表和问题两种形式。

第三步是设计问卷说明、问卷格式、项目分类和编排、翻译和试测。日文版的终稿完成后，再分别译成汉语和波斯语（波斯语版本在引进版中略）。为了保证翻译质量，研究团队还对译文进行了回译，以确保不同语言版本的质量。不过，笔者在此很遗憾地提醒读者，尽管作者团队自称在翻译时采取了这些措施，但汉语版本的问卷仍不尽如人意（见下节讨论）。

最后是确定终稿和项目分析，包括事后项目分析。读者从这一章中可以详细地了解"英语学习者问卷"的设计和使用过程。

附录："英语学习者的问卷调查"问卷

附录部分给出了Dörnyei团队使用过的不同语种的英语学习者调查问卷，特别值得一提的是其中的中文版本。该问卷为中英双语问卷，作者称附上英语原文的目的是为了让受访者更好地理解问卷内容，但在笔者看来这是一厢情愿的事情，甚至有些不负责任。使用双语不仅增加了受访者的负担，而且受访者一般不会自始至终都认真地阅读英语问题（如果是为了学习英语会有更多更好的途径），只会阅读汉语部分。如果问卷的汉语翻译不符合受访者的表达习惯，即使项目内容符合他们的真实情况，他们也可能因为措辞原因而倾向于选择不同意。遗憾的是，该中文问卷中不少项目存在着理解不当或翻译生硬的问题，如果用该问卷收

集数据，相信不能很好地反映受访者的真实情况。国内读者如果要使用
这个问卷最好自己动手将其从英文版本译成中文版。以下笔者随手摘录
了一些译文不当的例子（原译文中的下划线为导读作者所加），并给出
了建议译文，供国内读者使用时参考。

原文和原译文	建议译文
2. My parents/family believe that I must study English to be an educated person. 我家人认为要成为受教育良好的人，我必须学英语。	我的父母或家人要求我学好英语，以成为一个受到良好教育的人。
6. I can imagine myself living abroad and having a discussion in English. 我可以想象自己在国外生活并用英语和当地人交流。	我希望将来能在国外生活并能用英语与人交流。
7. I have to study English because I don't want to get bad marks in it. 我不得不学习英语是因为不想考试分数底。 （原文有别字，"底"应为"低"。）	我必须学习英语是因为不想考试成绩不好。
10.Studying English is important to me because English proficiency is necessary for promotion in the future. 对我来说学习英语很重要是因为精通英语对我将来的提升是必不可少的。	学好英语对我来说重要，因为这有助于自己将来在职场上获得提升。
27.Studying English is important to me in order to gain the approval of my peers/teachers/family/boss. 学习英语很重要完全是为了获得同学、老师、家人和老板对我的认可。	学好英语对我来说重要，因为可以获得同学、老师、家人或上司对我的认可。

28. The things I want to do in the future require me to use English. 我将来要做的事要求我使用英语。	我未来的生活或工作离不开英语。
29. I can imagine myself speaking English as if I were a native speaker of English. 我可以想像我用英语像自己母语一样交流。 （原文有别字，"想像"应为"想象"。）	我希望自己的英语能够讲得跟英语本族语者一样地好。
38. I can imagine myself speaking English with international friends or colleagues. 我可以想象和国外朋友或同事用英语交流。	我希望能用英语与国际友人或同行交流。
40. My family put a lot of pressure on me to study English. 我的家人在学习英语上给我很多压力。	我的家人极力敦促我学好英语。
46. Whenever I think of my future career, I imagine myself using English. 无论将来的职业是什么，我可以想象用英语交流。	无论自己将来从事何种职业，我都希望能够用英语交流。
47. I study English because with English I can enjoy travelling abroad. 我学习英语是因为我可以享受国外旅行。	我学习英语是为了方便以后出国旅行。

三、中国外语教学问卷调查研究现状

国内外语教学问卷调查研究涉及的内容大体上与国外研究相同，甚至范围更广，并呈如下趋势（参见秦晓晴，2009，pp. 1-2）：

首先是学习者因素方面的研究。国内研究者比较关注学习策略、学习信念、学习动机（如交流意愿、学习目的、目标设置、成绩归因、课堂焦虑等）、性格以及学习风格等学习者因素在外语学习中的作用。其中，热点研究问题是对学习策略的调查研究。这方面的研究过去主要是对总体学习策略的研究，现在越来越集中于对诸如词汇学习策略、写作策略、听力策略、词典运用策略、交际策略等具体的语言技能策略，以及学习策略的影响因素和学习策略培训等具体方面的研究。

其次是师生的学习和教学观念或态度研究，包括学生的语言学习观念、大学英语教师的外语教育观念、网络环境下的学习信念、师生对母语在语言学习过程中作用的态度、师生教学观念的一致性、教师对具体教学方法的看法、学生对教材和教法的态度，以及师生对多媒体辅助外语教学的态度等。

第三是对学生和教师的知识和能力掌握情况的调查。在学生方面，不少文献探讨了学生自主意识和自主学习能力、网络与计算机操作技能、语言现象的使用情况、网络英语的运用、语用能力、元认知策略的使用能力和言语行为能力等。教师方面的研究主要包括对教师课堂话语特点、大学英语教师的专业知识、教师的教学和科研能力，以及教师对有关教学理论和教师发展理论的掌握程度等方面的探讨。

第四是教学现状调查和教学评价。教学现状调查包括课外阅读情况调查、课外视听现状、专门用途英语教学现状、写作教学现状、中小学英语教学现状、母语在课堂上的使用情况、课程设置情况，以及英语专业学士论文写作现状等方面。教学评价方面的问卷调查研究涉及大学英语的教学效果、教材在外语教学过程中的地位与作用、网络教学效果、英语课程改革的评价、人才培养模式评价、教师对试卷质量的评价、学生对考试的评价、学生对具体教学实验的评价，以及学生对不同类型课堂或教学现状的满意度等方面。

第五是探讨教学或学习效果的影响因素，包括理工科学生英语阅读效率的影响因素、英语课堂教学效果的影响因素、大学英语教师素质、口语流利表达的成因分析、写作能力的影响因素等。

第六是教学需求或学习需求分析，如社会发展对大学英语教学的影响分析及需求预测、大学生英语听力需求分析、学生对英语教材文化内容的需求等等。

此外，学者还用问卷方法进行翻译方面的研究，如对翻译标准理解的一致性、不同译者对译文的评价一致性，以及译者对记忆与口译之间的关系的看法等等。[2]

以上是对近年来国内外语教学问卷调查研究趋势的总结。然而仔细检视国内过去发表的问卷调查研究，虽不乏高质量的研究，但有不少问卷研究存在着比较突出的问题：

1) 测量抽象结构时只依赖单项目问卷，相当多的研究不使用多项目问卷，单项目问卷的最大弊端是其结果的信度可能存在问题。

2) 研究者在自己设计问卷项目时存在着本书2.6.2节中所谈及的种种问题。

3) 不注重问卷实施过程，如对实施过程的具体环节考虑不周，或者在论文中不注重对数据收集方法和过程的汇报。不提供关于研究过程的足够的信息的话，读者就无从知道其结果的有效性，后人也无法进行重复研究。

4) 不进行信度和效度分析就直接使用和汇报假设检验结果的文献不在少数。外语类核心期刊上有不少问卷研究没有汇报信度和效度指标及措施，还有个别研究甚至选择了不当的数据分析方法等。

5) 国内不少论文没有汇报描述统计结果，尤其是在采用参数检验方法时也不汇报数据是否达到参数检验的要求（如数据是否呈正态分布）。

6) 除问卷法外，同时使用诸如访谈法或刺激回忆法等其他研究方法的研究少。

总之，设计不出好的问卷、没有合理的问卷调查实施方案或者没有采用恰当的数据处理方法，再好的研究其效度也会大打折扣，最终影响到整个研究的质量。所幸的是，外研社引进的《第二语言研究中的问卷调查方法》（第二版）一书非常系统地介绍了问卷法的使用。读者通读本书可以对问卷法的特点以及设计步骤有总体的把握，为有效地评价他人的问卷调查研究和设计好自己的研究打下基础；读者还可以对照自己在使用问卷法中的体会或不足有针对性地选读相关的章节，提高自己未来问卷调查研究的质量。

---

2. 限于篇幅，本节略去了所论及的众多国内问卷研究的文献信息。

参考文献

Brown, J. D. 2001. *Using Surveys in Language Programs* [M]. Cambridge: Cambridge University Press.

Dewaele, J.-M. 2005. Questionnaires in second language research, construction, administration, and processing [J]. *International Journal of Bilingual Education & Bilingualism*, 8 (1), 98-100.

Dörnyei, Z. 2003. *Questionnaires in Second Language Research: Construction, Administration, and Processing* (1st ed.) [M]. Mahwah, N.J.: Lawrence Erlbaum Associates.

Dörnyei, Z., Csizér, K., & Németh, N. 2006. *Motivation, Language Attitudes and Globalisation: A Hungarian Perspective* [M]. Clevedon: Multilingual Matters.

Montee, M. 2011. Zoltán Dörnyei and Tatsuya Taguchi, Questionnaires in second language research: Construction, administration, and processing (2nd ed.), Routledge, New York, USA and Abingdon, Oxon, UK (2010) viii + 185 pp. [J]. *System*, forthcoming.

Schrauf, R. W. 2006. Questionnaires in second language research: Construction, administration, and processing [J]. *Journal of Linguistic Anthropology*, 16 (2), 294-295.

Wilson, R., & Dewaele, J.-M. 2010. The use of web questionnaires in second language acquisition and bilingualism research [J]. *Second Language Research*, 26 (1), 103-123.

高一虹、赵媛、程英、周燕，2003，中国大学本科生英语学习动机类型 [J]，《现代外语》26 (1)：28-38。

秦晓晴，2009，《外语教学问卷调查法》[M]。北京：外语教学与研究出版社。

秦晓晴

华中师范大学

2011年7月

Preface to the Second Edition

In the Introduction to the first edition of *Questionnaires in Second Language Research*, I argued that in spite of the wide application of questionnaires in applied linguistics, there did not seem to be suffcient awareness in the profession about the theory of questionnaire design. The positive reception of the book confirmed that it successfully catered to the need for a relatively non-technical and accessible text that describes systematically how to construct, administer, and process questionnaires. So why write a second edition?

The reason for this new edition is not that the material in the first edition has become outdated—research methods texts usually have a much longer shelf life than books describing research results. Rather, over the past seven years I have thought of several ways of how the book could be improved by adding extra material and by filling certain gaps. The most significant change in this revised edition involves adding a whole new chapter to the book—Chapter 5, "Illustration: Developing a Motivation Questionnaire"—to provide a detailed, illustrative analysis of how an actual scientific research instrument was developed from scratch following the theoretical guidelines. This chapter was co-authored by my Ph.D. student, Tatsuya Taguchi, who has been directing a major test design program at the University of Nottingham under my guidance. Tatsuya has also helped me to update the references and improve several other parts of the material, particularly the addition of a section on translating questionnaire items in Chapter 2 and the discussion of how to collect survey data on the Internet in Chapter 3. We also added the full form of the Japanese instrument, along with Chinese and Iranian versions, in the Appendices.

Besides these more substantial changes, I have made numerous smaller additions, and improved the style and accuracy of the text in many places. All in all, the first edition has been given a thorough facelift! One thing has not changed, though: I still believe that conducting questionnaire surveys can be an exciting and rewarding activity, and I do hope that readers will find in this book all the technical information that they need to be able to obtain valid and reliable results. Have fun!

Zoltán Dörnyei

Introduction

One of the most common methods of data collection in second language (L2) research is to use *questionnaires* of various kinds. The popularity of questionnaires is due to the fact that they are easy to construct, extremely versatile, and uniquely capable of gathering a large amount of information quickly in a form that is readily processable. Indeed, the frequency of use of self-completed questionnaires as a research tool in the L2 field is surpassed only by that of language proficiency tests.

In spite of the wide application of questionnaires in L2 research, there does not seem to be sufficient awareness in the profession about the theory of questionnaire design and processing. The usual—and in most cases false—perception is that anybody with a bit of common sense can construct a good questionnaire. This situation resembles somewhat the "pre-scientific" phase of language testing (i.e., the period before the 1950s) when language tests were used without paying enough attention to their psychometric qualities, and every language teacher was, by definition, assumed to be capable of devising and grading tests and exams without any special training. It is my impression that many questionnaire users are unaware of the fact that there is considerable relevant knowledge and experience accumulated in various branches of the social sciences (e.g., psychometrics, social psychology, sociology). This is why it is all too common to find studies which start out with exciting research questions but are flawed by a badly designed or inadequately processed questionnaire.

In one sentence . . .
The essential point is that good research cannot be built on poorly collected data . . .

(Gillham, 2008, p. 1)

This book is intended to be practical in nature. During the past 20 years I have found questionnaire theory to be very helpful in my own research. I designed my first questionnaire in the mid-1980s for my Ph.D. work and, because my specialization area—the study of L2 motivation—is very closely linked to the use of questionnaires, I have since then taken part as a principal researcher, participant, or supervisor in numerous studies surveying over 20,000 language learners. The idea to share my experience in the use of questionnaires with a broader audience occurred to me when I was working on the research section of a book on motivation (Dörnyei, 2001), and, thanks to the encouragement I received from Susan Gass, right from the beginning, the initial idea eventually led to this book.

Although questionnaire design and, more generally, survey research, have a substantial literature in the social sciences, this has not been sufficiently reflected in L2 methodology texts. With the emphasis typically placed on research methods and statistical procedures in them, there was simply not enough room for discussing specific research instruments (with the sole exception of language tests), and the issue of "questionnaires" has usually been summarized in a maximum of three to four pages. It was therefore a real surprise that, while already working on this book, I learned about another book in the making on a related topic: J. D. Brown's (2001) *Using Surveys in Language Programs*. As it happened, the two books are largely complementary, with few overlaps. I was fortunate to have J. D.'s manuscript in my hands when preparing the final draft of this book (thanks once again, J. D.!) and I will refer it at times for a more detailed discussion of certain topics.

The structure of the book is straightforward. After an initial chapter that discusses the nature, the merits, and the shortcomings of questionnaires, separate chapters cover the construction and the administration of the questionnaire, as well as the processing of questionnaire data. Chapter 5 offers a detailed illustration of the theories by describing how we have developed a research instrument for the purpose of surveying language learning motivation in Japan. This questionnaire, which can be found in Appendix B, has been used successfully since then, and our research team has also produced Chinese and Iranian versions of it (see Taguchi, Magid, & Papi, 2009); all the items of the three instruments are listed in Appendix A. The book is concluded by a detailed checklist that summarizes the main principles and recommendations.

CHAPTER 1

Questionnaires in Second Language Research

Asking questions is one of the most natural ways of gathering information and, indeed, as soon as babies have mastered the basics of their mother tongue they launch into a continuous flow of questions, and keep going throughout the rest of their lives. Some people such as reporters actually make a living of this activity and survey/polling organizations can base highly successful businesses on it.

Because the essence of *scientific research* is trying to find answers to questions in a systematic manner, it is no wonder that the *questionnaire* has become one of the most popular research instruments applied in the social sciences. Questionnaires are certainly *the* most often employed data collection devices in statistical work, with the most well-known questionnaire type—the *census*—being the flagship of every national statistical office.

The main strength of questionnaires is the ease of their construction. In an age of computers and sophisticated word processing software it is possible to draw up something that looks respectable in a few hours. After all, as Gillham (2008) reminds us, we all know what questionnaires look like: Hardly a week goes by without some coming our way. Ironically, the strength of questionnaires is at the same time also their main weakness. People appear to take it for granted that everybody with reasonable intelligence can put together a questionnaire that works. Unfortunately, this is not true: Just like in everyday life, where not every question elicits the right answer, it is all too common in scientific investigations to come across questionnaires that fail. In fact, I believe that *most* questionnaires applied in L2 research are somewhat *ad hoc* instruments, and questionnaires with sufficient (and well-documented) psychometric reliability and validity are not that easy to come by in our field. This is of course no accident: In spite of the growing methodological awareness that has characterized applied linguistics over the past two decades, the practice of questionnaire design/use has remained largely uninformed by the principles of survey research accumulated in the social sciences. I sometimes wonder what proportion of questionnaire constructors are actually aware that such principles exist . . .

> **Not indeed . . .**
> The world is full of well-meaning people who believe that everyone who can write plain English and has a modicum of common sense can produce a good questionnaire. This book is not for them.
>
> (Oppenheim, 1992, p. 1)

As already mentioned in the Introduction, my interest in questionnaires is pragmatic and practice-driven. I use them all the time and I would like the measures obtained by them to meet high research standards. Having fallen into many of the existing pitfalls several times, I intend for this book to offer concrete suggestions on how to use questionnaires to best effect and how to save ourselves a lot of trouble. Drawing on my own experience and a review of the literature, I will summarize the main principles of constructing and administering questionnaires, and outline the key issues in processing and reporting questionnaire data.

I would like to emphasize right at the onset that this is a "questionnaire book," which means that I will not go into much detail about issues that go beyond the immediate scope of the subject; for example, I will not elaborate on topics such as overall survey design, statistical procedures, or qualitative data analysis. Readers who are interested in these areas may refer to my recent overview of *Research Methods in Applied Linguistics* (Dörnyei, 2007), in which these topics are extensively discussed. In the "Further Reading" section below I have also listed a number of good summaries of questionnaire theory that I have found particularly useful in the past.

Further Reading

There is no shortage of books on questionnaires; many relevant and useful works have been written on the topic in such diverse disciplines as psychology, measurement theory, statistics, sociology, educational studies, and market research. In the L2 field, J. D. Brown (2001) provides a comprehensive account of survey research (which uses questionnaires as one of the main data-gathering instruments), offering a detailed account of how to process questionnaire data either statistically or qualitatively. In the field of psychological measurement, two companion volumes by Aiken (1996, 1997) provide up-to-date overviews of questionnaires, inventories, rating scales, and checklists. A new edition of DeVellis's work (2003) concisely explains the theoretical and technical aspects of scale development. Of the many books specifically focusing on questionnaire design I would like to highlight three: Oppenheim's (1992) summary is the revised version of his classic work from 1966, and Sudman and Bradburn's (1983) monograph is also a seminal volume in the area. Finally, Gillham's (2008) slim monograph is refreshing, with its readable and entertaining style.

1.1 What Are "Questionnaires" and What Do They Measure?

Although the term "questionnaire" is one that most of us are familiar with, it is not a straightforward task to provide a precise definition for it. To start with, the term is partly a misnomer because many questionnaires do *not* contain any, or many, real questions that end with a question mark. Indeed, questionnaires are often referred to under different names, such as "inventories," "forms," "opinionnaires," "tests," "batteries," "checklists," "scales," "surveys," "schedules," "studies," "profiles," "indexes/indicators," or even simply "sheets" (Aiken, 1997).

Second, the general rubric of "questionnaire" has been used by researchers in at least two broad senses:

(a) *Interview schedules*, like the ones used in opinion polls, when some-one actually conducts a live interview with the respondent, reading out a set of fixed questions and marking the respondent's answers on an answer sheet.

(b) *Self-administered pencil-and-paper questionnaires*, like the "con-sumer surveys" that we often find in our mailbox or the short forms we are asked to fill in when, for example, checking out of a hotel to evaluate the services.

In this book—in accordance with Brown's (2001) definition below— I will concentrate on the second type only; that is, on the self-completed, written questionnaire that respondents fill in by themselves. More specific-ally, the focus will be on questionnaires employed as research instruments for measurement purposes to collect reliable and valid data.

A Definition for "Questionnaires"

Questionnaires are any written instruments that present respondents with a series of questions or statements to which they are to react either by writing out their answers or selecting from among existing answers.

(Brown, 2001, p. 6)

1.1.1 What a Questionnaire Is Not

Tests Are Not Questionnaires

Most scholars know that tests and questionnaires are assessment tools of a completely different nature, but because some novice researchers might find written, self-completed (or self-report) questionnaires and written tests rather similar, let me highlight the main difference between them. A "test" takes a sample of the respondent's behavior/knowledge and, on the basis of this sample, inferences are made about the degree of the development of the individual's more general underlying competence/abilities/skills (e.g., overall L2 proficiency). Thus, a test measures how *well* someone can do something. In contrast, questionnaires do not have good or bad answers; they ask for information about the respondents (or "informants") in a non-evaluative manner, without gauging their performance against a set of criteria or against the performance of a norm group. Thus, although some commercially available questionnaires are actually called "tests," these are not tests in the same sense as achievement or aptitude tests.

"Production Questionnaires" (DCTs) Are Not Questionnaires

The term *"production questionnaire"* is a relatively new name for a popular instrument—traditionally referred to as a DCT or "discourse completion task"—that has been the most commonly used elicitation technique in the field of interlanguage pragmatics (see Bardovi-Harlig, 1999; Johnston, Kasper, & Ross, 1998). Although several versions exist, the common feature of production questionnaires is that they require the informant to produce some sort of authentic language data as a response to situational prompts. For example:

> Rushing to get to class on time, you run round the corner and bump into one of your fellow students who was waiting there, almost knocking him down.
> You: _ _ _ _ _ _ _ _ _ _ _ _ _ _ _ _ _
> The student: Never mind, no damage done.
>
> (Johnston *et al.*, 1998, p. 176)

It is clear that these "questionnaires" are not questionnaires in the same psychometric sense as the instruments discussed in this book. They are written, structured language elicitation instruments and, as such, they sample the respondent's competence in performing certain tasks, which makes them similar to language tests.

1.1.2 What Do Questionnaires Measure?

Broadly speaking, questionnaires can yield three types of data about the respondent: *factual*, *behavioral*, and *attitudinal*.

1. *Factual questions* (also called "classification" questions or "subject descriptors") are used to find out about who the respondents are. They typically cover demographic characteristics (e.g., age, gender, and race), residential location, marital and socioeconomic status, level of education, religion, occupation, as well as any other background information that may be relevant to interpreting the findings of the survey. Such additional data in L2 studies often include facts about the learners' language learning history, amount of time spent in an L2 environment, level of parents' L2 proficiency, or the L2 coursebook used.

2. *Behavioral questions* are used to find out what the respondents are doing or have done in the past. They typically ask about people's actions, lifestyles, habits, and personal history. Perhaps the most well-known questions of this type in L2 studies are the items in language learning strategy inventories that ask about the frequency of the use of a particular strategy in the past.

3. *Attitudinal questions* are used to find out what people think. This is a broad category that concerns *attitudes*, *opinions*, *beliefs*, *interests*, and *values*. These five interrelated terms are not always distinguished or defined very clearly in the literature.

   - *Attitudes* concern evaluative responses to a particular target (e.g., people, institution, situation). They are deeply embedded in the human mind, and are very often not the product of rational deliberation of facts—they can be rooted back in our past or modeled by certain significant people around us. For this reason, they are rather pervasive and resistant to change.

   - *Opinions* are just as subjective as attitudes, but they are perceived as being more factually based and more changeable. People are always aware of their opinions but they may not be fully conscious of their attitudes (Aiken, 1996).

- *Beliefs* have a stronger factual support than opinions and often concern the question as to whether something is true, false, or "right."
- *Interests* are preferences for particular activities.
- *Values*, on the one hand, concern preferences for "life goals" and "ways of life" (e.g., Christian values); on the other hand, they are also used to describe the utility, importance, or worth attached to particular activities, concepts, or objects (e.g., instrumental/utilitarian value of L2 proficiency).

1.2 Using Questionnaires: Pros and Cons

1.2.1 Advantages

The main attraction of questionnaires is their unprecedented effciency in terms of (a) researcher time, (b) researcher effort, and (c) financial resources. By administering a questionnaire to a group of people, one can collect a huge amount of information in less than an hour, and the personal investment required will be a fraction of what would have been needed for, say, interviewing the same number of people. Furthermore, if the questionnaire is well constructed, processing the data can also be fast and relatively straightforward, especially by using some modern computer software. These cost-benefit considerations are very important, particularly for all those who are doing research in addition to having a full-time job (Gillham, 2008).

Cost-effectiveness is not the only advantage of questionnaires. They are also very *versatile*, which means that they can be used successfully with a variety of people in a variety of situations targeting a variety of topics. In fact, as Bryman (2008) points out, they can even tap into attitudes that the respondents are not completely aware of, and a well-constructed questionnaire can reduce the bias of interviewer effects and thus increase the consistency and reliability of the results. In the light of all these merits, it is no wonder that the vast majority of research projects in the behavioral and social sciences involve at one stage or another collecting some sort of questionnaire data.

1.2.2 Disadvantages

Although the previous description of the virtues of questionnaires might suggest that they are perfect research instruments, this is not quite so. Questionnaires have some serious limitations, and some of these have led some researchers to claim that questionnaire data are not reliable or valid. I do not agree with this claim in general, but there is no doubt that it is very easy to produce unreliable and invalid data by means of ill-constructed questionnaires. In fact, as Gillham (2008, p. 1) points out, in research methodology "no single method has been so much abused" as questionnaires. Let us look at the main problem sources.

Simplicity and Superficiality of Answers
Because respondents are left to their own devices when filling in self-completed questionnaires, the questions need to be sufficiently simple and straightforward to be understood by everybody. Thus, questionnaires are unsuitable for probing deeply into an issue (Moser & Kalton, 1971) because they often result in rather superficial data. The necessary simplicity of the questions is further augmented by the fact that the amount of time respondents are usually willing to spend working on a questionnaire is rather short, which again limits the depth of the investigation.

Unreliable and Unmotivated Respondents
Most people are not very thorough in a research sense, and this is all the more true about dealing with questionnaires—an activity which they typically do not enjoy or benefit from in any way. Thus, the quality of the results may vary greatly from one individual to another, depending on the time and care they choose or are able to give (Hopkins, Stanley, & Hopkins, 1990). Respondents are also prone to leave out some questions, either by mistake or because they did not like them, and Low (1999) presents empirical evidence that respondents also often simply misread or misinterpret questions (which of course renders the answers false). If returning the questionnaires to the survey administrator is left to the respondents (e.g., in a mail survey), they very often fail to do so, even when they have completed it. Or, what is even worse, in such "distant" modes, the majority of the respondents may not even bother to have a go at the questionnaire. After all, don't we all think, from time to time, that the questionnaires we receive are an absolute nuisance?

Respondent Literacy Problems
Questionnaire research makes the inherent assumption that the respondents can read and write well. Even in the industrialized world this is not necessarily the case with regard to the whole population: Statistics of about 5%-7% are regularly quoted when estimating the proportion of people who have difficulty reading, and the number of those who are uncomfortable with writing is even bigger. The situation may be more serious when a questionnaire is administered in languages that the respondents are learning, which is often the case in applied linguistic research. It is therefore

understandable that for respondents with literacy problems or with limited L2 proficiency, filling in a questionnaire can appear an intimidating or overwhelming task.

Little or No Opportunity to Correct the Respondents' Mistakes

Questionnaire items focus on information which the respondents know best, and therefore the researcher has little opportunity to double-check the validity of the answers. Sometimes respondents deviate from the truth intentionally (see below), but it is also common that—as just mentioned—they simply misunderstand or forget something, or do not remember it correctly. Another fairly common situation is when respondents do not know the exact response to a question, yet answer it without indicating their lack of knowledge. Without any personal contact between the researcher and the informant, little can be done to check the seriousness of the answers and to correct the erroneous responses.

Social Desirability (or Prestige) Bias

The final big problem with regard to questionnaires is that people do not always provide true answers about themselves; that is, the results represent what the respondents *report* to feel or believe, rather than what they *actually* feel or believe. There are several possible reasons for this, and the most salient one is what is usually termed the *social desirability* or *prestige bias*. Questionnaire items are often "transparent," that is, respondents can have a fairly good guess about what the desirable/acceptable/expected answer is, and some of them will provide this response even if it is not true. The most extreme example of a "transparent" question I have come across was in the offcial U.S. visa application form (DS 156):

Have you ever participated in genocide?

Although most questionnaire items are more subtle than this, trying to present ourselves in a good light is a natural human tendency, and this is very bad news for the survey researcher: The resulting bias poses a serious threat to the validity of the data. We should note that this threat is not necessarily confined to "subjective" attitudinal items only. As Oppenheim (1992) warns us, even factual questions are often loaded with prestige: People might claim that they read more than they do, bathe more often than is true, spend more time with their children, or give more to charity than actually happens, etc. In general, questions concerning age, race, income, state of health, marital status, educational background, sporting achievements, social standing, criminal behavior, sexual activity, and bad habits such as smoking or drinking, are all vulnerable (Newell, 1993; Wilson & McClean, 1994).

Self-Deception

Self-deception is related to social desirability but in this case respondents do not deviate from the truth consciously but rather because they also deceive themselves (and not just the researcher). As Hopkins *et al.* (1990, p. 312) point out, human defense mechanisms "cushion failures, minimize faults, and maximize virtues so that we maintain a sense of personal worth." People with personality problems might simply be unable to give an accurate self-description, but the problem of self-delusion may be present on a more general scale, though to a lesser degree, affecting many other people.

Acquiescence Bias

Another common threat inherent to self-completed questionnaires is *acquiescence*, which refers to the tendency for people to agree with sentences when they are unsure or ambivalent. Acquiescent people include "yeasayers," who are ready to go along with "anything that sounds good" (Robinson, Shaver, & Wrightsman, 1991, p. 8), and the term also covers those who are reluctant to look at the negative side of any issue and are unwilling to provide strong negative responses.

Halo Effect

The *halo effect* concerns the human tendency to (over)generalize. If our overall impression of a person or a topic is positive, we may be disinclined to say anything less than positive about them even if it comes to specific details. For many students, for example, a teacher they like is "perfect" in everything he/she does—which is obviously not true. And similarly, if we do not like someone, we—quite unfairly—tend to underestimate all his/her characteristics.

Fatigue Effects

Finally, if a questionnaire is too long or monotonous, respondents may begin to respond inaccurately as a result of tiredness or boredom. This effect is called the *fatigue effect*, and it is obviously more likely to influence responses toward the end of the questionnaire.

1.3 Questionnaires in Quantitative and Qualitative Research

The typical questionnaire is a highly structured data collection instrument, with most items either asking about very specific pieces of information (e.g., one's address or food preference) or giving various response options for the respondent to choose from, for example, by ticking a box. This makes questionnaire data particularly suited for *quantitative*, statistical analysis. After all, the essential characteristic of quantitative research is that it employs categories, viewpoints, and models that have been precisely defined by the researcher in advance, and numerical or directly quantifiable data are collected to determine the relationship between these categories and to test the research hypotheses.

In theory, it would be possible to devise a questionnaire that is entirely made up of truly open-ended items (e.g., "Describe your dreams for the future . . ."). Such an instrument would provide data that are *qualitative* and *exploratory* in nature, but this practice is usually discouraged by theoreticians. The problem with questionnaires from a qualitative perspective is that—as argued earlier—they inherently involve a somewhat superficial and relatively brief engagement with the topic on the part of the respondent. Therefore, no matter how creatively we formulate the items, those are unlikely to yield the kind of rich and sensitive description of events and participant perspectives that qualitative interpretations are grounded in. In fact, as Sudman and Bradburn (1983) assert, requests for long responses (i.e., more than a sentence as a minimum) often lead to refusals to answer the question or the entire questionnaire, and even if we get longer written answers, many of these will need to be discarded because they are uncodable or inappropriate. So, if we are seeking long and detailed personal accounts, other research methods such as a personal interview are likely to be more suitable for our purpose. Having said that, I do believe that some partially open-ended questions can play an important role in questionnaires (see Section 2.5 for a discussion), but if we want to significantly enrich questionnaire data, the most effective strategy is usually not the inclusion of too many open-ended questions but to combine the questionnaire survey with other data collection procedures (see Section 4.7).

True . . .
The desire to use open-ended questions appears to be almost universal in novice researchers, but is usually rapidly extinguished with experience.

(Robson, 2002, p. 245)

CHAPTER 2

Constructing the Questionnaire

Section 1.2.2 contained a long list of potential problems with self-completed questionnaires. My goal was not to dissuade people from using such instruments but rather to raise awareness of these possible shortcomings. It is true that respondents are often unmotivated, slapdash, hasty, and insincere, yet it is also an established fact that careful and creative questionnaire construction can result in an instrument that motivates people to give relatively truthful and thoughtful answers, which can then be processed in a scientifically sound manner. The relevant professional literature contains a significant body of accumulated experience and research evidence as to how we can achieve this. Some of the points highlighted by researchers are seemingly trivial in the sense that they concern small details, but I have come to believe that it is to a great extent the systematic handling of such small details and nuances that will eventually turn an *ad hoc* set of questions into an effective research instrument.

> **I agree . . .**
> Questionnaires can be designed to minimize, but not eliminate, dishonest, and careless reporting.
>
> (Aiken, 1997, p. 58)

Constructing a good questionnaire involves a series of steps and procedures, including:

- Deciding on the general features of the questionnaire, such as the length, the format, and the main parts.

- Writing effective items/questions and drawing up an item pool.
- Selecting and sequencing the items.
- Writing appropriate instructions and examples.
- Translating the questionnaire into a target language if it was not originally written in that language.
- Piloting the questionnaire and conducting item analysis.

This chapter will provide an overview of these issues, offering many practical do's and don'ts to facilitate effective questionnaire construction.

Indeed . . .
Questionnaires are so easy to do quickly and badly that, in a way, they invite carelessness.

(Gillham, 2008, p. 11)

2.1 General Features

Between the initial idea of preparing a questionnaire for the purpose of our research and actually getting down to writing the first draft, we need to take a number of important decisions regarding the general features of the would-be instrument. First of all, we need to specify the maximum *length of time* that the completion of the questionnaire could take; then we need to consider general *format characteristics*; and finally we need to think about the issue of *anonymity*, particularly if we are going to target sensitive/confidential topics.

2.1.1 Length

When we design a questionnaire, the general temptation is always to cover too much ground by asking everything that might turn out to be interesting. This must be resisted: In questionnaire design less is often more, because long questionnaires can become counterproductive.

How long is the optimal length? It depends on how important the topic of the questionnaire is for the respondents. If we feel very strongly about something, we are usually willing to spend several hours answering questions. However, most questionnaires in the L2 field concern topics that have a low salience from the respondents' perspective, and in such cases the optimal length is rather short. Most researchers agree that anything that is more than four to six pages long and requires over half an hour to complete may be considered too much of an imposition. As a principle, I have always tried to stay within a four-page limit: It is remarkable how many items can be included within four well-designed pages and I have also found that a questionnaire of three to four pages does not tend to exceed the 30-minute completion limit.

A further factor to consider is that if we are restricted in the time we can have access to the respondents—for example, when we administer a questionnaire to learners during their teaching hours—the maximum length should be set with the *slowest* readers in mind. For example, in a national survey that involved the group-administration of a questionnaire in hundreds of primary school classes in various locations in Hungary (see Dörnyei, Csizér, & Németh, 2006), we could only negotiate a maximum of 30 minutes' access to the children. This meant that the questionnaire had to be cut down to three pages and an estimated 20-minute completion time in order to give everybody a chance to finish within the allotted time.

To Summarize

In my experience, only in exceptional cases should a questionnaire:
- be more than four pages long;
- take more than 30 minutes to complete.

2.1.2 Layout

Sanchez (1992) points out that the design of the *questionnaire layout* is frequently overlooked as an important aspect of the development of the instrument. This is a mistake: Because in surveys employing self-completed questionnaires the main interface between the researcher and the respondent is the hard copy of the questionnaire; the format and graphic layout carry a special significance and have an important impact on the responses. Over the past 20 years I have increasingly come to the belief that producing an attractive and professional design is half the battle in eliciting reliable and valid data (for a discussion of the role of the layout in increasing respondent motivation, see Section 3.3.9).

What does an "attractive and professional design" involve? The following list summarizes the five most important points:

- *Booklet format.* Not only does the questionnaire have to be short but it also has to *look* short. I have found that the format that feels most compact is that of a *booklet*. It can be achieved by taking a double-sized sheet (A3 size in Europe), photocopying two normalsized pages on each of the sides, and then folding the sheet into two. This format also makes it easy to read and to turn pages (and, what is just as important, it also prevents lost pages . . .).

- *Appropriate density*. With regard to how much material we put on a page, a compromise needs to be achieved: On the one hand, we want to make the pages full, because respondents are much more willing to fill in a two-page rather than a four-page questionnaire even if the two instruments have exactly the same number of items. On the other hand, we must not make the pages look crowded (for example, by economizing on the spaces separating different sections of the questionnaire). Effective ways of achieving this trade-off involve reducing the *margins*, using a *space-economical font* (e.g., 11 or 12 point Times New Roman), and utilizing the whole *width* of the page, for example, by printing the response options next to the questions and not below (as illustrated in the following example).

	Strongly disagree	Disagree	Slightly disagree	Partly agree	Agree	Strongly agree
1. Language learning is a burden for me.						
2. Foreign languages are an important part of the school curriculum.						
3. I like the sound of English.						

On Length and Crowdedness

Perhaps the most common mistake of the beginner in questionnaire construction is to crowd questions together in the hope of making the questionnaire look short . . . While length is important, the respondent's perception of the difficulty of the task is even more important on self-administered questionnaires. A less crowded questionnaire with substantial white space looks easier and generally results in higher cooperation and fewer errors.

(Sudman & Bradburn, 1983, p. 244)

- *Orderly layout*. Even if the page is dense, a well-designed, orderly layout that utilizes various typefaces and highlighting options (e.g., bold characters or italics) can create a good impression, whereas an unsystematic layout, even if it is more spacious, can appear chaotic. It is also essential that the final version be nicely printed—as Newell (1993) points out, in these days of sophisticated word processors, people are used to receiving good-quality hard copies. So try and find a laser printer and a good photocopier!

- *Paper quality*. Even the quality and color of the paper might make a difference. Newell (1993) describes a colleague who has always produced documents on thick, beige paper because she believes that "(1) it stands out from the mass of other paper which might be received, (2) it is pleasant to handle, and (3) people will not have the heart to throw away such an attractive document. She says it works" (p. 109). Other researchers suggest that it may be useful to separate the various parts of the questionnaires with a certain color-code of the paper used as it clarifies the structure (Robson, 2002); for example, the paper of the cover page or the instructions can be of a different color.
- *Sequence marking*. I normally mark each main section of the questionnaire with Roman numbers, each question with consecutive Arab figures, and then letter all the subparts of a question; as a result, I may have Question 1a or 27d within Section I or III (see the example on pages 15-16). This creates a sense of structuredness. It is also beneficial to include a phrase such as "Continued on back" or "Please turn over" at the bottom of the first side of a page that is printed on both sides. Finally, it is probably obvious, but still worth mentioning, that a question should not be split between two pages.

2.1.3 Sensitive Topics and Anonymity

It was mentioned in Section 1.2.2 that respondents are sometimes reluctant to give honest answers to sensitive questions. Questionnaire items differ greatly in terms of how threatening/imposing/sensitive/embarrassing they feel. It is clear that we need to approach the issue of constructing and administering the questionnaire in a very different way if it concerns, for example, the evaluation of the L2 teacher or the school rather than one's interest in traveling abroad.

Example of Sequence Marking

I. Attitudes toward language learning
  1. Language learning is an exciting activity.
  2. Language learning often makes me happy.

II. Language choice

3. If you could choose, which foreign languages would you choose to learn next year at school? Please mark three languages in order of importance.

(a) ....

(b) ....

(c) ....

Continued on back . . .

Sensitive Topics

"Sensitive" topics are not confined to explicitly illegal or embarrassing subjects but also include basic demographic items such as age or marital status. Indeed, various facts of life can carry such a prominent social and emotional loading that questions targeting them often fall prey to the respondents' "social desirability" bias (see Section 1.2.2). Depending on our core values, we are likely to overreport on what we conceive as a positive aspect and underreport on a negative one. Questionnaire designers need to be aware of this tendency and a good initial rule of thumb is that we should *not* ask any sensitive questions unless absolutely necessary for the project. In cross-cultural surveys we need to be particularly careful to check that none of the questions interfere with some hidden sensitivities, for example because they touch upon some basic religious or cultural principles unknown to us.

In Section 2.6.3, I will discuss several item-writing strategies that might make such questions more palatable, and in Section 3.4 we will look at questionnaire administration techniques that may help to "sell" these items. Here I would like to highlight the usefulness of an explicit statement or promise of confidentiality in overcoming possible apprehensions. Oppenheim (1992, pp. 104-105) suggests that something along the following line be displayed prominently on the front of the questionnaire:

> The contents of this form are *absolutely* confidential. Information iden-
> tifying the respondent will not be disclosed under any circumstances.

In the general instructions of a language learning motivation questionnaire which included the appraisal of the L2 teacher and course (and was therefore particularly sensitive from the students' point of view), Gliksman, Gardner, and Smythe (1982, p. 637) provided the following detailed description of how confidentiality was observed in spite of asking the students to state their names:

Your answers to any or all questions will be treated with the strictest confidence. Although we ask for your name on the cover page, we do so only because we must be able to associate your answers to this questionnaire with those of other questionnaires which you will be asked to answer. It is important for you to know, however, that before the questionnaires are examined, your questionnaire will be numbered, the same number will be put on the section containing your name, and then that section will be removed. By following a similar procedure with the other questionnaires we will be able to match the questionnaires through matching numbers and avoid having to associate your name directly with the questionnaire.

Anonymity

One frequent method used to diffuse sensitive items is to make the questionnaire *anonymous*. For example, in a student questionnaire that asked the learners to evaluate their language teacher and the course (Clément, Dörnyei, & Noels, 1994) using similar items to the ones employed in the Gliksman *et al.* (1982) study just mentioned, we felt it unlikely that the 16- or 17-year-old teenagers in the sample were going to agree to give us honest answers without being assured about the anonymity of the questionnaires. Following the same reasoning—and particularly when legal considerations, such as local research ethical regulations, also necessitate it—researchers often feel "forced" to make the survey anonymous. The main argument to support this practice is that anonymous respondents are likely to give answers that are less self-protective and presumably more accurate than respondents who believe they can be identified (Kearney, Hopkins, Mauss, & Weisheit, 1984). Anonymity, however, raises two issues:

- Opinions differ widely as to whether respondent anonymity actually fulfills its purpose in encouraging honesty and willingness to disclose. As Aiken (1997) summarizes, most adults will probably give the same answers to questionnaire items whether or not their responses are anonymous. For example, Sudman and Bradburn (1983) report on a large-scale postal survey of college graduates, in which the researchers placed the mailing label (which naturally contained the respondent's name) on the back cover of the questionnaires and sent these out in window envelopes. Out of the 40,000 recipients, only five objected to this procedure and scratched out their names. On the other hand, in situations when an honest answer might cause embarrassment or pose an actual threat to the respondent, anonymity does obviously matter. Thus, the question to consider is whether our questionnaires really fall into this category.

- Anonymity may not serve the purpose of the investigation. More often than not the researcher would like to link the data from the questionnaires to data coming from other sources; for example, motivational data obtained by questionnaires is often correlated to achievement scores coming from end-of-term course grades or proficiency tests. Without any identity marking on the questionnaires, we simply cannot link someone's scores in the two datasets. Similarly, if we are conducting a longitudinal investigation we would not be able to follow a person's development if all the answers gathered from the multiple subjects at a time were anonymous.

In sum, sensitive items and anonymity are a serious issue that needs to be considered right from the beginning. In Section 3.4.3, I will present some approaches that have been successfully used in the past to try and reconcile confidentiality with the need for identification for research purposes.

2.2 The Main Parts of a Questionnaire

Bearing in mind the general considerations just discussed, we are now set to start drawing up the first draft of the questionnaire. Before we get down to describing the various item types, let me briefly summarize the main components of a questionnaire.

2.2.1 Title

Just like any other piece of writing, a questionnaire should have a title to identify the domain of the investigation, to provide the respondent with initial orientation, and to activate relevant background knowledge and content expectations. Because uninformative titles fail to achieve these objectives, Aiken (1997) suggests that we should try and avoid title words like "questionnaire" or "survey." For better identification, the title might be accompanied by the date of the survey administration and the name of the organization conducting or sponsoring the study.

2.2.2 Instructions

The title of the questionnaire is followed by instructions. These cannot be too long, and yet need to be informative and well pitched because they play an important role in determining the respondents' feelings toward the questionnaire and in specifying how they should go about answering the items. Instructions are of two types:

- *General instruction* (or "opening greeting") at the beginning of the questionnaire.
- *Specific instructions* introducing each new task.

General Instruction

As a minimum, the general instruction (or "opening greeting") should cover the following points (see also Section 3.2.1, for special instructions for mail surveys):

- What the study is about and why it is important or socially useful.
- The organization responsible for conducting the study.
- Emphasizing that there are no right or wrong answers; requesting honest answers and trying to elicit integrity in general.
- Promising confidentiality.
- Saying "thank you."

For better readability and emphasis, the instructions should be graphically highlighted, such as being printed in boldface type, and the main pieces of information can also be given in a format such as bulleted points. I would expect that the sample instruction in Sample 2.1 would be suitable for most purposes.

Sample 2.1 General Instruction

We would like to ask you to help us by answering the following questions concerning foreign language learning. This survey is conducted by the Language Research Group of the University of X to better understand . . . This is not a test so there are no "right" or "wrong" answers and you don't even have to write your name on it. We are interested in your personal opinion. Please give your answers sincerely, as only this will guarantee the success of the investigation. Thank you very much for your help.

Specific Instructions

Specific instructions explain and demonstrate how respondents should go about answering the questions (e.g., whether respondents need to place a tick by, or circle, their chosen response and whether they should choose only one answer or more than one answer). It is obvious that this is a crucial part. Each new task type requires instructions, and in order to separate these instructions from the rest of the text they should be graphically highlighted, for example, by printing them in bold (just like the general instruction).

A very important role of the instructions is to explain how various rating scales (see Section 2.4.1) work and what the various rating criteria are. For example, if we ask the respondents to produce evaluations on a five-point rating scale (e.g., giving marks ranging from 1 to 5), we need to explain very clearly what each of the five categories stands for. Then, to avoid misunderstandings and mistakes, a short summary of this explanation will need to be repeated at least twice on each new page. Samples 2.2 and 2.3 provide examples of instructions for two common rating scale types (see also Sample 2.4 on page 31).

Sample 2.2 Instructions for Numerical Rating Scales

In the following section we would like you to answer some questions by simply giving marks from 1 to 5.

    1 = not at all
    2 = not really
    3 = so-so
    4 = quite a lot
    5 = very much

For example, consider the following item. If you like hamburgers very much, write "5" in the space in front of the question:

    _____How much do you like hamburgers?

Please write one (and only one) whole number in front of each question and don't leave out any of them. Thanks.

2.2.3 Questionnaire Items

After the instructions comes the central part of the questionnaire, the actual items. They will be discussed in detail in Sections 2.3-2.7. Two points need to be made here:

- Questionnaire items rarely take the form of actual questions that end with a question mark. The item type found in Sample 2.3, for example, is far more common than that in Sample 2.2 (which is a real question).
- The items need to be very clearly separated from the instructions. This is where different typefaces and font styles come in handy.

Sample 2.3 Instructions for Likert Scales

Following are a number of statements with which some people agree and others disagree. We would like you to indicate your opinion after each statement by putting an "X" in the box that best indicates the extent to which you agree or disagree with the statement. Thank you very much for your help.

For example:

Pickled cucumbers are unhealthy.

☐	☐	☐	☐	☐	☐
Strongly disagree	Disagree	Slightly disagree	Partly agree	Agree	Strongly agree

If you think, for example, that there is something true about this statement but it is somewhat exaggerated, you can put an "X" in the fourth or the fifth box.

2.2.4 Additional Information

Depending on circumstances, the questionnaire may contain, usually at the end, a short additional information section in which the author can address the respondent concerning a number of issues:

- Unless the researcher or a representative is present during the completion of the questionnaire, it might be worth including a contact name (e.g., the researcher's or an administrator's) with a telephone number or (email) address—in North America this is, in fact, mandatory—and some explicit encouragement to get in touch if there are any questions.
- In "distant" situations, it might also be worth summarizing briely how the questionnaires should be returned, and even when a return envelope is provided we should print on the questionnaire the name and the address of the person to whom the completed questionnaire is to be sent (see Section 3.2.1 for further details).
- It is a nice gesture (unfortunately too rarely used) to include a brief note promising to send the respondent a summary of the findings if interested (see Section 3.3.10 for a discussion of this point).
- Sometimes questionnaires can also end with an invitation to volunteer for a follow-up interview.

2.2.5 Final "Thank You"

It is basic courtesy, yet it is all too often overlooked, that the respondents should be thanked for their cooperation at the very end of the questionnaire. After all, they have done us a favor. Although I usually do not include any drawings in my questionnaires, if I did it would be located here: a smiling face or some little figure that can be seen as a nice gesture. Modern word processing packages offer many graphic designs, such as:

2.3 Appropriate Sampling of the Questionnaire Content and the Significance of "Multi-Item Scales"

The first step in preparing the questionnaire items is to specify their content in explicit terms. Although this may sound obvious, it does not always happen, and vague content specifications can pose a serious threat to the validity and reliability of the instrument, particularly in two areas:

- the appropriate *sampling of the content*;
- the preparation of *multi-item scales*.

2.3.1 Appropriate Sampling of the Content

Ad hoc questionnaire design involves jotting down a number of relevant questions without any rigorous procedure to ensure that the coverage is comprehensive. The problem with this method, as Davidson (1996, p. 10) highlights, is that "You cannot analyze what you do not measure." That is, not even the most sophisticated data analysis techniques will be able to compensate for your leaving out some important questions from the data collection by accident. Certain omissions are bound to occur even in otherwise very thorough studies (as attested by the countless anecdotes one hears at professional conferences) but when the sampling of the content is not theory-driven the chances for something irrecoverable to happen are obviously much greater.

On the other hand, forewarned by the potential threat of a lack of comprehensiveness, researchers may be tempted to make the questionnaire too long by covering every possible angle. Although this is undesirable, without any explicit content specifications it is almost impossible to decide what limit to put on the range of questions. So, the initial stage of questionnaire design should focus on clarifying the research problem and identifying what critical concepts need to be addressed by the questionnaire. To facilitate this, it is often recommended that the questionnaire design phase be preceded by a small-scale qualitative study (e.g., focus group interviews) to provide information on the relevant points and issues (see Section 2.6.1).

Quite so!
The temptation is always to cover too much, to ask everything that might turn out to be interesting. This must be resisted.

(Moser & Kalton, 1971, p. 309)

Once a theoretically sound shortlist of specific content areas has been drawn up, it becomes possible to eliminate all the questions that are only of peripheral interest but not directly related to the variables and hypotheses that the questionnaire has been designed to investigate. Such a shortlist is also necessary to be able to produce "multi-item scales" (see below), without which no questionnaire can be reliable.

To illustrate this process, let us take a concrete example: the design of a short questionnaire to assess student attitudes toward the language teacher. Which aspects of the teacher shall we concentrate on? Without any theoretical guidelines we could be producing an infinite number of items, all seemingly targeting important teacher characteristics. In a study where we faced this problem (Clément *et al.*, 1994), in order to follow a more systematic approach we first conducted a review of the relevant literature and identified four main dimensions of teacher appraisal: *competence, rapport* (with the students), *motivation,* and *teaching style/personality.* We then used this list to guide us in generating the item pool.

2.3.2 Using Multi-Item Scales

The notion of *multi-item scales* is the central component in scientific questionnaire design, yet this concept is surprisingly little known in the L2 profession. The core of the issue is that when it comes to assessing abstract, mental variables not readily observable by direct means (e.g., attitudes, beliefs, opinions, interests, values, aspirations, expectations, and other personal variables), the actual wording of the questions assumes an unexpected amount of importance: Minor differences in how a question is formulated and framed can produce radically different levels of agreement or disagreement, or a completely different selection of answers (Gillham, 2008). We do not have such problems with factual questions: If you are interested in the gender of the respondent, you can safely ask about this using a single item, and the chances are that you will get a reliable answer (although the item *"Your sex:"* might elicit creative responses in a teenage sample . . .). However, with non-factual answers it is not unusual to find that responses given by the same people to two virtually identical items differ by as much as 20% or more (Oppenheim, 1992). Here is an illustration.

Converse and Presser (1986, p. 41) report on a case when simply changing "forbid" to "not allow" in the wording produced significantly different responses in the item *"Do you think the United States should [forbid/ not allow] public speeches against democracy?"* Significantly more people were willing to "not allow" speeches against democracy than were willing to "forbid" them. Although it may be true that on an impressionistic level "not allow" somehow does not sound as harsh as "forbid," the fact is that "allow" and "forbid" are exact logical opposites and therefore it was not unreasonable for the researchers to assume that the actual content of the two versions of the question was identical. Yet, as the differing response pattern indicated, this was not the case. Given that in this example only one word was changed and that the alternative version had an almost identical meaning, this is a good illustration that item wording in general has a substantial impact on the responses. The problem, then, is that there seems to be no reliable way of knowing exactly what kind of effect to expect with any specific wording.

A problem indeed . . .

When we sometimes despair about the use of language as a tool for measuring or at least uncovering awareness, attitude, percepts and belief systems, it is mainly because we do not yet know why questions that look so similar actually produce such very different sets of results, or how we can predict contextual effects on a question, or in what ways we can ensure that respondents will all use the same frame of reference in answering an attitude question.

(Oppenheim, 1992, p. 149)

So, what is the solution? Do we have to conclude that questionnaires simply cannot achieve the kind of accuracy that is needed for scientific measurement purposes? We would have to if measurement theoreticians — and particularly Rensis Likert in the 1930s — had not discovered an ingenious way of getting around the problem: by using *multi-item scales*. These scales refer to a cluster of differently worded items that focus on the same target (e.g., five items targeting attitudes toward language labs). The item scores for the similar questions are summed or averaged, resulting in a total scale score (which is why these scales are sometimes referred to as *summative scales*), and the underlying assumption is that any idiosyncratic interpretation of an item will be ironed out during the summation of the item scores. In other words, if we use multi-item scales, "no individual item carries an excessive load, and an inconsistent response to one item would cause limited damage" (Skehan, 1989, p. 11). For example, the question "*Do you learn vocabulary items easily?*" is bound to be interpreted differently by different people, depending on how easy they consider "easily," but if we include several more items asking about how good the respondents' word-learning and memorization skills are, the overall score is likely to reflect the actual level of the development of this skill. Thus, multi-item scales maximize the stable component that the cluster of individual items in a scale share.

In addition to reducing the extraneous influence of item wording, multi-item scales are also better equipped to capture the targeted content domain than single items (see, e.g., DeVellis, 2003; Fabrigar, Krosnick, & MacDougall, 2005). The problem with single items is that even if they appear to focus on a target issue perfectly, they will activate in most people too narrow or too broad content domains. For example, if we intend to measure the learners' "interest in the L2 culture," the question "*Are you interested in the L2 culture?*" is likely to elicit inconsistent results depending on how broadly respondents interpret the term "culture." On the other hand, narrowing down the concept to a more specific target—for example, "*Are you interested in L2 films?*"—raises the question of how much the respondents' answers are affected by interference from other aspects of the L2 culture. Multi-item scales deal with this categorization issue effectively by allowing us to address a range of aspects associated with the target concept (e.g., TV programs, books, magazines, videos, music, fashion, etc. in our specific example) so that the commonality among the items captures the core issue we are after.

Of course, we need to use common sense in how far we broaden the target domain, because if a multi-item scale loses its uni-dimensionality it will be like a cart pulled by several horses into different directions. Thus, adding items to a scale not only lengthens the whole instrument—which is not necessarily good news in itself—but can also create sub-content domains in a single-concept domain (see e.g., John & Benet-Martínez, 2000; Hair, Black, Babin, Anderson, & Tatham, 2006). The technicalities of how to produce reliable multi-item scales will be discussed below in the section on "rating scales" (Section 2.4.1), and we will come back to the internal consistency reliability issue in Section 4.3.5.

In conclusion, because of the fallibility of single items, there is a general consensus among survey specialists that more than one item is needed to address each identified content area, all aimed at the same target but drawing upon slightly different aspects of it. How many is "more than one?" Professional attitude questionnaires focusing on a single target area (e.g., racial attitudes) can contain as many as 20 items, but in batteries which aim to target several issues far fewer items are used per scale. For example, one of the best-known standardized questionnaires in the L2 field, Robert Gardner's (1985) Attitude/Motivation Test Battery (AMTB), contains 4-10 items to measure each constituent multi-item scale. Generally speaking, it is risky to go below 3-4 items per sub-domain because if the *post hoc* item analysis (see Section 2.10.3) reveals that certain items did not work in the particular sample, their exclusion will result in too short (or single-item) scales.

Of course, nothing is perfect. While multi-item scales do a good job in terms of psychometric reliability, they may not necessarily appeal to the respondents. Ellard and Rogers (1993) report that respondents sometimes react negatively to items that appear to be asking the same question, because this gives them the impression that we are trying to "trick them or check their honesty" (p. 19). This problem, however, can be greatly reduced by using effective item-writing strategies (see Section 2.6 for a summary).

2.4 "Closed-Ended" Questionnaire Items

Let us start our exploration of the various types of questionnaire items by first examining the most frequent question type: *closed-ended* (or simply "closed") *questions*. Although this category subsumes several very different item types, these all share in common the fact that the respondent is provided with ready-made response options to choose from, normally by encircling or ticking one of them or by putting an "X" in the appropriate slot/box. That is, these items do not require the respondents to produce any free writing; instead, they are to choose one of the given alternatives, regardless of whether their preferred answer is among those or not.

The major advantage of closed-ended questions is that their coding and tabulation is straightforward and leaves no room for rater subjectivity. Accordingly, these questions are sometimes referred to as "objective" items. They are particularly suited for quantitative, statistical analyses (see Section 4.3) because the response options can easily be coded numerically and then entered into a computer database.

2.4.1 Rating Scales

Rating scales are undoubtedly the most popular items in research questionnaires. They require the respondent to make an evaluative judgment of the target by marking one of a series of categories organized into a *scale*. (Note that the term "scale" has, unfortunately, two meanings in measurement theory: one referring to a cluster of items measuring the same thing— see Section 2.3.2 on "multi-item scales"—and the other, discussed in this section, referring to a measurement procedure utilizing an ordered series of response categories.) The various points on the continuum of the scale indicate different degrees of a certain category; this can be of a diverse nature, ranging from various attributes (e.g., good → bad; frequent → rare) to intensity (e.g., very much → not at all) and opinion (e.g., strongly agree → strongly disagree). The points on the scale are subsequently assigned successive numbers, which makes their computer coding a simple task.

The big asset of rating scales is that they can be used for evaluating almost anything, and accordingly, as Aiken (1996) points out, these scales are second only to teacher-made achievement tests in the frequency of usage of all psychological measurement procedures. Indeed, I believe that few people in the teaching profession are unfamiliar with this item format: We are regularly asked to complete rating scales in various evaluation forms (of students, teachers, coursebooks, or courses), and outside the school context we also come across them frequently, for example, when asked about our opinions of certain services (e.g., in hotels, transport).

Likert Scales

The most commonly used scaling technique is the *Likert scale*, which has been named after its inventor, Rensis Likert. Over the past 70-plus years (Likert's original article came out in 1932) the number of research studies employing this technique has certainly reached a six-digit figure, which is due to the fact that the method is simple, versatile, and reliable.

Likert scales consist of a series of statements all of which are related to a particular target (which can be, among others, an individual person, a group of people, an institution, or a concept); respondents are asked to indicate the extent to which they *agree* or *disagree* with these items by marking (e.g., circling) one of the responses ranging from "strongly agree" to "strongly disagree." For example:

Hungarians are genuinely nice people.

Strongly disagree	Disagree	Neither agree nor disagree	Agree	Strongly agree

After the scale has been administered, each response option is assigned a number for scoring purposes (e.g., "strongly disagree" = 1, "strongly agree" = 5). With negatively worded items—that is, items which address the opposite of the target concept (see Section 2.6.2)—the scores are reversed before analysis (i.e., 5 becomes 1, 4 becomes 2, etc.). Finally, the scores for the items addressing the same target are summed up or averaged. Thus, Likert scales are multi-item scales, following a "summative model."

The statements on Likert scales should be *characteristic*, that is, expressing either a positive/favorable or a negative/unfavorable attitude toward the object of interest. Neutral items (e.g., *"I think Hungarians are all right"*) do not work well on a Likert scale because they do not evoke salient evaluative reactions; extreme items (e.g., *"Hungarians are absolutely brilliant!"*) are also to be avoided.

An important concern of questionnaire designers is to decide the *number of steps* or response options each scale contains. Original Likert scales contained five response options (as illustrated above), but subsequent research has also used two-, three-, four-, six-, and seven-response options successfully. It is fair to say that there is no absolute standard for the number of response options to be used on Likert scales (and on rating scales in general). However, too many scale points on a Likert scale will lead to unreliable responses for many respondents because they won't be able to clearly distinguish different levels of agreement/disagreement. The most common step numbers have been five or six, which raises a second important question: Shall we use an even or an odd number of steps?

Some researchers prefer using an even number of response options because of the concern that certain respondents might use the middle category ("neither agree nor disagree," "not sure," or "neutral") to avoid making a real choice. Providing an accurate answer often involves a fair amount of cognitive work, and therefore individuals who are less motivated to expend cognitive effort tend to take such a "satisfying" strategy (see Krosnick, 1999; Krosnick, Judd, & Wittenbrink, 2005). Besides, the middle category choice can also be related to the cultural characteristics of respondents. Chen, Lee, and Stevenson (1995), for example, report that Asian students tend to use the midpoint more often than their North American counterparts. In light of these considerations, my personal preference in the past has been to omit the "undecided" category and to use a six-point scale such as the one illustrated in Sample 2.3 (on page 21).

The final question regarding Likert scales concerns the format of the respondents' answers: How do various physical appearances such as encircling options or ticking boxes compare to each other? Nunnally (1978) states that such variations appear to make little difference in the important psychometric properties of ratings as long as the layout of the questionnaire is clear and there are sufficient instructions and examples to orientate the respondents.

Likert scales have been used successfully with younger children as well; in such cases the number of the response options is often reduced to three in order to mitigate the cognitive load and the options themselves are presented in a pictorial format instead of words. For example, in a three-point "smilegram" children are asked to check the box under the face that best expresses how they feel toward a target:

Variations on Likert Scales
Likert scales use response options representing the degree of agreement. This standard set of responses (i.e., strongly agree → strongly disagree) can be easily replaced by other descriptive terms that are relevant to the target. For example, Oxford's (1990) "Strategy Inventory for Language Learning" uses categories ranging from "Never or almost never true of me" to "Always or almost always true of me." Or, in Dörnyei and Clément's (2001) "Language Orientation Questionnaire" a five-point scale ranging from "Not at all true" to "Absolutely true" has been used to assess attitudes toward language learning.

While these variations usually work well, we need to be careful about how to aggregate item scores to obtain multi-item scale scores. Likert scale items that measure the same attitude can simply be summed up because they refer to the same target and it is assumed that a higher total score reflects a stronger endorsement of the target attitude. However, not every variation on Likert scales is summative in the psychometric sense. For example, in Oxford's (1990) learning strategy inventory mentioned above, the various items within a group ask about the frequency of the use of different strategies. In this case, summing up the items would imply that the more strategies a person uses, the more developed his/her strategic skills are in the particular area. However, with regard to learning strategies this is *not* the case, since it is the *quality* rather than the quantity of the strategies a person utilizes that matters: One can be a very competent strategy user by consistently employing one single strategy that particularly suits his/her abilities and learning style. Thus, in this case, the summation of different item scores is not related linearly to the underlying trait. (For a detailed discussion of this issue, see Tseng, Dörnyei, & Schmitt, 2006.)

Semantic Differential Scales

Instead of Likert scales we can also use *semantic differential scales* for certain measurement purposes. These are very useful in that by using them we can avoid writing statements (which is not always easy); instead, respondents are asked to indicate their answers by marking a continuum (with a tick or an "X") between two bipolar adjectives on the extremes. For example:

Listening comprehension tasks are:

difficult _____ : _____ : _____ : _____ : _____ : _X_ : _____ easy
useless _____ : _X_ : _____ : _____ : _____ : _____ : _____ useful

These scales are based on the recognition that most adjectives have logical opposites and, where an opposing adjective is not obviously available, one can easily be generated with "in-" or "un-" or by simply writing "not . . ." Although the scope of semantic differential scales is more limited than that of Likert scales, the ease of their construction and the fact that the method is easily adaptable to study virtually any concept, activity, or person may compensate for this. Oppenheim (1992) raises an interesting point concerning the content of semantic differential scales. He argues that it is possible and often useful to include adjective pairs that are seemingly inappropriate to the concept under consideration, such as masculine/feminine (with respect to a brand of cigarettes, for example) or rough/smooth (with respect to, say, Socialism): "By their more imaginative approach, such scales can be used to cover aspects that respondents can hardly put into words, though they do reflect an attitude or feeling" (p. 239). An additional bonus of semantic differential scales is that, because they involve little reading, very little testing time is required.

Semantic differential scales are similar to Likert scales in that several items are used to evaluate the same target, and multi-item scores are computed by summing up the individual item scores. An important technical point concerning the construction of such bipolar scales is that the position of the "negative" and "positive" poles, if they can be designated as such, should be varied (i.e., the positive pole should alternate between being on the right and the left sides) to avoid superficial responding or a position response set (Aiken, 1996).

Semantic differential scales have been around for almost 50 years and during this time several factor analytic studies have examined their content structure. The general conclusion is that there are three major factors of meaning involved in them:

- *evaluation*, referring to the overall positive meaning associated with the target (e.g., good-bad, wise-foolish, honest-dishonest);
- *potency*, referring to the target's overall strength or importance (e.g., strong-weak, hard-soft, useful-useless);
- *activity*, referring to the extent to which the target is associated with action (active-passive, tense-relaxed, quick-slow).

Scales are normally constructed to contain items focusing on each of the three dimensions; however, the items measuring the three evaluative aspects tend to correlate with each other.

Sample 2.4 Instructions for Semantic Differential Scales

The following section of the questionnaire aims at finding out about your ideas and impressions about SOMETHING. In answering the questions we would like to ask you to rate these concepts on a number of scales. These all have pairs of opposites at each end, and between these there are seven dashes. You are to place an "X" on one of the seven positions, indicating how you feel about the particular concept in view of the two poles. For example, if the scales refer to "listening comprehension tasks" and you find these rather useless and fairly easy, you can place the "X"s as follows:

Listening comprehension tasks are:

difficult ____ : ____ : ____ : ____ : ____ : _X_ : ____ easy
useless ____ : _X_ : ____ : ____ : ____ : ____: ____ useful

In the following items please place the "X"s rapidly and don't stop to think about each scale. We are interested in your immediate impression. Remember: This is not a test and there are no right or wrong answers. The "right" answer is the one that is true for you. Be sure to put an "X" on each scale. Thank you!

Numerical Rating Scales

Teenagers sometimes play a rating game whereby they evaluate on a scale of 1-10 the appearance and "sexiness" of the various girls/boys they see passing by in the street. They would be surprised to hear that what they are doing is applying *numerical rating scales*. These scales involve "giving so many marks out of so many," that is, assigning one of several numbers corresponding to a series of ordered categories describing a feature of the target. The popularity of this scaling technique is due to the fact that the rating continuum can refer to a wide range of adjectives (e.g., excellent → poor; conscientious → slapdash) or adverbs (e.g., always → never); in fact, numerical ratings can easily be turned into semantic differential scales and vice versa. Sample 2.2 on page 20 provides an example.

True-False Items

In some scales the designers only set two response options: true versus false (or "yes" or "no"), resulting in what is usually referred to as a *true-false item*. While generally it is true that the more options an item contains, the more accurate evaluation it yields, there might be cases when only such a polarized, yes-no decision can be considered reliable. For example, little children are sometimes seen as incapable of providing more elaborate ratings, and some personality test items also follow a true-false rating to ensure reliability in domains where the respondent may not be able to properly evaluate the degree to which a particular feature is present/true or not. In addition, with certain specific areas such as study habits, it may also be more appropriate to apply true/false items when the questions ask about occurrences of various behaviors in the past.

The key sentence (i.e., the one to be judged) in a good true-false item is relatively short and contains a single idea that is not subject to debate (i.e., it is either true or false). Due to the nature of the responses, the *acquiescence bias* (see Section 1.2.2)—that is, the tendency to respond in the affirmative direction when in doubt—may be a problem (Aiken, 1997). Because offering a polarized, black-and-white judgment can often be perceived as too forced, some scales include a middle position, involving an "undecided," "neutral," or "don't know" option.

Mixing Scale Types

Over the past 20 years I have seen in student manuscripts and journal submissions the use of many creative mixtures of scale types; for example, Likert scales in which the response options are offered in a semantic differential scale format ranging between "strongly disagree" and "strongly agree." Are such hybrids legitimate? The main principle underlying scale construction is to give respondents a way of marking their answers with the least possible cognitive effort and distraction involved so that the transformation process from their internal rating/response to the marked option in the questionnaire does not cause, or is not subject to, any systematic interference. Semantic differential scales offer a very effective visual marking option, but in order for this method to work it requires two powerful anchors at the two ends of the scale. In my view, the "strongly agree"-"strongly disagree" contrast is not quite robust enough to hang an item on, which is why proper Likert scales list all the response options (i.e., strongly disagree, disagree, etc.). Indeed, Krosnick (1999) also argues that the labeling of all the rating points tends to improve the validity of a scale.

On the other hand, in many countries that use numerical grading in the school system (e.g., instead of "A"s or "B"s they are given "5"s and "4"s), a numerical rating scale corresponding to the school rating scale may be an established and well-internalized way of appraisal in general, and it can therefore be combined with other assessment techniques to good effect. This is particularly so if the respondent population is cognitively mature and thus can cope with the process of transforming their responses into the specific rating scale options. In sum, we have quite a bit of flexibility in designing the exact scale format for our specific survey situation as long as we realize that the "pure" scale types have become so popular not because past scholars lacked the creativity to think of more cleverly blended mixtures but because of these scales' own considerable merits.

2.4.2 Multiple-Choice Items

Language researchers will be very familiar with the multiple-choice item format because of its popularity in standardized L2 proficiency testing. The item type can also be used in questionnaires with respondents being asked to mark—depending on the question—one or more options. If none of the items apply, the respondent may have the option to leave the question unanswered, but because this makes it difficult to decide later whether the omission of a mark was a conscious decision or just an accident it is better to include a "Don't know" and a "Not applicable" category (and sometimes even a "No response" option). Also, it is often desirable to ensure that an exhaustive list of categories is provided, and for this purpose it may be necessary to include an "Other" category, typically followed by an open-ended question of the "Please specify" sort (see Section 2.5.2).

Multiple choice items are relatively straightforward. It makes them more reader-friendly if we can make the response options shorter by including as much information as we can in the stem without repeating this every time. It also makes it easier to answer them if the response options have a natural order; otherwise they should be arranged in a random or alphabetical order. It is an obvious yet often violated rule that all options should be grammatically correct with respect to the stem. Finally, the use of negative expressions, such as "not," should be avoided in both the stem and the response options — a rule that generally applies to all question types (see Section 2.6.2).

Interestingly, multiple-choice items can also produce ordinal rather than nominal (categorical) data (see Section 4.3.4); that is, if the item is properly constructed, the various alternatives can represent *degrees* of an attitude, interest, and belief. Respondents are, then, instructed to choose only one of these options and their answers will be coded according to the value of the particular option they chose (e.g., Option A may be assigned "3" and Option D "1" depending on their content). Obviously the value of each option cannot be set in advance on a purely theoretical basis but can only be deduced from extensive pilot testing (see Section 2.10) whereby the items are administered to a group of respondents and the value of each response option is calculated on the basis of their answers (for examples of such "graded" multiple-choice items, see Sample 2.5).

Sample 2.5 Multiple-choice Attitude Items from the "Attitude/Motivation Test Battery" (Gardner, 1985, p. 181)

Scoring
Key

During French Class, I would like:

2   (a) to have a combination of French and English spoken.
1   (b) to have as much English as possible spoken.
3   (c) to have only French spoken.

If there were a French Club in my school, I would:

2   (a) attend meetings once in a while.
3   (b) be most interested in joining.
1   (c) definitely not join.

2.4.3 Rank Order Items

It is a common human mental activity to rank order people, objects, or even abstract concepts, according to some criterion, and *rank order items* in questionnaires capitalize on our familiarity with this process. As the name suggests, these items contain some sort of a list and respondents are asked to order the items by assigning a number to them according to their preferences. Wilson and McClean (1994) warn us that it may be very demanding to arrange items in order of importance whenever there are more than five ranks requested, and it has also been found, more generally, that rank order items impose a more difficult task on the respondent than single-response items. Furthermore, unlike in a rating scale in which a person can assign the same value to several items (e.g., one can mark "strongly agree" in all the items in a multi-item scale), in rank order items each sub-component must have a different value even though such a forced choice may not be natural in every case.

In my own research, I have tended to avoid rank order items because it is not easy to process them statistically. We cannot simply count the mean of the ranks for each item across the sample because the numerical values assigned to the items are not the same as in rating scales: They are only an easy technical method to indicate *order* rather than the *extent* of endorsement. That is, if something is ranked third, the value "3" does not necessarily mean that the degree of one's attitude is 3 out of, say, 5 (which would be the case in a Likert scale); it only means that the particular target's relevance/importance is, in the respondent's estimation, somewhere between the things ranked second and fourth; the actual value can be very near to the second and miles away from the fourth or vice versa. To illustrate this, let us take a short list of items that we may need for traveling abroad:

- passport;
- credit card;
- tickets;
- plumbing manual.

A "plumbing manual" would probably be ranked by everybody as the least necessary item in the list, but by assigning a value of "4" or "1" to it (depending on which end we start counting from) its value would be only one less (or more) than the next one in the list, whereas in reality its value for traveling purposes is next to zero (unless you are a plumber . . .).

2.4.4 Numeric Items

One item type that is seemingly open-ended but is, in effect, closed-ended can be labeled as a *numeric item*. These items ask for a specific numeric value, such as the respondent's age in years, or the number of foreign languages spoken by a person. What makes these items similar to closed questions is that we can anticipate the range of the possible answers and the respondent's task is to specify a particular value within the anticipated range. We could, in fact, list, for example for the "age" item, all the possible numbers (e.g., between 5 and 100) for the respondent to choose from (in a multiple-choice fashion) but this would not be space-economical. However, computerized, online questionnaires often do provide these options in a pull-down menu for the respondent to click on the selected answer.

While answering items of this type is straightforward, we sometimes need to carefully think about the way the respondent responds. Although being required to specify their value by a fixed unit, say month, some respondents tend to write the value in a different unit like week (e.g., an item asking about the length of stay abroad). In addition, some people hesitate to write their age in a blank; they usually prefer choosing a response, particularly one with a wider range. Thus, depending on research purposes and target subjects, we might consider replacing numeric items with predetermined response categories.

2.4.5 Checklists

Checklists are similar to rank order items in that they consist of a list of descriptive terms, attributes, or even objects, and respondents are instructed to mark the items on the list that apply to the particular question. For example, students might be asked to mark all the adjectives in a list of personality characteristics that describe their teacher. This evaluation would, then, yield a score for the teacher on each characteristic, indicating how many raters checked the particular adjective; that is, the person's score on each item can be set equal to the number of judges who checked it. In the teacher's case, a score of "0" on the "fairness" item would mean that nobody thinks that the teacher is fair (which would be problematic). Because—unless otherwise instructed—different respondents may check a different number of items (e.g., someone may check almost all the adjectives, whereas another rater might check only one), this response set can have a pronounced effect on the scores and therefore some sort of grouping or statistical control is frequently used (Aiken, 1996).

2.5 Open-Ended Questions

Open-ended questions include items where the actual question is not followed by response options for the respondent to choose from but rather by some blank space (e.g., dotted lines) for the respondent to fill. As we have seen in the previous chapter (in Section 1.3), questionnaires are not particularly suited for truly qualitative, exploratory research. Accordingly, they tend to have few open-ended questions and even the ones included are relatively short, with their "openness" somehow restricted. Questionnaires are not the right place for essay questions!

In spite of this inherent limitation of the questionnaire as a research instrument (namely that due to the relatively short and superficial engagement of the respondents it cannot aim at obtaining more than a superficial, "thin" description of the target), open-ended questions still have merits. Although we cannot expect any soul-searching self-disclosure in the responses, by permitting greater freedom of expression, open-format items can provide a greater "richness" than fully quantitative data. Open responses can yield graphic examples, illustrative quotes, and can also lead us to identify issues not previously anticipated. Furthermore, sometimes we need open-ended items for the simple reason that we do not know the range of possible answers and therefore cannot provide pre-prepared response categories. Oppenheim (1992) adds that in some cases there may actually be good reasons for asking the same question both in an open and closed form.

The other side of the coin is that open-ended questions have serious disadvantages, most notably the following two:

- They take up precious "respondent-availability time" and thus restrict the range of topics the questionnaire can contain.
- They are difficult to code in a reliable manner.

Because of these considerations, professional questionnaires tend not to include any real open-ended items; yet, my recommendation is that it might be worth experimenting with including some. I agree with Fowler (2002) that respondents often like to have an opportunity to express their opinions more freely and may find it frustrating to be completely limited to choosing from ready-made options (see Section 2.5.4 below).

I agree . . .

A few well-chosen quotations from our respondents can convey the flavor of responses far better than any other rhetorical device.

(Aldridge & Levine, 2001, p. 102)

Researchers agree that truly open questions (i.e., the ones that require quite a bit of writing) should be placed at the end rather than at the beginning of the questionnaire. In this way, they are not answered at the expense of the closed items: They do not discourage people from completing the questionnaire and do not prevent those who get bogged down with them from answering the other questions.

In my experience, open-ended questions work particularly well if they are not completely open but contain certain guidance. In the following we will look at four techniques to provide such guidance: *specific open questions, clarification questions, sentence completion items*, and *short-answer questions*.

2.5.1 Specific Open Questions

As the label suggests, *specific open questions* ask about concrete pieces of information, such as facts about the respondent, past activities, or personal preferences (e.g., *"Which is your favorite television program/weekend activity?" "What languages have you studied in the past?"*). They can normally be answered in one line, which is usually explicitly marked on the questionnaire (e.g., with dots). The answers can sometimes be followed up with a "Why?" question.

2.5.2 Clarification Questions

Certain answers may be potentially so important that it is worth attaching a clarification question to them, for example in a "routed" form:

> If you rated the coursebook you are using as "poor" or "very poor,"
> please briefly explain why. Write your answer here:
>
> -
> -

Clarification questions are also appropriate when there is an "Other" category in a multiple-choice item. Typically, "Please specify" is used and some space is left for the respondent to provide a statement.

2.5.3 Sentence Completion Items

A simple question is often less effective in eliciting a meaningful answer than an unfinished sentence beginning that the respondent needs to complete. I have successfully used this technique on various feedback forms in particular. A good sentence completion item should be worded so that it directs the respondent's attention to a well-defined issue/area. Sometimes respondents are asked not to "agonize" over the answers but jot down the first thing that comes to mind. For example:

One thing I liked about this activity is _____

_____

One thing I didn't like about this activity is _____

_____

I found this activity _____

_____

2.5.4 Short-Answer Questions

The term *short-answer questions* is sometimes used to distinguish these questions from "essay questions" (which are not recommended in ordinary questionnaires and therefore will not be discussed). Short-answer questions involve a real exploratory inquiry about an issue; that is, they require a more free-ranging and unpredictable response than the techniques described above. As Gillham (2008, p. 34) concludes, these questions:

> can be motivating for the respondent, and they enable the researcher to trawl for the unknown and the unexpected. One or two questions of this type can be a good way of finishing a questionnaire, which can otherwise easily leave respondents with the impression that their personal opinions or experiences have to fit the straitjacket of prescribed answers.

Gillham even recommends the inclusion of a completely open concluding question, such as, "*We have tried to make this questionnaire as com-prehensive as possible but you may feel that there are things we have missed out. Please write what you think below, using an extra page if necessary*" (pp. 34-35).

Good short-answer questions are worded in such a focused way that the question can be answered succinctly, with a "short answer"—this is usually more than a phrase and less than a paragraph (and certainly no more than two paragraphs). That is, short-answer questions do not ask about things in general, but deal with only one concept or idea. For example, rather than asking, "*What did you like about the workshop?*" it might be better to narrow down the question by asking, "*What was it you found most useful about the workshop?*"

One type of questionnaire that is almost always concluded by a few open-ended questions is college forms for students to evaluate their teachers/courses. A typical final sequence of questions is as follows: "*What were the most effective aspects of this course?*" "*What were the least effective aspects of this course?*" "*How could this course be further improved?*"

2.6 How to Write Good Items

Over the past 50 years, survey researchers have accumulated a considerable body of knowledge and experience about what makes a questionnaire item good and what the potential pitfalls are. However, most specialists also emphasize that question design is not a 100% scientific activity, because in order to write good items one also needs a certain amount of creativity and lots of common sense. Furthermore, alternative versions of questions must be rigorously piloted because, in the absence of hard and fast theoretical rules, "tests of practicability must play a crucial role in questionnaire construction" (Moser & Kalton, 1971, p. 350).

> **Well said . . .**
> The writing of successful attitude statements demands careful pilot work, experience, intuition and a certain amount of flair.
>
> (Oppenheim, 1992, p. 180)

In the following I will summarize the do's and don'ts of item writing. Most of the material will concern the most common question types, rating scale items.

2.6.1 Drawing Up an "Item Pool"

It is generally recommended by survey specialists that, when we get down to writing the actual items, we should start doing so without restricting ourselves to any number limitations. Let our imagination go free and create as many potential items as we can think of—the resulting collection of items is referred to as the *item pool*. This should include many more items than the final scales: Nunnally (1978) recommends at least one and a half to twice as many items, while DeVellis (2003) points out that in less established content areas an item pool with three or four times as many items as the final scale is not unusual.

During the generation of the item pool, successful item designers rely heavily on their own verbal creativity, but they also draw on two additional sources:

1. *Qualitative, exploratory data* gathered from respondents, such as *notes* taken during talks and brainstorming in focus or discussion groups; recorded unstructured/semi-structured *interviews*; and *student essays* written around the subject of the enquiry (see e.g., Tseng *et al.*, 2006). The best items are often the ones that sound as if they had been said by someone—so why not include phrases and sentences that *have*

indeed been said by real interviewees? (I will come back to this issue in Section 4.7.2, which addresses complementing questionnaire research with interview studies.)

2. *Borrowing questions* from established questionnaires. Questions that have been used frequently before must have been through extensive piloting and therefore the chances are that "most of the bugs will have been ironed out of them" (Sudman & Bradburn, 1983, p. 120). Of course, you will need to acknowledge the sources precisely. An important point to note here is that, even if we adopt most items from existing instruments, our questionnaire will still need to be piloted for the specific population that we intend to use it for (see Section 2.10).

Provided you acknowledge the sources . . .
The best advice we can offer to those starting out to write attitude questions is to plagiarize. While plagiarism is regarded as a vice in most matters, it is a virtue in questionnaire writing—assuming, of course, that you plagiarize good quality questions.

(Sudman & Bradburn, 1983, p. 119)

2.6.2 Rules About Writing Items
The questionnaire items are the principal means for the researcher to communicate with the respondents and, therefore, at the end of the day everything is dependent on the quality of item design. Here is a list of strategies of producing items that work.

Aim for Short and Simple Items
Whenever possible, questionnaire items should be short, rarely exceeding 20 words. They should preferably be written in simple sentences rather than compound or complex sentences, and each should contain only one complete thought.

Quite so!
Short questions are good questions.

(Brown, 2001, p. 45)

Use Simple and Natural Language
As a rule, in questionnaire items we should always choose the simplest way to say something. Items need to be kept clear and direct, without any acronyms, abbreviations, colloquialisms, proverbs, jargon, or technical terms. We should try to speak the "common language" and find synonyms for the

"polysyllabic and Latinate constructions that come easily to the tongue of the college educated" (Converse & Presser, 1986, p. 10).

Oppenheim (1992) argues that the most important rule in writing rating scale statements is to make them *meaningful* and *interesting* to the respondents. As he points out, "There are many attitude scales which falter because the items have been composed in the office according to some theoretical plan and fail to arouse much interest in the respondents" (p. 179). The best items are the ones that sound as if they had been taken from actual interviews, and Oppenheim encourages item writers not to refrain from using contentiously worded statements that include phrases relating to feelings, wishes, fears, and happiness.

Avoid Ambiguous or Loaded Words and Sentences
It goes without saying that any elements that might make the language of the items unclear or ambiguous need to be avoided. The most notorious of such elements are:

- Non-specific adjectives or adverbs (e.g., "good," "easy," "many," "sometimes," "often").
- Items containing universals such as "all," "none," "never."
- Modifying words such as "only," "just," "merely"—these should be used with moderation.
- Words having more than one meaning.
- Loaded words (e.g., "democratic," "modern," "natural," "free," etc.), because they may elicit an emotional reaction that may bias the answer.

It is also obvious that pointed or loaded questions such as *"Isn't it reasonable to suppose that . . .?"* or *"Don't you believe that . . .?"* are likely to bias the respondent toward giving a desired answer and should be rephrased in a neutral way.

Avoid Negative Constructions
Items that contain a negative construction (i.e., including "not," "doesn't," or "don't") are deceptive because, although they read OK, responding to them can be problematic. Let us take a simple statement such as *"Our language classes don't prepare us for everyday communication."* Even a straightforward agreement with this claim is less than straightforward, because in a conversation we would probably concur using a negative construction (*"No, they don't"*), whereas in the questionnaire we need to agree affirmatively. However, computing in our heads the meaning of various degrees of disagreements with a negative statement is cognitively quite demandring (e.g., what exactly does moderate disagreement with a negative

item mean?), which means that some respondents will inevitably get it wrong. This, in turn, will reduce the item's reliability. In order to avoid any such difficulties, the best solution is to simply avoid the use of negatives altogether. In most cases negative items can be restated in a positive way by using verbs or adjectives that express the opposite meaning (e.g., "dislike" instead of "not like").

Avoid Double-Barreled Questions

Double-barreled questions are those that ask two (or more) questions in one, while expecting a single answer. For example, the question *"How are your parents?"* asks about one's mother and father, and cannot be answered simply if one of them is well and the other unwell, or if there are step-parents involved. Indeed, questions dealing with pluralisms (children, students) often yield double-barreled questions, but compound questions also often fall into this category (e.g., *"Do you always write your homework and do it thoroughly?"*). Even if respondents do provide an answer to a double-barreled question, there is no way of knowing which part of the question the answer concerned.

Avoid Items That Are Likely to Be Answered the Same Way by Everybody

In rating scales we should avoid statements that are likely to be endorsed by almost everyone or almost no one. In most cases these items are not informative and they are certainly difficult if not impossible to process statistically. Here is an example from my own research (Dörnyei & Clément, 2001): A questionnaire item asked students to rate the international role/ importance of six countries, including the United States. As can be imagined, most respondents gave the US the top score. However, as we found out in the analyses, this did not provide enough variance to compute certain statistical results involving this item, and in some cases—when in a particular subgroup (e.g., a class group) every single person gave the top score—the computer treated the responses as missing data because of the total lack of variance.

Include Both Positively and Negatively Worded Items

In order to avoid a response set in which the respondents mark only one side of a rating scale, it is worth including in the questionnaire both positively and negatively worded items. In addition, a balanced mixture might also reduce the harmful effects of the "acquiescence bias" (see Section 1.2.2). The term "negatively worded item" means that it focuses on negative rather than positive aspects of the target (e.g., instead of *"I don't enjoy learning English,"* we can write *"Learning English is a burden for me"*). Warning: It is all too easy to fall into the trap of trying to express a negative aspect by using a negative construction, which is a practice that I have argued against above. Furthermore, I have found that even some carefully designed and seemingly fine "negatively worded items" had to be excluded from the questionnaire because an item analysis (see Section 2.10.3) revealed that they did not work in a reliable manner.

Write Translatable Items

It often happens in L2 studies that researchers construct a questionnaire in one language first and then translate it into the mother tongue of the particular respondent sample (e.g., in cross-cultural comparisons or with multi-ethnic research teams). It soon becomes clear during this process that some items lend themselves to be converted into the target language more than others. While the issue of translation will be addressed later, in Section 2.8, let us look at a set of guidelines by Brislin (1986) on how to write translatable English items. Of course, all the general rules of item design discussed above apply here too, but Brislin also mentions the following special suggestions:

- Employ the active rather than the passive voice so that meanings become clearer.
- Repeat nouns instead of using pronouns to avoid vague referents.
- Avoid metaphors and colloquialisms.
- Avoid the subjective mood (e.g., "could," "would"), because these terms are less likely to be readily available in other languages.
- Use specific rather than general terms (e.g., "cows" and "chickens" rather than "livestock."

Ellard and Rogers' (1993, p. 17) "Ten Commandments of Question Writing"

I. Thou shalt not create double-barreled items.
II. Thou shalt not use "no" and "not" or words beginning with "un."
III. Thou shalt match the vocabulary used in items to the vocabulary of those who will respond to them.
IV. Thou shalt not use complex grammatical forms.
V. Thou shalt have 40% to 60% true- or agree-keyed items.
VI. Thou shalt not use redundant or irrelevant items.
VII. Thou shalt not permit any loaded questions to appear in your questionnaire.
VIII. Thou shalt not mix response formats within a set of questions.

IX.   Thou shalt not permit a non-committal response.

X.   Thou shalt pre-test questions before collecting data.

2.6.3 Writing Sensitive Items

If the previous section has (hopefully) shown that writing effective questionnaire items requires special attention to detail, then this is even more so when writing *sensitive items*; that is, questions targeting issues that are not easy to talk about because they may ask about *confidential personal information, undesirable social behavior*, or information that might pose a *potential threat* to the respondent.

Confidential Personal Information

With regard to questions that ask about *personal information* that is usually considered private, the best advice is that the fewer of them, the better. If they are really necessary for the survey, then some sort of a justification and a renewed promise of confidentiality are in order (e.g., *"Finally, in order to help us to better interpret and classify your answers, would you mind telling us more about your personal and language learning background?"*). A story I heard from someone a couple of days ago underlines the stakes here: This person described how he had diligently filled in a lengthy questionnaire just to throw it in the bin when he got to the final section and found that some of the questions asked about his personal life.

> **Quite so!**
> Classification questions . . . need a special introduction. After all, a respondent who agrees to answer questions about his leisure pursuits or to give his opinion about television may legitimately wonder why he should supply details about his family, his age, his education, his occupation, and even his income.
>
> (Moser & Kalton, 1971, p. 316)

Undesirable Social Behavior

With regard to answers that the respondent considers likely to meet with *disapproval*, several strategies have been suggested in the literature. Wilson and McClean (1994) recommend that they can be diffused by the use of ready-made categories for the respondents to tick. In their seminal book on questionnaire design, Sudman and Bradburn (1983) devote a great deal of space to discussing sensitive items. Their practical suggestions to mitigate the undesirable nature of certain behaviors include:

- Wording the question in a way that it suggests that the behavior is rather common (e.g., *"Even the most conscientious teachers sometimes . . .".*).
- Assuming the occurrence of the behavior and asking about frequencies or other details rather than whether the behavior has occurred (e.g., *"When was the last time that you were late for school?"*).
- Using authority to justify behavior (e.g., *"Many researchers now think . . ."*).
- Adopting a "casual approach" (e.g., *"Did you happen to . . .?"*).
- Including reasons that explain the behavior (e.g., *"Does your busy schedule sometimes prevent you from . . .?"* or *"Have you had time to . . . recently?"*).

Aiken (1997) further suggests that phrasing the question in a way that it refers to "other people" can encourage truthful responses, and the perceived importance of sensitive questions can also be reduced if they are embedded among other questions dealing with both sensitive and non-sensitive topics.

Potential Threat

With regard to items in which an honest answer can pose some *real threat* to the respondent (e.g., questions about illegal activities, or asking students to evaluate their language teacher), the main task is to convince the respondents that their answers will remain confidential. Obviously, offering complete anonymity in such cases might be helpful, but this may not be feasible in certain complex research projects where we need to match the data with information obtained from other sources (see Section 2.1.3). In such cases the important point to emphasize is that the responses will be treated in complete confidentiality, with no chance for them to be seen by unwanted people. In a classroom study already mentioned (Clément *et al.*, 1994), where a questionnaire was administered to secondary school students that asked them to evaluate both their L2 teacher and the L2 course, we successfully applied three confidence-building strategies:

- The questionnaire administrator was a representative of the university and thus external to the school — a fact that was sufficiently emphasized.
- We handed out envelopes in which students put their completed questionnaires and which they then sealed.
- The questionnaire administrator went around the classroom and stamped the envelopes with a university stamp on the seals.

Some questions can pose a threat not only to the respondent but also to the people or institutions that the questionnaire is about. For example, few teachers are likely to be happy to allow the administration of a questionnaire in their classes that explicitly asks the students to evaluate the quality of their teaching. Interestingly, Gardner and Smythe (1981) report that educational institutions found semantic differential scales (see Section 2.4) less objectionable than complete evaluative statements when talking about such sensitive issues. It seems that the fact that these items do not spell out the issues in detail but only provide pairs of bipolar adjectives make them less offensive.

2.7 Grouping and Sequencing Items

Once all the items to be included in the questionnaire have been written or collected, we need to decide on their order. Item sequence is a significant factor because the context of a question can have an impact on its interpretation and the response given to it. Indeed, the meaning of almost any question can be altered by the adjacent questions. However, it is usually acknowledged that research has not as yet generated any specific theoretical rules for ordering questions, beyond some broad suggestions (Robson, 2002). Let us have a look at the four main ordering principles.

2.7.1 Clear and Orderly Structure

The most important aspect of sequencing questions is to ensure that the respondents' overall impression is that the structure is well organized and orderly. If the ordering of questions is unpredictable or seemingly haphazard, it will frustrate respondents and make the study appear ill-considered and amateurish (Newell, 1993). Neither the content nor the style of the questionnaire should "jump around" (Aiken, 1997)—the items should seem as a series of logically organized sequences. To achieve this, we need to follow certain organizing principles.

One organizing principle should be the *item format*. If the questionnaire contains items of different types, these need to be clustered together into well-marked sub-sections, separated from each other by a clear set of instructions to highlight the format change for the respondent. Similarly, questions that deal with the same *broad topic* should be grouped together. In order to make the progression from topic to topic smoother, we may include short linking sentences such as *"In this section we'll move on to look at another aspect of . . ."* Content-based organization, however, does not mean that the items in a multi-item scale (see Section 2.3.2) should be next to each other—the repetitive content may frustrate the respondents. The items from different scales need to be mixed up as much as possible to create a sense of variety and to prevent respondents from simply repeating previous answers. What I usually do is take four or five content areas that are related to each other and then mix up the constituent items randomly.

2.7.2 Opening Questions

Similar to any other piece of writing, the initial section of a questionnaire is particularly important in that it sets the tone. This is partly the reason that instructions (see Sections 2.2.2 and 3.3.8) play a significant role, and this is also why the first few "opening" questions should be carefully selected. In particular, we need to be careful not to force the respondents to take fundamental decisions at such an early stage because that would affect all the subsequent answers (see the "halo effect" in Section 1.2.2). In order to create a pleasant first impression, the starter questions need to be interesting, somewhat simple, focused on a relatively mild or neutral aspect, and certainly not threatening or sensitive.

2.7.3 Factual (or "Personal" or "Classification") Questions at the End

As Oppenheim (1992) concludes, novice researchers typically start to design a questionnaire by putting a rather forbidding set of questions at the top of a blank sheet of paper, such as asking for the participant's name, address, gender, profession, highest level of education, and so on. These personal/ classification questions tend to be very off-putting: Having been through the various introductory phases, respondents are now ready to look at some interesting questions dealing with the topic of the study. Instead, they are faced with a set of "personal" questions not unlike those contained in the many bureaucratic forms we have to fill in when, for example, applying for a passport or registering in a hotel. This can result in a kind of anticlimax in the respondents and it may be difficult to rekindle their enthusiasm again. Thus, such personal questions are best left at the end of the questionnaire.

There is also a second reason why factual questions should not be introduced too early, and this concerns their sensitive nature. As discussed earlier (in Sections 2.1.3 and 2.6.3), in many cultures issues like age, level of education, or marital status are personal and private matters, and if we ask them near the beginning of the questionnaire they might create some resistance in the respondents ("*What business of yours is this . . .?*"), or, in cases where respondents are asked to provide their name, this might remind them of the non-anonymous nature of the survey, which in turn may inhibit some of their answers.

2.7.4 Open-Ended Questions at the End

We saw in Section 2.5 that if we include real open-ended questions that require substantial and creative writing, it is preferable to place them near the end rather than at the beginning of the questionnaire. In this way, their potential negative consequences—for example, the required work can put some people off and others might get bogged down and spend most of the available time and mental energy agonizing over what they should write—will not affect the previous items. In addition, some people find it psychologically more acceptable to put in the necessary work to answer an open question if they have already invested in the questionnaire and if they know that this is the final task. Even so, however, we should be prepared that the ratio of appropriate completion of open-ended questions tends to be relatively low compared with closed-ended items; therefore, such questions should be seen as additional "bonuses" to the dataset rather than an integral part of the expected results.

2.8 Translating the Questionnaire

The issue of how to translate questionnaires from one language to another has typically been marginalized and treated as an addendum in questionnaire design. This is also evidenced by the (regrettable) fact that the first edition of this book did not contain a section addressing this issue. In contrast, translating questionnaires as a practice is surprisingly common, due to the fact that (a) many of the available established L2 questionnaires are published in English; (b) cross-cultural studies often require the administration of the same instrument to samples of different ethnolinguistic origin; and (c) there are many multi-national research teams (including supervisor-research student teams) that prepare the original version of a questionnaire in one language (often English) before it is translated into the language(s) of the participants.

Quite so!

The effort and cost of producing and testing translations are small, compared to the financial investment made in developing and fielding instruments. In contrast, the price to be paid for poor translation can be high.

(Harkness, 2008a, p. 68)

49

The basic assumption underlying this widespread translation practice is the belief that the quality of the obtained data increases if the questionnaire is presented in the respondents' own mother tongue. It follows from this that the translated version of a questionnaire is usually the only version that the respondents see. I suspect that this point is frequently overlooked or insufficiently reflected by the amount of attention we pay to producing the translation. Thus, I have come to believe that translation issues should be taken more seriously than they typically are, and I am in full agreement with Harkness's claim that "Poor translations can rob researchers of the chance to ask the questions they intend and need to ask" (p. 68).

Well . . .
Because survey questions often look deceptively simple, the temptation
to do-it-yourself may also be high.

(Harkness, 2008a, p. 68)

In L2 studies, most research teams have at least one member who speaks the L2 of the participant sample they want to investigate, and the usual practice is for this person to prepare the final translation of the instrument. Once this has been done, the questionnaire is administered without any further ado. This practice is understandable: We are reluctant to invest effort, time, and money in the translation process since our resources are limited, particularly because this "do-it-yourself" practice appears to work well. However, once the data have been collected, problems often start to emerge with some items—and often even whole scales—not working as well as expected, and *post hoc* analyses often find the source of the issue at the level of translation. Unfortunately, at that stage there is very little the researchers can do beyond excluding the items in question. In the following, I present an elaborate team-based approach developed in a European project that can be seen as a model for best practice, and then discuss some general principles and techniques to be applied even if we have (as most of us do) limited resources only.

2.8.1 Translation as a Team-Based Approach

In a detailed description of the translation strategies and procedures used in a large-scale European research project, "The European Social Survey" (www.europeansocialsurvey.org/), Harkness (2008b) recommends a *committee-based translation approach* in producing the final version of a translated questionnaire. The proposed committee structure consists of three different sets of people:

- *Translators*, who are skilled practitioners with training in translating questionnaires and who are preferably native speakers.
- *Reviewers*, who also have good translation skills as well as familiarity with questionnaire design principles and with the research topic (if we cannot find a single person with these skills, two could cover the different aspects).
- *Adjudicators*, who are responsible for the final decisions about which translation options to adopt. They, too, need to understand the research subject, know about the survey design, and be proficient in the languages involved.

The translation framework adopted by the European Social Survey includes five interrelated procedures: translation, review, adjudication, pretesting, and documentation (or "TRAPD"). The central component of the process is that each questionnaire is translated by at least two translators in a parallel manner; their output is then discussed at a "reconciliation meeting" attended by a reviewer, and finally the adjudicator (who can also be a reviewer) signs off the final agreed version. Thus, the process is designed to include several people with well-defined roles going though the text more than once and then producing a negotiated final product (for further details, see Harkness, 2008b).

2.8.2 Translation with Limited Resources

While a structured team-based approach provides ideal opportunities to handle potential problems and translation blind spots such as idiosyncratic interpretation and unnaturalness of the translated language, in most research projects we simply do not have such multiple expertise available and thus need to make compromises. The main challenge in translating a questionnaire is to reconcile two somewhat contradictory criteria: (a) the need to produce a close translation of the original text so that we can claim that the two versions are equivalent, and (b) the need to produce natural-sounding texts in the target language, similar to the words people would actually say (see Section 2.6.2). For most parts of the questionnaire we are likely to find easy solutions to this challenge, but there will be a few places where a close or literal translation will not express the real meaning and the pragmatic function of the text well. This is the point where team-based brainstorming and negotiation would be particular useful, and even in small-scale projects we should make an effort to recruit some competent (temporary) help to deal with these problem issues.

After the initial translation is completed, it is necessary to ensure the equivalence of the two versions. We have two basic options to do so: To consult *external reviewers* or to recruit an independent translator to *back-translate* the target language version into the source language (Brislin, 1970). The first option can be combined with the initial piloting of the questionnaire (see Section 2.10.1): One group of people, who are specialists in both the target and the source language, assess the equivalence of the original and the translated questionnaires, while another group of people, ideally people similar to the target population, check the naturalness of the translation. The second option, back-translation, involves an independent translator turning the L2 version of the questionnaire back into the source language and then comparing the two texts: If the back-translated version corresponds with the source language version, this is an indication that both instruments are asking the same questions, which attests to the accuracy of the translation (for an example of back-translated items, see Illustration 5.6 on p. 127).

2.9 Computer Programs for Constructing Questionnaires

Because market research—a booming business area—utilizes questionnaires for various types of surveys, several software companies have developed commercial computer programs to cater to these needs: Currently there are over 30 available desktop packages that combine questionnaire design, data collection, and data analysis. However, as Macer (1999) summarizes, few packages rise to the challenge of each stage in the process with the same degree of accomplishment, and development effort often tends to gravitate to some areas at the expense of others. For comprehensive listings and descriptions of the programs on the market, see for example the Research Software Central database (www.meaning.uk.com/rscentral/index.html) or the database of the Association for Survey Computing (UK), which contains a classified listing of over 130 software packages related to survey research, with attributes and suppliers (www.asc.org.uk/Register/index.htm).

Here I introduce one computer program that I am familiar with: *Sphinx Survey* (www.sphinxsurvey.com/en/home/home_sphinx.php), which is an integrated, PC-based Windows package for conducting questionnaire-based surveys (for a review, see Macer, 1999). It has built-in functions to help the user to design and print professional questionnaires with ease. The program can handle a variety of question types, including open and closed questions. Similar questions can be grouped and conditional jumps can be defined to permit complex question routings (e.g., if people answer "yes" to Question

X, they should move to Question Y). In addition, extensive question libraries can be developed and used to aid the preparation of an item pool.

Sphinx Survey is certainly a useful tool in providing a computerized framework for quick and professional questionnaire construction (the data processing functions of the program will be analyzed in Section 4.5). The novice researcher will find various ready-made options to choose from by simply clicking on items in the menu. The display format is quite flexible and the final result is fairly attractive. Because of the paramount importance of the appropriate layout (see Section 2.1.2), I would still design the final version of a questionnaire on a more powerful word processor, but in many situations the available formats are sufficient.

In addition to computer software designed to create paper-and-pencil questionnaires, there is a growing number of online, web-based survey services that researchers can use for a subscription fee (even *Sphinx Survey* has developed its online version since the first edition of this book). Wright (2005) offers a review of the following 20 of the more prominent packages and services, along with their URL addresses: Active Websurvey, Apian Software, CreateSurvey, EZSurvey, FormSite, HostedSurvey, InfoPoll, InstantSurvey, KeySurvey, Perseus, PollPro, Quask, Ridgecrest, SumQuest, SuperSurvey, SurveyCrafter, SurveyMonkey, SurveySite, WebSurveyor, Zoomerang. For a comprehensive list please refer to a dedicated website of the University of Ljubljana, Slovenia—www.websm.org—which lists more than 350 products related to web surveys as well an excellent up-to-date bibliography on the topic.

While the general features of web-based questionnaires are the same as those of their paper-and-pencil-based counterparts, online instruments have certain advantages: They can be more compact because of the use of pull-down menus of possible responses and they can be programmed to prevent the respondent from skipping a response, thereby excluding any missing data. This, however, can backfire because some respondents might not answer the questions seriously in order to get to the end as soon as possible or, alternatively, might even abandon the whole questionnaire. Web-based instruments can also incorporate rich visual content (e.g., images, diagrams, video clips, etc.) which would be almost impossible to integrate into a paper-based questionnaire (Tourangeau, 2004). Potaka (2008) offers a very useful overview of the various design options available for researchers. (I will come back to the question of online administration of surveys in Section 3.2.4.)

2.10 Piloting the Questionnaire and Conducting Item Analysis

Because, as we have seen, in questionnaires so much depends on the actual wording of the items (even minor differences can change the response pattern), an integral part of questionnaire construction is "field testing," that is, *piloting* the questionnaire at various stages of its development on a sample of people who are similar to the target sample the instrument has been designed for. These trial runs allow the researcher to collect feedback about how the instrument works and whether it performs the job it has been designed for. Based on this information, we can make alterations and fine-tune the final version of the questionnaire.

> **Well . . .**
> If you do not have the resources to pilot-test your questionnaire, don't do the study.
>
> (Sudman & Bradburn, 1983, p. 283)

The pilot test can highlight questions:

- whose wording may be ambiguous;
- which are too difficult for the respondents to reply to;
- which may, or should be, eliminated because, contrary to the initial expectations, they do not provide any unique information or because they turn out to measure something irrelevant;
- which—in the case of open-ended questions—are problematic for coding into a small set of meaningful categories.

Piloting can also indicate problems or potential pitfalls concerning:

- the administration of the questionnaire;
- the scoring and processing of the answers.

Valuable feedback can also be gained about:

- the overall appearance of the questionnaire;
- the clarity of the instructions;
- the appropriateness of the cover letter (if there is one);
- the length of time necessary to complete the instrument.

Finally, this is also the phase when omissions in the coverage of content can be identified.

The importance of the piloting is in sharp contrast with reality; in fact, many researchers completely omit the pilot stage from their research design.

Although this is understandable from a personal point of view because researchers at this stage are eager to get down to the survey and see the results, from a measurement perspective this practice is untenable. Regardless of how experienced the questionnaire designer is, any attempt to shortcut the piloting stage will seriously jeopardize the psychometric quality of the questionnaire. Furthermore, my personal experience is that patiently going through the careful editing procedures can save us a great deal of frustration and possible extra work later on.

Sometimes the omission of the pilot stage is not due to the lack of will or interest but rather to insufficient time. To do it well, piloting takes up a substantial period, which has often not been allowed for in the timing of the overall research design. As we will see below, piloting is a stepwise process that, when properly done, can take several weeks to complete. This is usually much more than was originally intended for this phase of the research.

Absolutely!
Questionnaires do not emerge fully-fledged; they have to be created or adapted, fashioned and developed to maturity after many abortive test flights. In fact, every aspect of a survey has to be tried out beforehand to make sure that it works as intended.

(Oppenheim, 1992, p. 47)

So when and what shall we pilot? While it is useful to have "ongoing piloting" by continuously discussing every aspect of the questionnaire design with a colleague or a friend, there are two key points where a more formal trial run is needed: (1) once the item pool has been completed, and (2) when a complete, almost final version of the questionnaire has been prepared.

2.10.1 Initial Piloting of the Item Pool
The first time in the questionnaire construction process that some external feedback is indispensable is when we have prepared an initial item pool, that is, an extensive list of possible items (see Section 2.6.1), and we are ready to reduce the number of questions to the intended final number. The initial piloting of the item pool usually consists of the following steps:

- Select three or four people who are motivated to spend some time to help you and whose opinion you value. Some of them should not be specialists in the field—they are very useful in locating unnecessary jargon; others may be people who are accustomed to survey research or who know the target population well. In any case, as Converse and Presser (1986) so realistically state, at this stage we are likely to end up with "that familiar source of forced labor—colleagues, friends, and family" (p. 53).

- Ask them to go through the items and answer them, and then to provide feedback about their reactions and the answers they have given. The best method to conduct this phase is for you to be present while they are working: This way you can observe their reactions (e.g., hesitations or uncertainties) and can note and respond to any spontaneous questions or comments.
- Once they have gone through all the items, you may ask for any general comments and can initiate a brainstorming session.

It may be useful to provide your pilot group with certain basic guidelines to focus on. These can include the following:

- They should mark any items whose wording they don't like; if they can suggest an improvement, so much the better!
- They should mark any items whose meaning is not 100% clear; again, suggestions are welcome.
- They should mark any items that they consider unnecessary.
- They should try and think of anything else that might be worth asking about.

Very important!
You may find that you have put so much personal time and effort into developing the questionnaire that it becomes "your baby." If someone is subsequently critical of it, you may find yourself reacting as if you have been personally attacked. Perhaps, rule number one in the critiquing/ revision process is that the creator should never take the criticism personally.

(Brown, 2001, p. 62)

2.10.2 Final Piloting ("Dress Rehearsal")

Based on the feedback received from the initial pilot group we can normally put together a near-final version of the questionnaire that "feels" OK and that does not have any obvious glitches. However, we still do not know how the items will work in actual practice, that is, whether the selected respondents will reply to the items in the manner intended by the questionnaire designers. There is only one way to find out: by administering the questionnaire to a group of respondents who are in every way similar to the target population the instrument was designed for. This is usually an "undeclared" pre-test whereby the respondents are not told that this is a questionnaire under construction (Converse & Presser, 1986).

How big should this final pilot group be? The typical sample size at this stage is around 100 (± 20), but for statistical reasons the pilot sample should not be smaller than 50. This number will allow the researcher to conduct some meaningful item analysis, which is the next, and final, step in the questionnaire construction process. If the sample size is too small, the results may be unstable due to the idiosyncratic composition of the respondent group, which may lead to the exclusion of potentially good items (DeVellis 2003). Of course, if this piloting phase does not result in any major changes in the instrument, it may be possible to use at least some of the obtained data for the purpose of the "real" investigation.

2.10.3 Item Analysis

Item analysis can be conducted at two different points in the survey process:

- After the final piloting stage—in this case, the results are used to fine-tune and finalize the questionnaire.
- After the administration of the final questionnaire—such a "*post hoc* analysis" is useful to screen out any items that have not worked properly.

The procedures in both cases are similar and usually involve checking three aspects of the response pattern:

1. *Missing responses* and possible signs that the instructions were not understood correctly. If some items are left out by several respondents, that should serve as an indication that something is not right: Perhaps the item is too difficult, too ambiguous, or too sensitive; or perhaps its location in the questionnaire is such that it is easily overlooked. Also, a careful visual examination of the completed questionnaires might reveal some further response irregularities, for example in the way respondents marked their answers.
2. The *range of the responses* elicited by each item. It was argued in Section 2.6.2 that we should avoid including items that are endorsed by almost everyone or by almost no one, because they are difficult if not impossible to process statistically (since statistical procedures require a certain amount of variation in the scores). Although, as Brown (2001)

remarks, the lack of variation may well be the true state of affairs in the group, it may be useful in many cases to increase item variation by adding additional response categories or rewording the question.

3. The *internal consistency* of multi-item scales. The gist of Section 2.3.2 was that—for the sake of reducing the unpredictable impact of any idiosyncratic item wording and ensuring comprehensive content coverage—questionnaires should contain multi-item scales, rather than single items, to focus on any particular content domain. It is obvious, however, that multi-item scales are only effective if the items within a scale work together in a homogeneous manner, that is, if they measure the same target area. In psychometric terms this means that each item on a scale should correlate with the other items and with the total scale score, which has been referred to as Likert's criterion of "Internal Consistency" (Anderson, 1985). Following this principle, a simple way of selecting items for a scale is to compute correlation coefficients for each potential item with the total scale score and to retain the items with the highest correlations. There are also other, more sophisticated statistical methods to check and improve internal consistency—these will be summarized in Section 4.3.5.

A word of caution: Before we discard an item on the basis of the item analysis, we should first consider how the particular item fits in with the overall content area of the whole scale. Automatic exclusion of an item suggested by the computer may lead to narrowing down the scope of the content area too much (see Section 2.3.2). If a problem item represents an important dimension of the targeted domain, we should try and alter its wording or replace it with an alternative item rather than simply delete it.

CHAPTER 3

Administering the Questionnaire

One area in which a questionnaire study can go very wrong concerns the procedures used to *administer* the questionnaire. Strangely enough, this aspect of survey research has hardly ever been discussed in the L2 literature—questionnaire administration is often considered a mere technical issue relegated to the discretion of the research assistants or voluntary helpers. This is wrong; there is ample evidence in the measurement literature that questionnaire administration procedures play a significant role in affecting the quality of the elicited responses. In this chapter, I will first look at the selection of an appropriate *sample*, then discuss the various *types* of questionnaire administration and the *strategies* that can be employed to promote positive questionnaire attitudes and involvement on the part of the respondents. Finally, I will address the issue of *confidentiality/anonymity* and other *ethical responsibilities* survey researchers have.

3.1 Selecting the Sample

The most frequent question asked by novice researchers who are planning to use questionnaires in their investigation is *"How many people do I need to survey?"* In measurement terms this question can be formulated as *"How large should my sample be?"* And a second question to follow is *"What sort of people shall I select?"* Or, in other words, *"Who shall my sample consist of?"* Let us start answering these key questions with the latter pair.

3.1.1 Sampling Procedures

Broadly speaking, the *sample* is the group of people whom researchers actually examine and the *population* is the group of people whom the survey is about. For example, the population in a study might be EFL learners in Taiwanese secondary schools and the actual sample might involve three Taiwanese secondary classes. That is, the target population of a study consists of all the people to whom the survey's findings are to be applied or generalized.

Why don't we include every member of the population in the survey? This is a valid question and, indeed, there is one particular survey type where we do just that: the "census." In most other cases, however, investigating the whole population is not necessary and would in fact be a waste of resources. By adopting appropriate *sampling procedures* to select a smaller number of people to be questioned we can save a considerable amount of time, cost, and effort and can still come up with accurate results—opinion polls, for example, succeed in providing national projections based on as few as 1,000-3,000 respondents. The key question, then, is what we mean by "appropriate sampling procedures."

A good sample is very similar to the target population in its most important general characteristics (e.g., age, gender, ethnicity, educational background, academic capability, social class, or socioeconomic status, etc.) and in all the more specific features that are known to be significantly related to the items included on the questionnaire (e.g., L2 learning background or the amount and type of L2 instruction received). That is, the sample is a subset of the population which is *representative* of the whole population. Sampling procedures have been designed to ensure this representativeness. The issue of representativeness is crucial, because the strength of the conclusions we can draw from the results obtained from a selected small group depends on how accurately the particular sample represents the larger population.

Broadly speaking, sampling strategies can be divided into two groups: (a) scientifically sound "probability sampling," which involves complex and expensive procedures that provide a truly representative sample; and (b) "non-probability sampling," which consists of a number of strategies that try to achieve a trade-off, that is, a reasonably representative sample using resources that are within the means of the ordinary researcher.

Selecting a truly representative sample is a painstaking and costly process, and several highly technical monographs have been written about the topic (e.g., Cochran, 1977; Levy & Lemeshow, 1999). In most L2 survey research (and, indeed, in any quantitative research) it is unrealistic or simply not feasible to aim for perfect representativeness in the psychometric sense. Therefore, in the following I will discuss only briefly the main principles of "random sampling," which is the key component of probability sampling, and will elaborate more on non-probability sampling procedures. (For more details on sampling procedures, please refer to Dörnyei, 2007, pp. 95-101.)

Random Sampling

Random sampling involves the selection of members of the population to be included in the sample on a completely random basis, a bit like drawing numbers from a hat (for example, by numbering each member and then asking the computer to generate random numbers). In this way the selection is based entirely on chance rather than on any extraneous or subjective factors. As a result, a sufficiently large sample is generally believed to contain subjects with characteristics similar to the population as a whole. Combining random sampling with some form of rational grouping is a particularly effective method for research with a specific focus. In "stratified random sampling" the population is divided into groups, or "strata," and a random sample of a proportionate size is selected from each group.

Convenience or Opportunity Sampling

The most common non-probability sampling type in L2 research is a *convenience* or *opportunity sampling*, where an important criterion of sample selection is the convenience for the researcher: Members of the target population are selected for the purpose of the study if they meet certain practical criteria, such as geographical proximity, availability at a certain time, or easy accessibility. Captive audiences such as students in the researcher's own institution are prime examples of convenience samples. To be fair, convenience samples are rarely completely convenience-based but are usually partially purposeful, which means that besides the relative ease of accessibility, participants also have to possess certain key characteristics that are related to the purpose of the investigation.

Snowball Sampling

Snowball sampling involves a "chain reaction" whereby the researcher identifies a few people who meet the criteria of the particular study and then asks these participants to identify further members of the population. This technique is useful when studying groups whose membership is not readily identifiable (e.g., teenage gang members).

Quota Sampling

In *quota sampling* the researcher defines certain distinct subgroups (e.g., boys and girls, or age cohorts) and determines the proportion of the population that belongs to each of these subgroups (e.g., when targeting language teachers, determining that the female-male ratio among them is 70%-30% in a particular setting). The actual sample, then, is selected in a way as to reflect these proportions (i.e., 70% of the sample will be women). Thus, quota sampling is similar to stratified random sampling without the "random" element.

Non-probability Sampling and Non-representativeness

We must not forget that no matter how principled a non-probability sample strives to be, the extent of generalizability in this type of sample is often negligible. Therefore, we need to describe in sufficient detail the limitations of such samples when we report the results, while also highlighting the characteristics that the particular sample shares with the defined target population. In a similar vein, we also have to be particularly careful about the claims we make about the more general relevance of our findings. We will come back to the issue of generalizability in Section 4.6.1 when we discuss how to summarize and report questionnaire data.

3.1.2 How Large Should the Sample Be?

When researchers ask the question, *"How large should the sample be?"* what they usually mean is *"How small a sample can I get away with?"* Therefore, the often quoted "the larger, the better" principle is singularly unhelpful for them. Unfortunately, there are no hard-and-fast rules in setting the optimal sample size; the final answer to the *"How large/small?"* question should be the outcome of the researcher considering several broad guidelines:

1. In the survey research literature a range of between 1%-10% of the population is usually mentioned as the "magic sampling fraction," depending on how careful the selection has been (i.e., the more scientific the sampling procedures applied, the smaller the sample size can be, which is why opinion polls can produce accurate predictions from samples as small as 0.1% of the population).

2. From a purely statistical point of view, a basic requirement is that the sample should have a *normal distribution*, and a rule of thumb to achieve this, offered by Hatch and Lazaraton (1991), is that the sample should include 30 or more people. However, Hatch and Lazaraton also emphasize that this is not an absolute rule, because smaller sample sizes can be compensated for by using certain special statistical procedures:

non-parametric procedures (see Dörnyei, 2007, Ch. 9, for non-parametric tests).

3. From the perspective of *statistical significance* (see Section 4.3.6), the principal concern is to sample enough learners for the expected results to be able to reach statistical significance. Because in L2 studies meaningful correlations reported in journal articles have often been as low as 0.30 and 0.40, a good rule of thumb is that we need around 50 participants to make sure that these coefficients are significant and we do not lose potentially important results. However, certain multivariate statistical procedures require more than 50 participants; for factor analysis, for example, we need a minimum of 100 (but preferably more) subjects.

4. A further important consideration is whether there are any distinct subgroups within the sample which may be expected to behave differently from the others. If we can identify such subgroups in advance (e.g., in most L2 studies of schoolchildren, girls have been found to perform differently from boys), we should set the sample size so that the minimum size applies to the *smallest subgroup* to allow for effective statistical procedures.

5. When setting the final sample size, it is advisable to leave a decent *margin* to provide for unforeseen or unplanned circumstances. For example, some participants are likely to drop out of at least some phases of the project; some questionnaires will always have to be disqualified for one reason or another; and—in relation to point 4 above—we may also detect unexpected subgroups that need to be treated separately.

3.1.3 The Problem of Respondent Self-Selection

To conclude the discussion of the various sampling issues for research purposes in general, we need to highlight a potential pitfall that might put the validity of the survey at risk: *the problem of participant self-selection*. This refers to cases when for various reasons the actual composition of the sample is not only the function of some systematic selection process but also of factors related to the respondents' own willingness to participate. Problems can arise, for example, when:

- Researchers invite *volunteers* to take part in a study (occasionally even offering money to compensate for the time spent).
- The design allows for a high degree of *dropout* (or "mortality"), in which case participants self-select themselves *out* of the sample.

- Participants are free to choose whether they fill in the questionnaire or not (e.g., in *postal surveys*).

Self-selection is inevitable to some extent because few questionnaire surveys can be made compulsory; however, in some cases it can reach such a degree that there is a good chance that the resulting sample will *not* be similar to the population. For example, volunteers may be different from non-volunteers in their aptitude, motivation, or some other basic characteristic, and dropouts also may share some common features that will be underrepresented in the sample with their departure (e.g., dropouts may be more demotivated than their peers and therefore their departure might make the remaining participants' general level of motivation unnaturally high). Consequently, the sample may lose its representative character, which of course would prevent any meaningful generalizability.

Quite so!

The problem is that the types of respondents who return questionnaires may be a specific type of "eager-beaver" or "gung-ho" respondent. Thus the results of the survey can only be generalized to "eager-beaver" or "gung-ho" people in the population rather than to the entire population.

(Brown, 2001, p. 85)

The scope of the self-selection problem can be illustrated by the fact that "impersonal" questionnaires (e.g., mail surveys) typically attract an initial response rate of only around 30%, and over 50% can already be seen as a good response (Gillham, 2008). Although there are several ways of increasing respondent motivation and subsequent return rate (see Sections 3.2.1, 3.2.4, and 3.3), with the exception of "captive groups" (e.g., students surveyed in a lecture hall as part of some scheduled instructional activity), we can always expect a considerable self-selection effect, which suggests that—given that in order to ensure sample representativeness a response rate of at least 80% is considered necessary—survey samples are frequently biased in some unknown manner (Aiken, 1997).

3.2 Main Types of Questionnaire Administration

In social research the most common form of administering questionnaires is *by mail*. Educational research is different in this respect because administration *by hand* is just as significant (if not more) as postal surveys. Within non-postal surveys, we can distinguish two distinct subtypes, one-to-one administration and group administration. In addition, a recent important development in survey research has been the increased use of *online* administration of questionnaires (e.g., email or web-based surveys). Because the administration method has a significant bearing on the format and to some extent also on the content of the questionnaire, we need to examine separately the special features of the different types of questionnaire administration.

3.2.1 Administration by Mail

The unique characteristic of *postal administration* is that the researcher has no contact with the respondent except for a cover letter he/she has written to accompany the questionnaire. In addition, mailed questionnaires are often in competition for the addressee's attention with various sorts of circulars, catalogues, and junk mail also received through the mail, and the two factors together largely explain why the return rate of such surveys is often well below 30%. Such a low return rate, of course, undermines the reliability of the sample (see Section 3.1.3) and therefore if we decide to conduct a survey by mail we need to adopt a number of special strategies that have been found to increase the respondents' willingness to complete and return the questionnaire.

The Cover Letter

In the absence of a "live" contact person, the *cover letter* has the difficult job to "sell" the survey, that is, to create rapport with the respondents and to convince them about the importance of the survey and of their role in contributing to it. In addition to this public relations function, the cover letter also needs to provide certain specific information and directions. To write a letter that meets all these requirements is not easy, particularly in view of the fact that it needs to be *short* at the same time. If it is more than a page, it is likely to be tossed aside and then find its way into the trash can unread. So writing this letter is something we do not want to rush.

Cover letters usually address the following points:

- who the writer is;
- the organization that is sponsoring or conducting the study;
- what the survey is about and why this is important or socially useful;
- why the recipient's opinion is important and how he/she was selected;
- assurance that all responses will be kept confidential;
- how to return the completed questionnaire;
- the date by which the completed questionnaire should be returned;
- what to do if questions arise (e.g., a contact name and telephone number);

- possible reward for participation;
- thank you!
- signature, preferably by a person of recognized stature.

Gillham (2008) warns us that, even though the questionnaire is sent out together with the cover letter, the two often get separated. Therefore, it is important that the questionnaire itself be self-contained and also include vital pieces of information such as the return address and the return date (which, in my experience, should be around 10 days after receiving the questionnaire).

Follow-up Letters

After you have posted the questionnaires, an anxious period of waiting begins. Based on his experience, Gillham (2008) provides a rule-of-thumb estimate that the response you have received by the end of 10 days will be about half of what you can expect to get back in the long run. In order to receive the other half, you need to send a follow-up letter (about two and a half to three weeks after the original mailing). This second mailing is well worth the effort, as it can increase the response rate by as much as 30%. With regard to the content of this letter, Gillham makes the following suggestions:

- We need not be too apologetic.
- We should reiterate the importance of the study and of the *participants' contribution.*
- There is no need to talk about the response rate to date.
- We should enclose a further copy of the questionnaire and another stamped addressed envelope "in case they did not receive or have mislaid the original one."

In another 10 days' time a second follow-up letter can be sent.

Guidelines for Increasing Mail Survey Return Rates

How can we increase the willingness of the recipients to take the time and trouble to complete and return the postal survey? The strategies most frequently mentioned in the measurement literature are as follows (see also Section 3.3, which offers general—i.e., not restricted to postal surveys in particular—strategies to promote respondent attitudes):

- *Pre-survey letters* give advance notice about the purpose and nature of the forthcoming questionnaire and can create a favorable climate for the survey.
- *Careful timing of the mailing.* First, it is advisable to avoid mailings at holiday periods or particularly busy times of the year. Second,

questionnaires that arrive in the second half of the week are more likely to be dealt with over the weekend.

- Make the opening and concluding questions in the questionnaire particularly *interesting*: the former to whet the respondents' appetite, and the latter to encourage the return of the questionnaire.
- Emphasize that the recipient's responses are *needed* and *valuable*.
- The final push for some recipients to get down to completing the questionnaire is often the reputation of a prestigious *organization* sponsoring the survey—this can be highlighted by using the organization's letterhead or logo. If some of the questions are related to the respondent's workplace, it is important that the organization in charge of the survey is seen as independent.
- With postal surveys, making the *layout* of the questionnaire (see Section 2.1.2) attractive is more important than with hand-delivered questionnaires.
- Use good-quality *paper* and *envelope*, and attach a *stamped, addressed* envelope.
- The *address* should be typed and special care needs to be taken that the person's name is spelled correctly and that the person's title is accurate—writing "Miss" instead of "Mrs." is seen as annoying by some and others do not like the title "Ms." Susan Gass (personal communication, January 18, 2002) has successfully used a "stopgap" strategy in the past in cases in which she was not sure about the exact title by only writing "M." She found that this is less disturbing for people with strong feelings about either Ms. or Miss than using the wrong title.
- Send the questionnaire by *first-class mail* or some equivalent, in order to emphasize that it is not one of those "bulk deliveries."
- Send a small *token of appreciation*; it might be helpful, because it evokes the human instinct of reciprocation.

Unfortunately, even if we observe all these guidelines we cannot expect high respondent motivation. A return rate of more than 50% can be considered satisfactory and response rates higher than 80% are rarely obtained (Aiken, 1997).

Regrettably . . .

An unexpectedly poor response to questionnaires can be a salutary experience for the novice researcher.

(Gillham, 2008, p. 9)

3.2.2 One-to-One Administration

One-to-one administration refers to a situation when someone delivers the questionnaire by hand to the designated person and arranges the completed form to be picked up later (e.g., handing out questionnaires to colleagues at work). This is a much more personal form of administration than mail surveys and therefore the chances for the questionnaires to be returned are significantly better. The personal contact also allows the questionnaire administrator to create a rapport with the respondent, to explain the purpose of the enquiry, and to encourage cooperation. Furthermore, with young children (i.e., less than 10 years old) the administrator can be present while they complete the questionnaire to be available if help is needed.

Oppenheim (1992) draws attention to a potential pitfall of one-to-one administration: When such a questionnaire administration strategy is adopted, researchers often utilize the help of someone in an official capacity on site who is not a skilled interviewer (e.g., a teacher or a manager or some other contact person in a targeted institution). However, there is a danger that without appropriate briefing such persons may, with the best intentions, introduce fatal biases. The face-to-face survey administrator needs to cover all the points that the cover letter does in postal surveys (see Section 3.2.1) and yet, when we ask mediators to hand out a few questionnaires in the contexts they move around in, how often do we train them to do this job properly? When it comes to *group administration* (see Section 3.2.3) researchers typically place more emphasis on standardizing the administration procedures, and with postal surveys a carefully composed cover letter can do the job; however, one-to-one administration somehow slips into the gap between the two and it is often assumed that exercising the "personal touch" with the respondents (which is the mediator's forte) can substitute for professional administration procedures. A possible remedy is to give the administrator a *cue card* with the main points to be covered briefly when handing out each questionnaire.

3.2.3 Group Administration

In L2 research, *group administration* is the most common method of having questionnaires completed. One reason for this is that the typical targets of the surveys are language learners studying within institutional contexts, and it is often possible to arrange to administer the instrument to them while they are assembled together, for example, as part of a lesson or slotted between certain other organized activities. The other reason for the popularity of this administration format is that it can overcome some of the problems just mentioned with regard to postal surveys or one-to-one administration. Groups of students are typically "captive groups" in the sense that a response rate of nearly 100% can be achieved with them, and because a few questionnaire administrators can collect a very large number of questionnaires it is easier to make sure that all of them are adequately trained for the job.

Group administration is the format I have used most in my past research and it is my overall experience that as long as the questionnaire is well designed and the administration situation well prepared in advance, very good results can be achieved. There are, however, some important points to consider:

- Because respondents have to work individually, Oppenheim (1992) reports that this format may not be appropriate for children under about age 10.
- With larger groups, or with groups of less mature kids, more than one field worker is needed at a time to help to answer questions and to distribute/collect the questionnaires.
- Oppenheim (1992) also warns us that in group administration "contamination" through copying, talking, or asking questions is a constant danger.
- The negative influence of deviant kids may create an inappropriate climate for sincere and thoughtful work.
- If the questionnaire is administered to students, there might be a need for some educational justification for taking up class time. Under these circumstances, using a bilingual version of the questionnaire may help. (Appendix B presents a questionnaire used in China that also contains the English text.)

In Section 3.3 below, I will list ten questionnaire administration strategies that can significantly increase the success of the survey, but before that let us look at a unique new development in survey methodology, the increased utilization of the Internet.

3.2.4 Online Administration

With computers and Internet access becoming more ubiquitous, it was inevitable that researchers would start considering online data collection methods. Indeed, given the increasingly available and continuously improving computer hardware and software, it is becoming relatively easy to set up online surveys. In L2 research, due to practical reasons, group administration is still the most popular way of reaching the participants (see Section 3.2.3) and not many online surveys have been conducted (for exceptions, see, e.g.,

Dewaele, Petrides, & Furnham, 2008; Levine, 2003). Nevertheless, surveys of this type are bound to become more prominent in the near future, as online administration can overcome several problems associated with traditional administration methods and can also offer some tempting benefits (for reviews, see, e.g., Birnbaum, 2004; Fox, Murray, & Warm, 2003; Michaelidou & Dibb, 2006; van Selm & Jankowski, 2006; Wright, 2005):

- *Target populations*. One advantage of online surveys is that we can get easy access to populations who would otherwise be difficult to reach. These can include small, scattered or specialized groups and individuals, as well as international participants living at a considerable geographical distance. As a result, we can start thinking of surveying much larger and more diverse participant samples worldwide than would have been possible before.

- *Time*. Web-based research helps us to save time because it does not require the administration of the instrument in person—once the recruitment posting has been made, administration is self-running. A comparative study of online and postal data collection by McDonald and Adam (2003) shows that obtaining a 40% cumulative response took 10 days in the postal mode while only one day in the online mode. Furthermore, if we use proper technology, we can make the coding and recording of the answers automatic, thus skipping the rather tedious and time-consuming data-entering stage.

- *Costs*. For many, the reduction of costs may be the most attractive feature of online surveys. Because most universities and research centers have the necessary computer facilities, setting up a computer-based project is no more expensive than initiating traditional research, and the running costs (e.g., postage, printing/photocopying, and traveling) are significantly lower. Akl, Maroun, Klocke, Montori, and Schünemann (2005) estimated that the expenditures for a web survey were one-third of those for a postal survey.

Online questionnaires can be divided into two main types: *email surveys* and *web-based surveys*.

Email Surveys
Email surveys entail embedding the questionnaire in, or attaching it to, an email message. The former involves including a questionnaire in the main body of the email text, with the recipients marking their answers in the space provided and then replying to the sender. In contrast, the latter method

requires the recipients to download the instrument, answer the questions, and then send the completed form back as an attachment. Both procedures are popular among research students for obvious reasons, but they also have shortcomings. As Dommeyer and Moriarty's (1999/2000) study shows, the administration procedures of the embedded form are simpler, which leads to a higher response rate, while the response rate of the attached form becomes lower because of the more complicated procedures to response and concerns about viruses. On the other hand, embedded questionnaires must be typed in "flat" or "plain" text and can have very limited formatting, making them a far cry from the professional appearance of attached documents.

The currently recommended practice of email surveys is a hybrid method that also involves web-based questionnaire administration: Email messages are sent to potential respondents inviting them to participate in the survey and pointing them to the appropriate URL address that is included in the message in the form of a hypertext (Michaelidou & Dibb, 2006).

Web-Based Surveys

Compared with its purely email-based counterpart, the web-based survey is more efficient and attractive. As described above (in Section 2.9), various software packages for creating web questionnaires enable the researcher to produce visually appealing instruments with special features to prevent certain problems (such as missing data).

With regards to the actual administration process, the procedures are similar to the ones used for email surveys but are more versatile: The investigators contact various Internet discussion groups, bulletin boards, chatrooms, and lists, and/or initiate some sort of snowball sampling by emailing potential participants, and then hope for a sizable sample. Yet, despite the attractive features, online survey response rates tend to be lower than return rates of traditional postal surveys (see Bryman, 2008; Shih & Fan, 2008): According to Shih and Fan's (2008) meta-analysis, although there is considerable variation from study to study, the average difference might be as much as 10%. Interestingly, their meta-analysis also indicates that certain populations, most notably college students, are exceptions to this general trend.

Guidelines for Increasing Online Survey Return Rates

While some of the response boosting strategies for mail surveys are applicable to online survey, the following are strategies specific to the online survey (see, e.g., Michaelidou & Dibb, 2006; Porter & Whitcomb, 2007; Shih & Fan, 2008; van Selm & Jankowski, 2006):

- *Incentives* such as being entered in a lottery, offering a software download, or receiving some tangible reward (e.g., a book token or money) can be used to encourage participants to complete the survey. (Of course, this strategy has been extensively abused by the spam messages we regularly receive telling us we have just won a million dollars.)
- The *length of web-based questionnaires* should be kept as short as possible. No longer than 20 minutes is preferable (Umbach, 2004) and we should pay special attention to designing the first few pages where the dropout rate is the highest (Ganassali, 2008).
- A *progress indicator* is useful in showing respondents how much is left to complete (Couper, Traugott, & Lamias, 2001). This can stop people from abandoning the questionnaire halfway through completion.
- *Multiple attempts* should be made to contact potential respondents (e.g., pre-notifications, reminders and replacement surveys, and thank-you notes). With regard to follow-up reminders, the timing to send them needs to be shorter than with traditional mail surveys (perhaps even as short as a week).
- A *mixed-mode strategy* (electronic and pencil-and-paper question-naire) might be useful to reach respondents without any Internet access and this approach might also be useful with highly heterogeneous target audiences (e.g., in terms of age or social characteristics). There is a danger, however, that even minor differences in the layout and formatting of the different versions may elicit different responses from the respondents (see Potaka, 2008, for ways of dealing with this issue in New Zealand's 2006 census).
- *Anonymity*: Although the general perception is that web-based research is truly anonymous, with email surveys the researcher can identify the respondents easily, and it is technically possible to trace back most participants in a web-based survey as well (particularly when the website requires a special PIN code or password to log in). Therefore, it is important to offer some convincing reassurance of confidentiality to potential participants.

The Sampling Problem in Online Surveys

In concluding the discussion of online surveys it is important to note that the most acute problem associated with this type of questionnaire administration is that it is usually not possible to apply any systematic, purposive sampling.

However, before we decide that this lack of control over who will eventually participate in the study should disqualify such projects from the category of scientific inquiry, we should recall that non-probability sampling (and especially convenience sampling) is the most common sampling strategy even in non-web-based surveys (see Section 3.1.1). So, the main problem does not necessarily concern the unprincipled selection procedures but rather the fact that the actual sample that completes the web-based survey may be much more heterogeneous than in traditional research, largely consisting of self-selected participants. As a result, even if we have thousands of responses, it may be difficult to decide how to generalize the findings.

3.3 Strategies to Increase the Quality and Quantity of Participant Response

The main message of this section can be summarized in three words: *Administration procedures matter!* It was emphasized more than once in the previous two chapters that the "Achilles heel" of questionnaires as measuring instruments is that it is difficult to get respondents to spend enough time and effort completing them. Educational researchers are in a slightly better position in this respect because schoolchildren are often willing to work hard on a task simply because it is assigned to them, but the older the students get, the less this is so. Adults—and also young adults—are usually perfectly aware of the fact that they have nothing to gain from participating in the survey and may also see the questionnaire as an intrusion both literally and metaphorically. Haven't we all thought at one time or another that a questionnaire we have received was nothing but a nuisance? As Gillham (2008, p. 10) rightly notes, "The market is questionnaire saturated," and even if someone completes and returns a questionnaire, the chances are that he/she will not have worked hard at the answers.

Regrettably . . .
People tend not to take questionnaires seriously; their answers may be frankly frivolous.

(Gillham, 2008, p. 13)

In view of these handicaps, the researcher's task to motivate the respondents to give truthful and thoughtful answers to all the relevant items on the questionnaire might seem daunting, if not impossible. The good news, however, is that people in general like to express their opinions and do not mind answering questions as long as they think that the survey is related to a worthy cause and that their opinion will be taken seriously. Thus, if we take sufficient care planning and executing the administration process, we can successfully build on these human characteristics and can secure the cooperation of our participants. The following strategies have been found effective in achieving this objective.

3.3.1 Advance Notice

Surprising as it may sound, the administration of the questionnaire really does not start when the survey administrator first appears on the scene with a bundle of sheets in his/her hand. In most cases several important things about the survey have been determined by the respondent by that time. For example, Sudman and Bradburn (1983) conclude that most refusals to cooperate occur before the interviewer has had a chance to explain fully the purposes of the survey. In a paper entirely devoted to analyzing test/questionnaire administration, Clemans (1971, p. 193) also emphasizes that "to a very considerable extent, the examinee's attitudes toward the test will have been formed before the day it is administered."

One important factor that influences the respondent's initial disposition is the person's attitude toward questionnaires in general. Some people simply cannot stand any kinds of self-completed forms and there isn't much we can do about it. What we *can* do, however, is to announce the questionnaire a few days in advance and to send each participant a printed leaflet that explains the purpose and nature of the questionnaire, contains a few sample items, and invites participation. This is an effective method of generating a positive climate for the administration and it also reduces the anxiety caused by the unexpected and unknown. Such advance notice also raises the "professional" feel of the survey, which in turn promotes positive participant attitudes.

3.3.2 Attitudes Conveyed by Teachers, Parents, and Other Authority Figures

Data gathering often takes place in someone's "home ground"; in school settings, for example, students usually hear about the survey first from their teachers. The important thing to note with respect to this is that participants are rather quick to pick up their superiors' (e.g., teachers' or bosses') attitude toward the survey and only acquiesce if the message they receive is unambiguously positive. Similarly, parental disposition can also have a major impact on students' willingness to respond. It is therefore an imperative to *win the support* of all these authority figures in advance.

An important aspect of securing the cooperation of the people who are in charge within the questionnaire administration context is to start at the top. Even if we have personal contacts in a particular school, it is advisable to approach the headteacher (or even the chief education officer of the region) first and ask for a formal consent to approach the designated teachers to discuss the possibility of conducting research among their pupils. The official request, which is usually a formal letter, should obviously outline the aims, the design, and the methods of the research, and should offer some rationale in terms of the survey's relevance to education (Oppenheim, 1992).

3.3.3 Respectable Sponsorship

A further factor that might work positively for survey administrators before they have even opened their mouths is some respectable and impressive *institutional sponsorship* of the study. If we can claim to represent an organization that is esteemed highly by the respondents, the positive reputation is likely to be projected onto the survey. If our institution is less known among the participants, a short leaflet describing its main features (and its strengths!) might tip the balance in favor of the survey. Similarly, a letter of introduction from someone influential can also boost questionnaire attitudes.

3.3.4 The Presence of a Survey Administrator

After all the preliminary considerations, we have finally arrived at the actual day of the survey. The first issue to consider is how important it is for a member of the survey team to be actually present during the administration of the instrument. With large-scale school surveys, the questionnaire is often distributed by the students' own teacher, which is understandable from a logistic point of view but not recommended from a motivational point of view. A study conducted by Strange *et al.* (2003) among schoolchildren, for example, indicated a definite preference for the presence of the researcher; as one girl commented, "It would have helped if we had had one of the actual researchers, we had to have our tutor which was a bit embarrassing and I didn't feel like asking him questions about the questionnaire" (p. 340). The study also showed that participants were more likely to provide personal information when the researcher was present.

3.3.5 The Behavior of the Survey Administrator

On the actual day of a group-based survey, the survey administrator is facing the participants and is about to launch into his/her pep talk. However, before we look at what he/she should say, we must realize that the administrator's behavior also conveys important messages to the respondents in line with the saying, "Actions speak louder than words." Survey administrators are, in

75

many ways, identified with the whole survey and, therefore, everything about them matters:

- Their *clothes* should be businesslike but certainly not more formal than what is typical in the given environment.
- The way they *introduce themselves* is important: friendliness is imperative and smiling usually breaks the ice effectively.
- Their *overall conduct* should be professional to represent the serious character of the survey without being stiff and unnatural.

A crucial aspect of the survey administrators' behavior is that it should exhibit *keen involvement* in the project and show an obvious *interest* in the outcome (Clemans, 1971). They should establish rapport and give encouragement, thereby projecting positive attitudes and "pulling along" the respondents. Skilled questionnaire administrators are able to sustain rapport and participant motivation throughout the whole questionnaire completion process.

3.3.6 Communicating the Purpose and Significance of the Survey

Although actions may speak louder than words, this does not mean that words don't matter. An important element in "selling" the survey to the participants is *communicating* to them the purpose of the survey and conveying to them the potential significance of the results. People tend not to mind answering questions if they see the point. We should also be aware of the fact that, as Gillham (2008) warns us, in our information-conscious age there is a general suspicion that much more data are stored about us than what we know of, and that even "anonymous" information can be identified. Therefore, unless researchers explain why the information is being collected and how it will be used, some people may be reluctant to complete the questionnaire or to provide true answers even if nothing sensitive is being targeted.

Indeed . . .

If respondents are clear about what you are trying to find out and why, they are much more likely to respond appropriately and helpfully or, indeed, at all. There is a curious convention that if you tell respondents what you are trying to find out this will "bias" them. It might simply make them more helpful. If you are mysterious about the purpose of the questionnaire they may be disinclined to answer or misunderstand the purpose, and so bias their answers in that way.

(Gillham, 2008, p. 38)

Just like the cover letter in a postal survey, the introductory speech of the questionnaire administrator needs to be carefully designed. It should briefly cover the following points:

- introduction;
- the sponsoring organization;
- purpose of the survey and its potential usefulness;
- why the particular participants have been selected;
- assurance of confidentiality;
- the usual duration of completing the questionnaire;
- any questions?
- thank you!

A word of caution: The manner in which the questionnaire is presented can have a considerable impact on the participants' performance. By means of illustration, Clemans (1971) reports on a study in which the same test was introduced to three different groups first as an "intelligence test," then as an "achievement test," and finally as a "routine test." Because of the different connotations and inherent motivating characteristics of these three conditions, there was a significant difference between the test results, with the "intelligence test" group doing best, followed by the "achievement test" group and finally by the "routine test" group.

3.3.7 Emphasizing Confidentiality

Questionnaires administered in educational settings often contain sensitive items such as the evaluation of the language course (see also Sections 2.1.3 and 2.6.3). Students cannot be expected to provide honest information and possibly make critical statements about such issues unless we manage to convince them about the confidentiality of the investigation. Simply saying that the data will be treated confidentially, or making the questionnaires anonymous, may not be a sufficient guarantee for some respondents. As already mentioned briefly, in a study that involved the appraisal of a range of situation-specific factors and motives (Clément et al., 1994), we made a big "fuss" about handing out envelopes to the participants and asking them to put the completed forms in these and then seal them. The administrator, who was external to the school, then stamped every single envelope in front of the students with a university stamp before collecting them. The strategy worked.

3.3.8 Reading Out the Questionnaire Instructions

It is a general experience in educational psychology that people do not tend to read written directions, and this also applies to the printed instructions of the questionnaire. Therefore, it is advisable for the administrator to read the initial instructions out loud while the respondents read the text silently.

3.3.9 The Style and Layout of the Questionnaire

As argued earlier, respondents are normally willing to spend time and effort on a questionnaire if they believe that they are contributing to a serious investigation. One factor that plays an important role in convincing them about this is the professional quality of the questionnaire. The tone and content of the printed instructions, the layout and typesetting of the items, and small details such as thanking the participants for their cooperation, can all contribute to the formation of a general good impression about the survey, which in turn affects the quality of the responses.

Well said . . .

In designing questionnaires it is not merely important for us also to look at things from the respondents' point of view; we must make them feel that we are doing so.

(Oppenheim, 1992, p. 122)

Thus, when designing the questionnaire we should not only strive for a psychometrically reliable and valid instrument but also for an *intrinsically involving* one. As Oppenheim (1992) emphasizes, besides eliciting answers, each question also has a covert function to motivate the respondent to continue to cooperate. So, it may be worthwhile sometimes to be a bit more long-winded, and instead of giving short prompts such as "age of starting L2 studies" we could state each question in full, including the word "please." Of course, as with so many things in questionnaire construction, a delicate balance needs to be struck here between considerations of style and length.

In Section 2.1.2, I argued that attractive layout is an important tool in making the questionnaire engaging. A variety of question styles can make the answering process less monotonous, and an interesting (but not confusing!) variety of graphic features (fonts, spacing) can create a fresh atmosphere. It was mentioned in an earlier section, for example, that a successful strategy someone used was to print documents on thick, beige paper in order for recipients to take them more seriously (Newell, 1993).

3.3.10 Promising Feedback on the Results

Christopher Ryan (personal communication) has always maintained that survey researchers can do great damage if they pursue what he called a "slash and burn" strategy. By this he meant that surveyors typically exploit their participants without offering anything in return—as soon as the data have been gathered, they disappear. On the other hand, if someone puts reasonable effort into answering the questions, this involvement will create a natural curiosity about the project and its outcome. It is therefore not only a nice gesture but it also prepares the grounds for future surveys if we offer to send respondents some sort of feedback on the results (e.g., an article or a copy of the research report). Not everybody will need this, though; in order to avoid any unnecessary waste of paper, we can include a box for people to check if they would like to receive further information. The natural place for this box is somewhere at the end of the questionnaire (see Section 2.2.4) but mentioning it at the beginning can serve as an incentive.

Absolutely!
Remember, if you make a promise to send them something, you really must remember to do it.

(Brown, 2001, p. 87)

3.4 Questionnaire Administration, Confidentiality, and Other Ethical Issues

To conclude this chapter on questionnaire administration and data collection, we need to consider aspects which, although unrelated to the psychometric qualities of the measuring instruments, concern the respondents as human beings. The hard fact is that survey research is inherently intrusive and the data we obtain can be abused. Therefore, investigators wishing to adopt this methodology need to be aware of and observe certain basic research ethical principles. As a preliminary, let me emphasize that in several countries detailed legal and institutional frameworks are in existence, governing every aspect of conducting research, including analyzing, reporting, and storing the obtained data. In the US, for example, researchers have to submit a detailed research plan for approval to an Institutional Review Board (IRB) prior to starting their investigations in order to comply with federal regulations that provide protection against human rights violations. These regulations also apply to graduate (M.A. or Ph.D.) research, and only in exceptional circumstances will Graduate Schools accept a thesis or dissertation without some sort of "human subjects" approval. There are elaborate procedures to go through, including filling in forms offered by each university's review board (for more details, see Duff, 2008; Mackey & Gass, 2005).

3.4.1 Basic Ethical Principles of Data Collection

Drawing on Oppenheim's (1992) and Sudman and Bradburn's (1983) discussion of ethical issues in survey research, the following five general principles can be compiled:

Principle 1: No harm should come to the respondents as a result of their participation in the research. This is the primary ethical principle governing data collection and it overrides all other considerations.

Principle 2: The respondent's right to privacy should always be respected, and no undue pressure should be brought to bear. That is, respondents are perfectly within their rights to refuse to answer questions without offering any explanation, and they have the right to decide to whom and under what conditions the information can be made available. No information can be published about identifiable persons or organizations without their permission.

Principle 3: Respondents should be provided with sufficient initial information about the survey to be able to give their informed consent concerning participation and the use of data. The key issue here is what we consider "sufficient"; I believe that providing true information about the extent to which answers will be held confidential as well as how and for what purpose the data will be used is a minimal requirement. In some contexts the respondents' consent must be confirmed with their signature; however, we should also note that a request for consent in too formalized a manner can raise undue suspicions that something is not quite right about the survey, and this can reduce the response rate (Sudman & Bradburn, 1983).

Principle 4: In the case of children, permission to conduct the survey should always be sought from some person who has sufficient authority. Relevant legal requirements vary from country to country, so we need to check these carefully, otherwise the obtained data can be invalidated. I will come back to this point in the following section (Section 3.4.2).

Principle 5: It is the researcher's moral and professional (and in some contexts legal) obligation to maintain the level of confidentiality that was promised to the respondents at the onset. We need to make sure that we do not promise a higher degree of confidentiality than we can achieve.

To reiterate, in many countries, observing these principles is also enforced by legal and institutional requirements, and university researchers may have to submit an application to an Institutional Review Board (IRB) prior to embarking on data collection. For a more detailed discussion of research ethics in applied linguistics, see Dörnyei (2007), Duff (2008), and Mackey & Gass (2005).

3.4.2 Obtaining Consent for Children

Many, if not most, educational studies are conducted within schools or other educational institutes, targeting schoolchildren, who may not be in a position to represent themselves appropriately. The main question is to decide who has sufficient authority to give consent in such cases: the legal guardian (particularly, parent), the children's teacher(s), or both. In this respect the existing legal and ethical research frameworks differ greatly across countries. It is my view that unless there exist legal requirements stating otherwise, it may not always be necessary to ask for parental consent when surveying schoolchildren. In the case of "neutral" questionnaires that do not contain any personally sensitive information, permission to conduct the survey can be granted by the children's teachers. Teachers are usually aware of the significance of legal matters and therefore if they have any doubts about who should authorize the project they will seek advice.

In case parental permission is needed for the research, a common procedure is to send an information leaflet along with a consent form to the children's parents to be signed. In order to avoid cases when the parent has nothing against the survey but simply forgets to return the consent form, an alternative way to go about this (provided, of course, there are no contradicting legal requirements) is to merely advise the parents about the proposed research and the fact that their child has been chosen (among others) to take part in it, and that parental permission will be assumed *unless the parents object* before the proposed starting date (Oppenheim, 1992).

3.4.3 Strategies for Getting Around Anonymity

We saw in Section 2.1.3 that—from the researcher's point of view— respondent anonymity is often undesirable in survey research, because without proper identification we cannot match survey data with other sources of information obtained about the same participants (e.g., course marks or other questionnaires). The other side of the coin, however, is that with certain sensitive questions anonymity may be desirable from the respondents' point of view because they may feel safer this way in providing less self-protective and presumably more accurate answers. Is there a way to "have the cake and eat it too?" That is, can we devise administration procedures that provide the assurance of anonymity and yet produce identifiable data? In the following I will describe two attempts to achieve this objective. One used is my own past research; the other, reported in the literature.

Identification Through the Seating Plan

There may be situations when, even though you do not promise anonymity, you do not want to include the rather salient and potentially loaded task of the respondents identifying themselves by name in the questionnaire. In certain group administration contexts this can be avoided by putting a pre-coded identification number on each questionnaire and then recording the respondents' exact seating plan during the questionnaire administration (with the help of the students' class teacher, for example). If we hand out the pre-coded questionnaires in a specific order, we will be able to match the code numbers with the respondents' names through the seating plan. In my experience no one has ever complained about, or even raised the issue of, the identification numbers on the questionnaires, and I make it absolutely certain that the names remain confidential.

A Self-Generated Identification Coding Procedure

The identification procedure just described does not ensure anonymity but only saves the salient act of students' writing their name on the question-naire. A more complex method of ensuring identifiable anonymity has been piloted by Kearney *et al.* (1984) with some success. This method involves students' generating for themselves a unique personal code number and including this on every document they complete—hence the possibility for data linkability. Of course, no one except them would know the identity behind the identification code—hence the assurance of anonymity.

Asking students to make up a code name for themselves has been tried in the past more than once, but the problem with this method is that in longitudinal studies some respondents will almost inevitably have difficulty remembering their ID codes over long intervals. The novel element in Kearney *et al.*'s (1984) technique is that respondents do not create an imaginary ID code or password but rather generate a code by providing specific code elements that are well known to them but not to the researchers, such as their own or their parents' initials or birth dates, or specific digits of their street addresses or telephone numbers. So, a template for the students' personal identification number would specify each digit separately. This is obviously not an unbreakable code because someone who knows the students well can have access to enough code elements to identify the students, but the procedure works well under many research conditions. Of course, there is also the danger of someone not knowing the required information, or some key events in one's life changing (e.g., moving to a new house or when a new brother/sister is born)—and indeed, Kearney *et al.* (1984) report only a 78.1% successful linkage rate for an interval of one year— but the method appears to be reliable for a cross-sectional study that does not involve a long interval between the various data collection procedures.

CHAPTER 4

Processing Questionnaire Data

Having designed a questionnaire and administered it to an appropriate sample is half the battle. Now comes the final phase of our research, the processing of the data. The starting point of this phase is the very salient presence of stacks of completed questionnaires taking up what little empty space there is in our office. Accordingly, our initial priority is to get rid of these stacks and transform the information that is hidden in these piles of questionnaires into a more useful form that we can easily store, access, sort, and analyze (Brown, 2001).

Indeed ...

Many books seem to deal with programming for particular statistical analyses, but few detail the painful experience of going from a stack of disorganized hard copy to on-line data that are trustworthy.

(Davidson, 1996, p. ix)

Questionnaire data are most usable if they are stored in a computer file. This is a prerequisite to any professional analysis of the data, but even if you are engaged in a small-scale investigation that is not intended to result in a research publication you can save a lot of time if you enter the data into a spreadsheet, for example. Modern computer programs tend to be so user-friendly that one can often learn to use them with less effort than would be required, for example, to calculate the mean (i.e., the average) scores of the questionnaire responses manually, using a pocket calculator.

This chapter will describe the consecutive steps in processing questionnaire data. We will start with methods of scoring and coding the responses and then entering the data into a computer file. Following this, I will discuss the analysis of closed- and open-ended items separately. The chapter will be concluded by summarizing the main types of computer software we can utilize for our research, the most important aspects of reporting questionnaire data, and finally the various ways we can complement our survey data with information obtained from other sources. It may be worth reiterating at this point that this chapter will not elaborate on statistical and qualitative techniques of data analysis. I have discussed these procedures in some detail in Dörnyei (2007).

4.1 Coding Questionnaire Data

Most data analysis software handles data in a numerical rather than in an alphabetic form, and even with programs that allow the storage of information recorded as letters, the procedures that are available for handling such data are limited compared to the vast arsenal of statistical techniques to be used with numerical responses. Therefore, the first step of data processing usually involves converting the respondents' answers to numbers by means of *coding procedures*. As we will see, these procedures are more straightforward with closed-ended questions; processing open-ended questionnaire items requires some sort of *content analysis*.

4.1.1 First Things First: Assigning Identification Codes

Before we get down to actual coding, there is an important task to carry out, which is too often omitted: Assigning to each questionnaire a unique *identification code*. In practice this involves taking each questionnaire one by one and numbering them sequentially by writing a code number in one of the top corners of the front page. Questionnaires coming from the same group (e.g., same school or class) should be kept together and marked with a special code; for example, the first one or two digits of the questionnaire code can refer to the school, the next one to the particular class within the school, and the final numbers identify the individual learners.

4.1.2 Coding Quantitative Data

Having marked each questionnaire with an identification number, we are ready to embark on the *coding* of the items. Except for extensive texts obtained by open-ended questions (which require special content analysis—see Section 4.4), the coding process for each item involves converting the answer into a *numerical score*. Because numbers are meaningless in and of themselves and are all too easy to mix up, a major element of the coding phase is to define each variable and then to compile coding specifications for every possible "value" that the particular variable can take. For example, gender data are usually labeled "sex" and it can take two numerical values: "male" is usually coded "1" and "female" "2."

With closed-ended items, such as Likert scales (see Section 2.4.1), coding is usually straightforward: Each predetermined response option is assigned a number (e.g., "strongly disagree" = 1, "disagree" = 2, "neutral" = 3, "agree" = 4, "strongly agree" = 5). For simple open-ended questionnaire items (e.g., a background information question such as *What foreign languages have you learned in the past?"*) the coding is more complex because it can have many categories (e.g., German = 1, French = 2, etc.), in fact, as many as the number of the different answers in all the questionnaires. Thus, with such items the coding specifications are continuously extended during the processing of the data, with every new language mentioned by the respondents being assigned a new number.

The coding of other open-ended questionnaire items that elicit more diverse or longer responses, however, may go beyond the mechanical conversion of a category into a number and may require a certain amount of subjective interpretation and summary on the part of the coder. For example, with a question such as *"What is your favorite leisure activity?"* the task is to condense the diverse information contained in the responses into a limited number of categories; ongoing decisions will need to be made about whether to label two similar but not completely identical responses (for example, "walking the dog" and "going for a walk") as the same or whether to mark the difference somehow. These decisions will be a function of qualitative interpretation by the researcher in light of the broader purpose and nature of the particular study.

In the past, researchers have had to compile a "codebook" that included the coding frames for each variable in their investigation (and thus the first edition of this book contained a section describing this). However, the data files in the latest versions of modern statistical software (such as SPSS) offer such convenient facilities to include detailed descriptions of all the variables and values that many researchers nowadays simply incorporate the codebook into the data file.

4.2 Inputting the Data

Having sorted out the coding specifications, we need to get down to the rather tedious and time-consuming process of entering the data into a computer file. However, before doing so we need to create and name the data file.

4.2.1 Creating and Naming the Data File

Creating a new data file is easy in modern statistical software. However, the nature of data files is such that we regularly make changes in them during the process of data analysis (e.g., recoding variables or computing new composite variables) and one of the recurring problems I have encountered with novice (and not-so-novice) researchers is that multiple versions of the data files are stored next to each other, with file names becoming confusing and the files getting mixed up. Furthermore, in most studies we are likely to return to the dataset at later stages, and without a foolproof naming/labeling system it might be a daunting task to sort out which file is what. Therefore, it is worth adopting a systematic process; my preferred practice involves giving the data file a simple generic name and whenever I make any changes in the file, I save the modified file under a new version name (usually by sequencing the file names; e.g., "Motivation_data_1," "Motivation_data_2," etc.). My rule of thumb is that no change in the data file should be saved under the old file name because this would make it very difficult (if not impossible) at a later stage to trace back what we have done.

4.2.2 Keying in the Data

All of us involved in survey research have spent countless number of hours in front of a computer screen typing seemingly endless rows of figures. However boring and mechanical this job may be, it is essential that we maintain concentration because every mistyped number will be a contamination of the dataset. In agreement with Brown (2001), I have found that one way of making the task more interesting and more accurate is to work with a partner, taking turns at dictating and typing.

When keying the data, we often come across a special category for cases when *no answer* has been given (e.g., because someone overlooked the item or intentionally avoided it)—such missing data are often treated by leaving the particular cell empty (rather than following the traditional practice of typing in a set number such as "99"). This ensures that we do not mix up real values with missing data values by accident, and there will be opportunities later for each statistical analysis to decide how to handle missing data.

Fred Davidson's Plea for Backing up Data

Law 1: Back it up. Law 2: Do it now.

—Anonymous

I have noticed that nobody seems to learn to back up data until he or she has a serious disaster with data that are personally quite important. Please prove me wrong and abide by these two laws as early in your data career as possible.

(Davidson, 1996, p. 15)

The traditional (and still frequently used) method of entering data into a computer file involves creating a rectangular *text file* (e.g., a word processing file saved in a "text only with line breaks" file format) in which each horizontal line contains the data from a particular questionnaire and each vertical column (or set of columns) represents a particular variable. So, the final text file would look something like this (note that missing values have been left blank):

```
214  673342  31  5452731  261615  262512  13 423
215  565554  54  545 521  261616  262526  143333
216  542221  21  5661312  251617  152526  134 33
217  474232  43  6352621  472617  261516  133424
218  6 3453  44  5371631  361615  261724  134354
```

During the past decade technology has come a long way and there are now several more user-friendly ways of keying in data; interestingly, some of these still follow the rectangular (rows for respondents, columns for variables) format:

- There are various computer spreadsheet programs (such as Excel) which allow for setting up rows and columns in an electronic form. These programs can even execute certain statistical procedures, and the data entered through them can usually be read, or converted for use, by other, more sophisticated statistical packages.
- "SPSS," which is one of the most frequently used statistical packages in the social sciences, has its own Data Editor screen, which provides a convenient, spreadsheet-like method for creating and editing data files.
- One of the main functions of specially designed software for survey research (see Sections 2.9 and 4.5) is to facilitate data entry. These packages also allow respondents to key in their answers directly, following an online version of the questionnaire (which means that no hard copy of the questionnaire record is created).
- Some specialist programs even allow structuring the computer screen for the purpose of data entry to look like the original questionnaire. This can make the link between the hard copy and the electronic file more straightforward, which helps to reduce any typing errors.

4.3 Processing Closed Questions

Closed-ended questions are the most common types of questionnaire items. The complete processing sequence of such questions involves a number of consecutive steps, starting with the initial data check and cleaning, and concluded by the statistical analyses of the data.

4.3.1 Data Cleaning

The initial data file will always contain mistakes. Some of these are the result of human error occurring during the data entry phase (e.g., typing the wrong number) and some are mistakes made by the respondent when filling in the questionnaire. *Data cleaning* involves correcting as many of these errors and inaccuracies as possible before the actual analyses are undertaken. This is an indispensable phase of preparing the data because some mistakes can completely distort our results. The main checks and techniques are as follows:

- *Correcting impossible data.* Most items have a specific range, determined by the given response options or by the inherent logic of the item. A quick frequency listing of all the items can expose out-of-range values; for example, with a six-point Likert-scale a value of 7 is obviously incorrect, and if someone's age is entered as 110, we can also suspect human inaccuracy. Once such impossible values have been detected, we need to check the hard copy of the particular questionnaires, and then reenter the correct values.

- *Correcting incorrectly entered values that conform to the permissible range.* It is easy to detect and correct a value of 7 with a six-point Likert-scale. But what about a typing error in the same scale when "5" has been recorded instead of "4?" The only way of detecting such a mistake is by means of a very laborious procedure, whereby the entire data bank is reentered in a second data file and then the two data files (which ought to be identical) are computer-checked for correspondence with each other.

- *Correcting contradicting data.* Some questionnaires have "routed" items, which means that some questions are to be answered only if the respondent gave a particular answer to a previous question. For example, if a language learner gives a negative answer to the question *"Have you ever stayed in the L2 environment for an extended period?"* and then answers "6 months" to the subsequent *"If so, for how long?"* question, something is obviously wrong. Depending on the type of questions asked, several other logical checks are also conceivable. In any case, when such inconsistencies are found, a closer inspection of the questionnaire can usually help us to remedy these, but sometimes the only way of getting rid of the contamination is to eliminate both parts of the contradicting or illogical combination.

- *Examining implausible data.* The data check may highlight values that are inconsistent with the rest of the dataset, for example, because they are way out of the usual range. If such "suspicious" values are not merely the result of a typing error, they are referred to as *outliers*. They can indicate an out-of-the-ordinary but true response but they can also be caused by respondent carelessness or intentional silliness (which does happen with some participants). If a close analysis of the response patterns in the particular questionnaire points to one of the latter two options, we should consider eradicating the spurious information so that it does not bias the results. If we cannot make an unambiguous decision, we may conduct the main analysis twice, with and without the outlier, and see if the outcome will provide a clue about how to handle the outlier.

4.3.2 Data Manipulation

Data manipulation involves making changes in the dataset prior to the analyses in order to make it more appropriate for certain statistical procedures; it does *not* involve biasing the results one way or another. Three issues in particular need attention: (a) *handling missing data*, (b) *recoding certain values*, and (c) considering *standardizing the data.*

Handling Missing Data

One issue that should definitely be resolved before starting the data analysis is deciding what to do with missing values. They are a nuisance in many ways. First, it is not always clear whether the lack of any useful response is meaningful or not. For example, if Rupert is asked about what foreign languages he speaks and he leaves the question unanswered, would this mean that (a) Rupert only speaks his mother tongue, (b) he has skipped the question by mistake, or (c) he has intentionally refused to answer?

Second, for the purpose of certain statistical procedures a single missing value can invalidate an otherwise complete questionnaire. For example, in multivariate statistics when many variables are examined at the same time, some programs (e.g., AMOS, a well-known program used for structural equation modeling) can set it as a basic requirement to have valid values for *every* variable for a case, or the case will be automatically excluded from the analyses. Given that, regrettably, it is quite common to have a few missing values in every questionnaire, we can end up losing as much as half of our sample this way, which is clearly undesirable. In such cases the program might offer some ways of imputing the missing data that are unlikely to change the results, for example by including item means or maximum likelihood estimates. Luckily, several statistical procedures allow for a choice between *listwise deletion* and *pairwise deletion*: The former refers to the "hard" line whereby one missing value deletes a whole case from all the analyses even if some of the available data could be used for certain calculations. The latter refers to the temporary deletion of a case from the analysis only when specific statistics are computed that would involve the particular missing value.

In sum, missing data are always something to bear in mind and it is advisable to go through all our variables prior to the statistical analyses to check whether missing values have been properly recorded and interpreted. If we have "0" values coded, we would also need to consider whether these should be assigned a missing value status.

Recoding Values
It has been recommended earlier (in Section 2.6.2) that in order to avoid a response set whereby the respondent marks only one side of a rating scale, it is worth including in the questionnaire both positively and negatively worded items; this may also reduce the harmful effects of the acquiescence bias. For example, a scale that targets positive attitudes toward the L2 class may include the following negatively worded item: "*I find my language classes boring.*" However, if we have such negatively worded items, we must not forget to reverse the scoring for these before including them in multi-item scales. This may sound like an obvious and trivial recommendation, but unless one makes the recoding of such scores a compulsory step before any real analyses, it is all too easy to forget about it.

Standardizing the Data
When we use pooled results from various subsamples (e.g., data from different language classes), one way of controlling for the heterogeneous nature of the subgroups is to use standardized scores. The standardization of raw scores involves a fairly straightforward statistical conversion carried out by the computer: The distribution of a variable within a sample is transformed in a way that its mean will be and the standard deviation 1 (for more details about these terms, see Section 4.3.6). Such a standardized score expresses how much the individual members' raw scores differ from

the mean score of the particular subsample, and, because the means have been equalized, scores obtained from different subsamples (e.g., different classes in the school) become readily comparable. Furthermore, because the key parameters of the score distributions (i.e., the means and the standard deviations) are set the same in all subsamples, the subsample scores can be meaningfully pooled. For a detailed argument in favor of standardizing heterogeneous questionnaire data, see Gardner (1985, pp. 78-80); he also provides a hypothetical illustration in which a motivation measure shows significant positive correlation with learning achievement in two school classes when computed separately, but the same correlation becomes non-significant when the data are pooled without standardization.

4.3.3 Reducing the Number of Variables in the Questionnaire

Once we have completed data cleaning and data manipulation, we are ready to embark on the examination of the obtained data. The first step in analyzing questionnaire data is always to *reduce to manageable proportions the number of variables* measured by the questionnaire so that the mass of details does not prevent us from seeing the forest through the trees. The rationale for this is that—in accordance with the arguments in Section 2.3.2—a well-designed questionnaire contains several items focused on each content area and therefore the parallel items need to be summed up in *multi-item scales* for the purpose of analysis. By so doing, we can create fewer but broader variables that carry almost as much information as the original variables. However, even if we have not consciously devised multiple items assessing the same target, the chances are that some questions will tap into the same underlying trait and will therefore have to be summed.

The procedure to compute a multi-item scale is simple: All it takes is to calculate the mean of the constituent items. The difficult part is to decide *which* items to merge. Most researchers apply one of two approaches (or a combination of these) to determine which items belong together:

- Based on the theoretical considerations guiding the construction of the questionnaire, we form clusters of items that are hypothesized to hang together and then conduct an internal consistency check (see Section 4.3.5) to determine whether our assumptions are borne out in practice. As we will see in Section 4.3.5, some modern computer software not only computes coefficients describing the homogeneity of the items in a scale but can also advise us to possibly exclude one or more items from the scale if the internal consistency of the scale would improve in this way.

- One statistical technique, *factor analysis*, is particularly suited to reduce the number of variables to a few values that still contain most of the information found in the original variables (Hatch & Lazaraton, 1991). Although the procedure is rather complex mathematically, it is straightforward conceptually: It explores the inter-relationships of the items and tries to find patterns of correspondence—that is, common underlying themes—among them. The outcome is a small set of underlying dimensions, referred to as *factors* or *components*. This "pattern finding capacity" makes factor analysis very useful in making large datasets more manageable and therefore it is often used in the preparatory phase in data processing (for more details, see Dörnyei, 2007, pp. 233-236).

4.3.4 Main Types of Questionnaire Data

Although questionnaires show a great variety, they elicit only four main types of data: *nominal* (categorical), *ordinal*, *interval*, and *textual*. As will be discussed in Section 4.4, the last type—open-ended and sometimes extensive verbal response—is usually converted to quantifiable categories, that is, to one of the first three data types. The main difference between the three types of quantitative data lies in the precision of the measurement:

- *Nominal* or *categorical data* come from scales that have no meaningful numerical value, such as gender or race. Here the assigned values are completely arbitrary; for example, for the gender variable male is usually coded "1" and female "2," which does not indicate any difference in size or salience.
- *Ordinal data* are similar to nominal data except that greater numbers refer to the order of the values on a continuum. In other words, ordinal data involves ranked numbers. For example, a multiple-choice item with options such as "once a day," "once a week," "once a month," "once a year," and "never" will produce ordinal data because the answers can be placed on a "frequency" continuum.
- *Interval data* can be seen as ordinal data in which the various values are at an equal distance—or intervals—from each other on a continuum. That is, equal numerical differences in the coding imply equal differences in the degree/salience/size of the variable being measured. An example of such data would be L2 proficiency test scores. It is useful to note that interval data can be transformed as ordinal data, depending on analytical purposes. For example, learners taking a 100-point language proficiency test can be grouped into, say, three groups by forming a low-scoring group whose scores range from

0 to 33, a medium-scoring group whose scores range from 34 to 66, and a high-scoring group whose scores range from 67 to 100. The new grouping variable (having a value of 1 for the first group, 2 for the second, and 3 for the third) is ordinal in nature.

The separation of these three types of measure becomes important when we select the statistical techniques to be used with our data. Certain types of data can be analyzed only by means of certain types of techniques: The big dividing line is between *parametric procedures*, which require interval data, and *non-parametric procedures*, which can be applied to ordinal and even nominal data. Statistical computer packages contain a variety of procedures belonging to both types.

4.3.5 Examining the Reliability and Validity of the Data

Reliability and *validity* are two key concepts in measurement theory, referring to the psychometric properties of the measurement techniques and the data obtained by them.

- The *reliability* of a psychometric instrument refers to the extent to which scores on the instrument are free from errors of measurement. For example, bathroom scales are not reliable if they show different figures depending on the amount of steam in the bathroom, and neither are proficiency test raters if their evaluation varies according to how tired they are.
- *Validity* is the extent to which a psychometric instrument measures what it has been designed to measure. For example, if a test that is claimed to assess overall language proficiency measures only grammatical knowledge, the test is not valid in terms of evaluating communicative competence, although it may be perfectly valid with regard to the appraisal of grammar (in which case it should be called a grammar test).

Because of the salience of these terms in educational and psychological measurement, tens of thousands of pages have been written about them and every research manual will provide a detailed discussion about how to compute reliability/validity indices.

Questionnaires are scientific measurement instruments and, accordingly, they must be able to yield scores of adequate reliability and validity. Standardized questionnaires need to undergo rigorous validation procedures for different populations, and the manuals usually present a variety of reliability and validity coefficients. For made-to-measure research instruments that we develop for our specific research purpose, however, it is not always feasible to provide indices of every aspect of validity and reliability. Yet, even in cases where there are no resources and opportunities for elaborate validation exercises, we should strive for a questionnaire that has appropriate and well-documented reliability in at least one aspect: *internal consistency*. This attribute refers to the homogeneity of the items making up the various multi-item scales within the questionnaire. If your instrument has it, you can feel fairly safe.

Internal Consistency Reliability
In order to meet internal consistency reliability requirements, a questionnaire must satisfy two conditions:

(a) Instead of single items, *multi-item scales* (see Section 2.3.2) are to be used wherever it is possible.
(b) Multi-item scales are only effective if the items work together in a homogeneous manner, that is, if they measure the same target area. In psychometric terms this means that each item on a scale should correlate with the other items and with the total scale score; as mentioned already, this condition has been referred to as Likert's criterion of "Internal Consistency" (Anderson, 1985).

Internal consistency is generally seen as the psychometric prerequisite for any scientific survey measurement. It does not guarantee the validity of a scale—as in extreme cases we can imagine a scale where all the items consistently measure something different from the scale's intended purpose—but the intuitive contention is that if several items *seem* to measure a construct and they can be proven to measure the *same thing*, then this "same thing" *must be* the targeted construct.

Nunnally (1978) points out that the term "internal consistency" is partly a misnomer, because the reliability coefficient is based not only on the average correlation among the items (i.e., internal consistency proper) but also on the number of items making up the scale. That is, it is much easier to achieve appropriate internal consistency reliability with 20 items than with 3. This, of course, makes good sense: With few items the wording of the individual items can make much more of a difference than with 20, and therefore short scales need to display more evidence of homogeneity than long ones to be seen as trustworthy. Although internal consistency admittedly covers only one aspect of overall reliability, Nunnally concludes that reliability estimated from internal consistency is usually surprisingly close to the reliability estimated from other sources, for example from correlations between alternative questionnaire forms.

Measuring and Ensuring Internal Consistency Reliability

Internal consistency reliability is measured by the *Cronbach Alpha coefficient* (named after its introducer, L. J. Cronbach). This is a figure ranging between 0 and +1 (although in extreme cases—for example, with very small samples and with items that measure rather different things—it can also be negative), and if it proves to be very low, either the particular scale is too short or the items have very little in common. Internal consistency estimates for well-developed attitude scales containing as few as 10 items ought to approach 0.80. Because of the complexity of the second language acquisition process, L2 researchers typically want to measure many different areas in one questionnaire, and therefore cannot use very long scales (or the completion of the questionnaire would take several hours). This means that somewhat lower Cronbach Alpha coefficients are to be expected, but even with short scales of 3-4 items we should aim at reliability coefficients in excess of 0.70; if the Cronbach Alpha of a scale does not reach 0.60, this should sound warning bells.

How do we obtain Cronbach Alpha coefficients? Modern statistical computer programs make it relatively easy to conduct item analysis. The "Reliability" procedure of SPSS, for example, not only provides the Cronbach Alpha for any given scale but also computes what the Alpha coefficient would be if a particular item were deleted from the scale. By looking at the list of these "would-be" Alphas for each item, we can immediately see which item reduces the internal consistency of the scale and should therefore be considered for omission. Sample 4.1 presents the results of the analysis of a seven-item scale focusing on *group cohesiveness*. The Cronbach Alpha coefficient of the total scale is 0.77, which is rather good. However, if we look at the Alpha statistics if each item were to be deleted, we can see that deleting Item 1 would add to the internal consistency of the scale, whereas deleting any of the other items would reduce the reliability.

A frequently asked question is, "How far should the deletion process go?" That is, "Is it advisable to keep deleting items from a scale even after the scale's Cronbach Alpha has reached 0.70?" If some substantial further improvement can achieved by deleting an item that is either somewhat questionable or is of secondary importance in the scale, I would probably discard it, but if the theoretical breadth or soundness of the scale would be compromised by the deletion of the item, then it is best to leave it.

Reliability analysis can also be used to reduce the number of items in the scale. It is sometimes necessary to discard some items from the scale, for example for the purpose of reducing the number of items in the item pool and making the questionnaire shorter. In this case, by relying on suggestions from the computer we can be more confident which items to leave out. An alternative method for making scales shorter and more homogeneous is using factor analysis to help to eliminate items (see, for example, Noels, Pelletier, Clément, & Vallerand, 2000, who followed this procedure). In this case, scale uni-dimensionality is achieved by selecting only those items that have the highest loadings on the factor that they were written to tap. Finally, the simplest and yet effective way of ensuring that the items making up a scale belong together is to compute correlation coefficients for each item with the total scale score and to retain the items with the highest correlations. Sample 4.1 shows very clearly that the item-total correlation for Item 1 is considerably lower than all the other correlations, which confirms the result of the reliability analysis, namely that the internal consistency of this scale would improve if this item was deleted.

Sample 4.1 Reliability Analysis for "Group Cohesiveness"
Item-total Statistics (based on real data)

Item	Corrected item-total correlation	Cronbach Alpha if item deleted
1. Sometimes there are tensions among the members of my group and these make learning more difficult.	.23	.80
2. Compared to other groups like mine, I feel that m y group is better than most.	.50	.75
3. There are some cliques in this group.	.44	.76
4. If I were to participate in another group like this one, I would want it to include people who are very similar to the ones in this group.	.63	.72
5. This group is composed of people who fit together.	.66	.72
6. There are some people in this group who do not really like each other.	.47	.75
7. I am dissatisfied with my group.	.58	.73

Cronbach Alpha for the seven items = .77

4.3.6 Statistical Procedures to Analyze Data

The standard method of analyzing quantitative questionnaire data involves submitting them to various statistical procedures. These include a range of different techniques, from calculating item means on a pocket calculator to running complex statistical analyses. As mentioned earlier, it is beyond the scope of this book to provide a detailed analysis of the available procedures (for non-technical discussions of statistics, see Dörnyei, 2007; Pallant, 2007). Instead, I would like to emphasize one crucial aspect of statistical data analysis that is so often misunderstood or ignored by novice researchers: the distinction between *descriptive statistics* and *inferential statistics*.

Descriptive Statistics

Descriptive statistics are used to summarize sets of numerical data in order to conserve time and space. It is obvious that providing the *mean* and the *range* (i.e., minimum and maximum values) of a variable is a more profes- sional way of describing the respondents' answers than listing all the scores that have been obtained. And if we also include the *standard deviation* of the results (which is an index of the average disparity among the scores), we have achieved a well-rounded description of the scores that would satisfy most purposes. Thus, descriptive statistics offer a tidy way of presenting the data we have. The important thing, however, is to note that these statistics do *not* allow drawing any general conclusions that would go beyond the sample. In practice this means that we ought to start every sentence which describes descriptive findings by "*In my sample* . . ." If we want to draw some more general lessons from the study—which is what we usually do when we write a journal article or give a conference presentation—we need to compute *inferential statistics*.

Inferential Statistics

Broadly speaking, inferential statistics are the same as descriptive statistics except that the computer also tests whether the results that we observed in our sample (e.g., mean differences or correlations) are powerful enough to generalize to the whole population. It makes intuitive sense that what we find needs to pass a certain threshold of magnitude to be of general significance— inferential statistics basically evaluates the results against such a threshold. Let us look at the following example. Descriptive statistics are useful to describe the achievement of a particular class of learners. What happens, however, if we notice that, say, the L2 learning achievement of boys and girls shows a remarkable difference in our sample, with girls outperforming boys (which is often the case)? Can we draw the inference that girls tend to be better language learners? No, we cannot. Based on descriptive statistics all we can say is that in this class girls did better than boys. In order to venture any generalization concerning the wider population and not just the particular sample, we need to show that the difference between girls and boys is *significant in the statistical sense*. To achieve this, we need to employ *inferential statistical procedures*.

> **Well said . . .**
> When an individual uses descriptive statistics, he talks about the data he has; but with inferential statistics, he talks about data he does not have.
>
> (Popham & Sirotnik, 1973, p. 40)

Statistical significance denotes whether a particular result is powerful enough to indicate a more generalizable phenomenon. If a result is non-significant, this means that we cannot be certain that it did not occur in the particular sample only because of chance (e.g., because of the unique composition of the respondents examined). In other words, even if we feel that the particular descriptive data reveal some true and more general tendency, we cannot exclude the possibility of a mere coincidence. For this reason, statistically non-significant results *must be ignored* in research studies. That is, we must not say things like *Although the mean difference between boys' and girls' scores did not reach significance, girls tended to do better than boys . . .*

One important feature of statistical significance is that it is the function of not only the magnitude of the result but also the *size of the sample* investigated. It is easy to see why this is so: If we assess, say, millions of people, even a relatively weak tendency can be regarded as typical of the whole population, whereas with only a handful of people we cannot be certain even about far stronger tendencies. Therefore, clever computers take the combined effect of magnitude and sample size into account when they calculate the significance of a result. If they mark a particular result as *significant*, we can utter a sigh of relief as this means that the observed phenomenon represents a significant departure from what might be expected by chance alone. That is, it can be assumed to be *real*. Having said that, we also need to stress here that statistical significance is *not* the final answer because even though a result may be statistically significant (i.e., reliable and true to the larger population), it may not be valuable. "Significance" in the statistical sense only means "probably true" rather than "important."

To sum it up, if researchers have some interesting data obtained from, say, a language class and they want to use these data as the basis for making certain more general claims, it is not enough to merely quote descriptive statistics that support their observation. They also have to run inferential statistical tests (such as T-tests, ANOVAs, or correlation analysis) to check if what they have noticed is powerful enough to qualify as being statistically significant.

4.4 Content Analysis of Open-Ended Questions

Although it was argued in Sections 1.3 and 2.5 that wide-open, essay-like questions do not work well in questionnaires and therefore should be avoided, questions that are slightly "less open" can have some merits and are well worth experimenting with as long as this does not get done at the expense of the closed questions (in terms of response time or willingness). Because open-ended questions do not have pre-coded response options, their processing is less straightforward than that of closed items.

Specific open questions (see Section 2.5.1) usually ask about factual information that is easy to summarize. With adequate coding specifications (see Section 4.1.2), the responses to these items can be turned into distinct categories and then treated as nominal, or possibly ordinal, data (see Section 4.3.4).

With *clarification questions*, *sentence completion tasks*, and *short-answer questions* (see Sections 2.5.2 to 2.5.4), the categorization process involves more potentially subjective elements on the part of the coder. In order to avoid the harmful effects of such rater subjectivity, these items are to be processed by means of some systematic "content analysis," whereby the pool of diverse responses is reduced to a handful of key issues in a reliable manner. This is usually achieved through a stepwise process that involves two broad phases (for a detailed discussion, see Brown, 2001; Dörnyei, 2007):

1. Taking each person's response in turn and marking in them any distinct content elements, substantive statements, or key points.
2. Based on the ideas and concepts highlighted in the texts (see Phase 1), forming broader categories to describe the content of the response in a way that allows for comparisons with other responses.

The categories obtained in Phase 2 can be numerically coded and then entered into the data file to be treated as quantitative data. Some of the key points highlighted in Phase 1 can also be quoted in the research report verbatim for the purpose of illustration and exemplification, or to retain some of the original flavor of the response.

Finally, although often omitted, qualitative data can also be checked for reliability, for example by computing inter-coder agreement coefficients that describe to what extent two raters agree on assigning categories to the responses (see Brown, 2001, pp. 231-240; Dörnyei, 2007, pp. 56-62).

Well said . . .

In practice, even the most direct forms of content analysis involve a good deal of to-ing and fro-ing and there are almost always some loose ends, unclassifiable elements which have to be reported as such.

(Gillham, 2008, p. 65)

4.5 Computer Programs for Processing Questionnaire Data

There are numerous statistical software packages that can be used to process quantitative questionnaire data. Personally, I have always used, and been satisfied with, SPSS (Statistical Package for the Social Sciences), which is the market leader in this category. There are also various computer programs to facilitate the qualitative analysis of transcribed texts (e.g., NVivo, SPSS Text Analysis for Surveys). From a survey researcher's point of view, programs that can handle quantitative and qualitative questionnaire data in an integrated manner are particularly valuable. There is no shortage of desktop packages specifically created to combine questionnaire design, data collection, and qualitative/quantitative data analysis (there are over 30 such programs available; for references, see Section 2.9). Although they show considerable variation in terms of the elaborateness of the various processing components, many packages can already perform most of what ordinary users will ever need. Furthermore, developments in this area are so fast that the improved versions available in a few years' time will have ironed out most of the currently existing shortcomings.

In Section 2.9, I introduced one particular program, *Sphinx Survey*, which is an integrated, PC-based Windows package for conducting questionnaire-based surveys (for a review, see Macer, 1999). One reason for selecting this software has been its unique and powerful qualitative data analysis module. All the available survey research programs on the market can perform standard statistical operations (and for advanced statistics, researchers can switch over to a specialized statistical software), but there is far less available in terms of analyzing the open-ended, longer verbal responses. The lexical module of *Sphinx Survey* provides a variety of indices about open responses, ranging from total number of words and the number of unique words, to the most frequently used words and lexical range. The program can reduce the vocabulary of each response by eliminating non-relevant words and terms, leaving a core lexicon that is readily analyzable for content. Other sophisticated functions offer *computer aided content analysis* of each text response by assigning categories to it, which can then be analyzed by means of quantitative methods. Such lexical examinations are still fairly novel in survey research and are definitely worth experimenting with.

For the purpose of analyzing open-ended questions in surveys, SPSS Inc. has produced a software program called SPSS Text Analysis for Surveys, to categorize verbatim questions. In the process of the analysis, this program makes it possible not only to provide statistics-based methods (i.e., frequency of terms and phrases) but also linguistics-based methods (i.e., grouping terms with similar meanings and identifying semantic networks smoothly). In addition, because it is strongly linked with the statistical modules of the SPSS software, data management for analysis by importing and exporting the text-based results becomes easier (for a review of this product, see Galt, 2008).

4.6 Summarizing and Reporting Questionnaire Data

Having collected and analyzed the data, the researcher's next job is to write up and disseminate the results. This is because, as Ortega (2005) argues, any research field in the social sciences, including applied linguistics, has as its ultimate goal the improvement of human life. Therefore, it is a researchers' responsibility to communicate their results and the practical significance of their research in clear, straightforward, and appropriate language.

Survey data can be used for a great variety of purposes and each of these might require somewhat different types of summaries and reports of the findings. It is obvious, for instance, that a Ph.D. dissertation will have to meet criteria that are very different from the presentation requirements of a summary of student achievement at a school staff meeting. Rather than attempting to provide templates for all the diverse applications (such templates are readily available in various writers' manuals and also in Chs. 12-13 in Dörnyei, 2007), in the following I will focus on three general aspects of survey reports:

- *General guidelines* about what to report and how.
- The *technical information* about the survey that needs to be included in a professional report to accompany the actual findings.
- *Presentation methods* that can make survey data more reader-friendly and digestible.

4.6.1 General Guidelines

There are two specific problem areas in reporting survey findings that I have often observed both in my own and my graduate students' writing: (a) the question of how much one should be allowed to generalize; and (b) the problem of the detached nature of the largely quantitative summaries from the real-life situations they concern.

How Much to Generalize

With regard to the issue of generalizing the findings, it is so easy to offer the broad and rather unhelpful guideline: *Do not overgeneralize!* However, research in most cases is all about the need to produce generalizable findings. After all, with the exception of "action research," researchers in the L2 field rarely investigate a sample with the sole purpose of wanting to know more about the particular people under investigation only. Instead, what we normally want to do is find out more about the *population* (see Section 3.1), that is, about all the similar people in the world. This means that the crucial question to decide is what "over" means in the term "overgeneralization."

It would again be easy to give a less than useful, though technically correct, definition of "overgeneralization," namely that it occurs when we generalize the findings to a population that our sample is not representative of. This states, in effect, that if we examine, say, primary school pupils, we should not generalize our findings to secondary or university students. There is no question about the truth in this claim, and yet it avoids the crux of the problem, which is that if we were to observe this guideline rigidly, few (if any) studies in the educational psychological literature could speak about "students" in general. It is clear that hardly any investigations are sufficiently large-scale to include representatives of every main age group, ethnicity, school type, and subject matter in a single study (just to list four key factors)—yet the discussions of the findings are rarely restricted to the particular subpopulation in question.

This does not mean, though, that I support overgeneralization. No, not in the least. However, in the absence of hard-and-fast rules about what constitutes *over*generalization, we need to strive to find a delicate balance between the following two considerations:

- On the one hand, we may wish to be able to say something of broader relevance (since it may severely reduce our audience if we limit our discussion to very specific subgroups).
- On the other hand, big claims can usually be made only on the basis of big studies.

Having said that, some classic studies in the research literature did confine their focus to extremely limited target issues, and some famous big claims were indeed made based on small studies.

So, the conclusion I can offer is that researchers need to exercise great caution when pitching the level of generalization in their research reports; this is particularly so in light of Lazaraton's (2005) warning that using high-powered parametric procedures may easily tempt scholars to overgeneralize their results and to make grand claims regarding their findings. On the other hand, along with the "Task Force on Statistical Inference" of the American Psychological Association (Wilkinson & TFSI, 1999, p. 602), I would encourage researchers not to be afraid "to extend your interpretations to a general class or population if you have reasons to assume that your results apply."

Detachment from Real Life

Researchers often note how ironical it is that months of hard labor can sometimes be summarized in one or two tables. While this may not be a problem in basic research—after all, Einstein's theory of relativity did not exactly take up several volumes either—in more applied studies when we are looking at concrete questions concerning real people, a primarily quantitative summary may lose some of the edge and flavor of the original issue. This is when a few open-ended items in the questionnaire might play a useful role in providing quotations that can help to retain or restore the real perspective. Furthermore, as Moser and Kalton (1971) remind us, to many readers statistical tables are dull and difficult to comprehend, and a certain amount of verbatim quotation of answers can effectively enliven the report (see Section 4.6.3, which describes a number of reader-friendly presentation techniques).

How true . . .!

If the basic research questions are complex (when are they not?) then your data are going to look pretty thin and superficial if all you can report are the results of a questionnaire. In a small-scale study this lack is going to be particularly apparent.

(Gillham, 2008, p. 99)

4.6.2 Technical Information to Accompany Survey Results

Novice researchers often make the mistake of concentrating only on the presentation of their actual findings in their survey reports, while paying little attention to describing their methodology. While this approach may appear logical, it fails to take into account the fact that in order to be able to interpret (and believe) the claims made, readers will have to be convinced that the methodology used to produce the particular findings was appropriate. This does not mean that we can only report results if our study did not have any methodological limitations but only that we must provide a concise and yet detailed summary of the main aspects of the survey, including any known limiting factors. There is no perfect study and it is up to the readers (and the journal editors) to decide on the value of the findings. The following list of the main points to be covered can be used as a checklist:

PARTICIPANTS (i.e., the sample)

- *Description of the sample*: The exact details to be supplied depend on the focus of the study but normally include as a minimum the participants':
  - total number (possibly accompanied by some justification and the total number of all the eligible people);
  - age;
  - gender;
  - ethnicity (possibly accompanied by information about the participants' first language);
  - any grouping variable (e.g., number of courses or classes they come from);
  - level of L2 proficiency;
  - L2 learning history;
  - L2 teaching institution (if applicable);
  - type of tuition received.
- Any necessary *additional details* (again, depending on the study), such as:
  - general aptitude (or academic ability);
  - socioeconomic background;

  – participants' occupation or (if the participants are students) areas of specialization;
  – L2 class size;
  – L2 teaching materials used;
  – amount of time spent in an L2 host environment.
- The *sampling method* used for the selection of the participants.
- If the sample consisted of several groups: *similarities* and *differences* among them.

QUESTIONNAIRE

- *Description* of and *rationale* for the main content areas covered.
- *Justification* of why some potentially important areas have been left out.
- *Factual description* of the instrument (with the actual questionnaire possibly attached in the Appendix), including:
  – number of main parts/sections;
  – number of items;
  – types of items (e.g., response types);
  – scoring procedures;
  – language of the actual instrument administered to the sample.
- Details about the *piloting* of the instrument.
- Any available data concerning the *reliability* and *validity* of the instrument.
- Details about how *confidentiality/anonymity* was handled.

QUESTIONNAIRE ADMINISTRATION

- *Procedures* used to administer the questionnaire, including:
  – any advance information provided;
  – characteristics of the questionnaire administrator(s) (including training/briefing, role, experience, education, etc.);
  – administration format (e.g., postal, one-to-one on-the-spot, one-to-one take-away, group, email, online);
  – any special circumstances or events.
- *Length of time* that was needed to complete the questionnaire.
- *Duration of the complete survey* (if it included several administration dates).
- Questionnaire *return rate*.

VARIABLES

- *Complete list* of the variables derived from the raw questionnaire data, including details of how they were operationalized.
- With *multi-item scales*: the number of constituent items and the Cronbach Alpha internal consistency reliability coefficient for each scale.

LIMITATIONS

- Any *circumstances* (foreseen or unforeseen) that may have affected the results in a systematic manner.
- Problems related to the *size* and *representativeness* of the sample.
- Any potential *biases of the sample* (related to composition, selection procedure, non-participation, or dropout rate, etc.).
- *Biases* stemming from missing *data*.
- Problems with the *research design*.

Well said . . .

Research workers writing for fellow scientists are generally careful to emphasize limitations; indeed they sometimes fall over backwards to argue that what they have been doing is worthless. But particularly when writing for a general audience, the temptation to soft-pedal limitations is strong; the writer feels that the significance of technical shortcomings will not be appreciated, and shortage of space further encourages him to skip them. There is little need to stress how serious such omissions can be.

(Moser & Kalton, 1971, p. 477)

4.6.3 Reader-Friendly Data Presentation Methods

Questionnaire studies typically produce a wealth of data, and therefore developing effective and digestible—that is, reader-friendly—ways of presenting the data is an essential skill for the survey researcher. A rule of thumb is that we should present as much of the information as possible in *figures* and *tables* rather than in the running text. Or, to go one step further: Whatever can be presented in tables and figures, should be.

Figures
Figures are methods to visualize various characteristics of the data. I have used two types of figures in the past, *charts/diagrams* and *schematic representations*.

Charts/diagrams offer a useful way of describing the size/strength of variables in relation to each other. *Bar charts* and *line charts* use a vertical *Y*-axis and a horizontal *X*-axis to present data (see Figures 4.1 and 4.2). The vertical axis usually represents the unit of measurement (or dependent variable) and the horizontal axis the independent variable(s). These charts are very flexible in terms of the type of data they can display, and they can effectively demonstrate comparisons or changes over time in a way that is easy to interpret (Fink, 1995).

Pie charts are used to describe proportions and percentages; they are usually used in presentations for non-specialist audiences rather than in academic publications. The first pie chart in Figure 4.3 can display, for example, the proportion of focusing on three L2 skills in a language course. If we want to highlight changes, we can use two pies. Thus, the second pie below can be seen, for example, to represent the revised curriculum after some significant educational reform. By changing the overall size of the second pie we can also indicate growth or shrinkage (Fink, 1995)—the pie charts

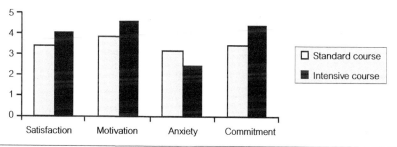

Figure 4.1 Sample bar chart

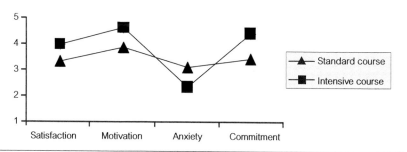

Figure 4.2 Sample line chart

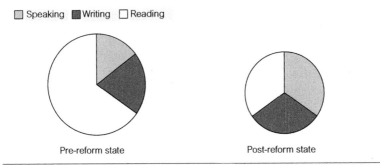

Figure 4.3 Sample pie charts

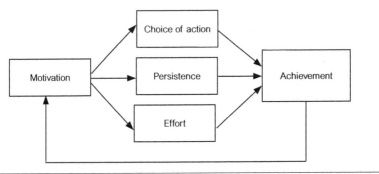

Figure 4.4 Sample schematic representation

in Figure 4.3 may suggest a decrease in the total amount of tuition after the reform.

Schematic representations offer a useful way to describe complex relationships between multiple variables, and typically utilize various boxes and arrows (see Figure 4.4). They can be used, for example, to describe the blueprint of mental processes or the componential structure of multi-level constructs.

Tables

Tables are used to summarize data about the respondents and their responses, and to present results of statistical analyses (see Table 4.1 as well as Sample 4.1 on page 96). They are typically made up of rows and columns of numbers, each marked with headings and subheadings. They can provide a more accurate and richer description than figures but they are less digestible because they lack the advantage of a visual impact. Tables are, therefore, more appropriate for articles in academic journals than for lectures to a non-specialist audience.

Table 4.1 Sample table reporting descriptive statistics

| | Language proficiency level | | | | | | | | |
| | Beginner | | | Intermediate | | | Advanced | | |
Sex	M	SD	n	M	SD	n	M	SD	n
Female	3.35	.38	353	3.20	.45	1.041	3.12	.52	274
Male	3.22	.47	257	3.04	.47	653	2.97	.52	152

Language Anxiety Scores of Hungarian Secondary School Learners of Finnish, Broken Down by Proficiency Level.

In reporting the results of tables, there are two points that need to be stressed. First, if we present statistics in tables, we should *not* include the figures also in the text, except for highlighting some particularly noteworthy results. Second, we should note that statistics tables have certain canonical features, both in content (i.e., what information to include) and format (for example, usually we do not use vertical lines). See Dörnyei (2007, Chs. 9 and 12) for concrete illustrations.

Indeed . . .

Page after page of ANOVA tables in a results section challenges even the most determined reader, who may still give up and head right for the discussion section.

(Lazaraton, 2005, p. 218)

4.7 Complementing Questionnaire Data with Other Information

Having discussed how to construct and administer questionnaires, and then how to analyze and report the data we have obtained, let me briefly address some ways of proceeding toward a fuller understanding of the content area targeted by our survey. As discussed in Chapter 1, although questionnaires offer a versatile and highly effective means of data collection, the kinds of insight they can generate are limited by several factors, most notably by the restricted time and effort that respondents are usually willing to invest in completing the instrument. In a more general sense, questionnaires are also limited by the shortcomings of quantitative research as a methodological approach, in that they offer little scope for explorative, in-depth analyses of complex relationships or for doing justice to the subjective variety of an individual life.

The good news about questionnaires, however, is that their flexible nature makes them ideal for use in complex research paradigms in concert with other data collection methods, particularly qualitative methods (e.g., interviews, observations, and diary studies). Such an integrated approach is often labeled as *mixed methods research*, and it involves the collection, analysis, and mixing of both quantitative and qualitative data in a project.

While several methodology mixtures are possible (see Creswell & Plano Clark, 2007; Dörnyei, 2007; Teddlie & Tashakkori, 2009, for further details), the most common combination of questionnaire research is with an interview study that either follows or precedes the survey (see below). However, questionnaires can also be integrated with several other research methods, for example to collect background information about the participants in an experimental study or to complement classroom observation data. In fact, the recent advocacy of the integrated use of multiple data collection methods, in line with the general concept of "triangulation," has created fertile ground for the increased use of professionally designed questionnaires as psychometrically sound measuring instruments.

4.7.1 Questionnaire Survey with Follow-up Interview or Retrospection

Statistical procedures allow us to examine the intricate interrelationship of the variables measured in a survey, but if we find some unexpected results (and there are always some unexpected results!) we cannot usually interpret those on the basis of the questionnaire data. And even if an observed relationship does make sense, the questionnaire data can typically reveal little about the exact nature of this relationship. Adding a subsequent qualitative component to the study can remedy this weakness: In a follow-up interview (either in an individual or focus group format), we can ask the respondents to explain or illustrate the obtained patterns and characteristics, thereby adding flesh to the bones. Creswell, Plano, Clark, Gutmann, and Hanson (2003) labeled this combination a "sequential explanatory design," which expresses its rationale well. This is a straightforward design that is easy to implement and analyze, yet which enriches the final findings considerably.

In a similar vein, Gillham (2008) also urges survey researchers to conduct semi-structured interviews to accompany questionnaire results in order to gain a better understanding of what the numerical responses actually mean. Interview data can both illustrate and illuminate questionnaire results and can "bring your research study to life" (p. 101). Questionnaires also lend themselves to follow-up *retrospective research* (see Gass & Mackey, 2000; Kasper, 1998; Kormos, 1998), in which participants are asked to go through their own responses with an interviewer and provide retrospective comments on the reason for their particular answer to each item. Thus, in this design the participants' own item responses serve as prompts for further open-ended reflection and, at the same time, the comprehensive coverage of all the items ensures systematicity.

4.7.2 Questionnaire Survey Facilitated by Preceding Interview

This design is related to the development of an item pool, discussed earlier in Section 2.6.1. As already mentioned there briefly, a frequently recommended procedure for designing a new questionnaire involves conducting a small-scale exploratory qualitative study first (usually a series of focus group interviews but one-to-one interviews can also serve the purpose) to provide background information on the context, to identify or narrow down the focus of the possible variables, and to act as a valuable source of ideas for preparing the item pool for the purpose of questionnaire scale construction. Such a design is effective in improving the content representation of the survey and thus the internal validity of the study. It is routinely used when researchers are building a new instrument.

CHAPTER 5

Illustration: Developing a Motivation Questionnaire

with TATSUYA TAGUCHI

The previous chapters have explained the main principles of constructing and administering questionnaires and processing questionnaire data. While it is important to understand these theoretical principles, relatively little has been said so far about how to put them into practice. Therefore, drawing on the experiences of a questionnaire development project at the University of Nottingham, this chapter provides a detailed, step-by-step illustration of how a concrete instrument was designed, piloted, and finalized. The questionnaire that we present has already been used in a large-scale comparative study in Japan, China, and Iran, and some of the results have appeared in Taguchi, Magid, and Papi (2009). In this chapter, the focus will be on the procedures for constructing the original, Japanese version, but we will also discuss how this instrument has been adapted for use in the other two countries. All the items of the three versions can be found in Appendix A and the final, formatted versions of the three instruments, along with their English translation, are presented in Appendix B. Finally, in Appendix C we have included references to many published questionnaires in the L2 field that we know of.

5.1 Construction of the Initial Questionnaire

Developing a questionnaire is a stepwise process, and the quality of the final instrument depends on the cumulative quality of each sub-process. The following description follows through these steps sequentially, and we will regularly refer back to the relevant theoretical parts in the first four chapters.

5.1.1 Deciding the Content Areas to be Covered in the Questionnaire

The first step in constructing any questionnaire is to decide what main concepts need to be addressed in the study (Section 2.3.1). One of the main research objectives of the project we are going to illustrate was to replicate in diverse language learning environments Dörnyei et al.'s (2006) Hungarian motivation studies, using the framework of Dörnyei's (2005) "L2 Motivational Self System," which is made up of three dimensions: the *Ideal L2 self*, the *Ought-to L2 self*, and the *L2 learning experience*. The target population of the study in Japan involved university students learning English as part of their studies. The specific content areas which we considered important in relation to the L2 Motivational Self System and the understanding of Japanese learners' motivation to learn English were selected on the basis of a review of previous studies (Clément & Baker, 2001; Dörnyei et al., 2006; Gardner, 1985; Mayumi, in progress; Noels et al., 2000; Ryan, 2008; Ushioda, 2001), and in the end we decided to cover the following 16 variables:

(a) *Criterion measures (related to intended effort)*; (b) *Ideal L2 self*; (c) *Ought-to L2 self*; (d) *Parental encouragement*; (e) *Instrumentality-promotion*; (f) *Instrumentality-prevention*; (g) *Linguistic self-confidence*; (h) *Attitudes toward learning English*; (i) *Travel orientation*; (j) *Fear of assimilation*; (k) *Ethnocentrism*; (l) *Interest in the English language*; (m) *English anxiety*; (n) *Integrativeness*; (o) *Cultural interest*; and (p) *Attitudes toward L2 community*.

The important point to emphasize here is that this initial stage needs to be fully theory-driven rather than choosing the variables to measure on the basis of what ready-made instrument is available. The stakes are high: If we do not include a particular content area in the questionnaire at this stage, it has no chance of emerging later on during the survey even if the specific variable is salient in the population. Thus, the initial selection of the content areas constitutes a significant constraint with regard to the final results.

5.1.2 Designing Items for the Item Pool

Once the specific content areas have been determined, the next task is to devise items assessing the concepts in the questionnaire, thereby forming an item pool for each variable. Because our instrument contained a wide range of factors to be assessed, the multi-item scales (Section 2.3.2) to be used needed to be short. We set the minimum number of items per content area at 3-4 items, but at this initial stage we did not know how the items would work in the real survey, so the initial item pools contained several extra items. Here is a list of the main issues that came up at this stage:

- As most of the specific content areas in this project were based on previous studies, many of the actual items in the item pool were adopted from established questionnaires (Section 2.6.1). However, even these items required certain modifications in order to make them suitable for the specific research context. Illustration 5.1 presents a selection of initial items and their modified version.

Illustration 5.1 Item Modifications

Original: Do you like Hollywood films?
Modified: Do you like English films?
Original: Do you like English magazines? (Write "X" if you don't know any.)
Modified: Do you like English magazines, newspapers, or books?
Original: I don't trust people with different customs and values to myself.
Modified: I am uncomfortable with people with customs and values different to mine.

- Because of our reliance on previously published English-language instruments, and also because the members of our team were of various nationalities, the whole initial questionnaire construction phase was conducted in English, knowing that the English version would need to be translated later into the respondents' mother tongue (Section 2.8).
- We decided to use two types of items, *statements* suitable for Likert scales and *questions* to make some of the items identical in format to the question-type items used by Dörnyei *et al.* (2006) in Hungary.
- Some content areas were theoretically new (e.g., *Ought-to L2 self* and *Instrumentality-prevention*) and thus required the design of new items. Here we largely relied on our own experience and creativity (Illustration 5.2 presents some newly written items).

Illustration 5.2 Some Newly Written Items

- Learning English is important for me because the people I respect expect me to study it. (*Ought-to L2 self*)
- My parents encourage me to attend extra English classes after school. (*Parental encouragement*)
- I have to learn English because without passing the English course I cannot graduate. (*Instrumentality-prevention*)
- Studying English is important for me because I don't want to get a poor score or a fail mark in English proficiency tests. (*Instrumentality-prevention*)

- After some deliberation, we decided not to include items assessing the language teachers—for the *L2 learning experience* dimension—because for our large-scale study we needed the willing cooperation of a large number of colleagues, many of whom would have been reluctant to allow the instrument to be administered in their classes if it had contained such sensitive items (Sections 2.1.3 and 2.6.3).

5.1.3 Designing Rating Scales

With regard to the type of rating scales to employ (Section 2.4.1), we adopted the scales used by Ryan (2008), because his scales had already been adjusted to Japanese learners of English after extensive piloting. Statement-type items were measured by six-point Likert scales, with the options ranging from *strongly disagree* to *strongly agree* (Section 2.4.1). We decided not to include a middle point, and because of the cultural reluctance of many Japanese respondents to give an explicit negative response, we emphasized the graded nature of the appraisal by assigning numbers to the response options and repeating these for each item (Illustration 5.3 presents a segment of the actual questionnaire to illustrate this). The question-type items were also assessed by a six-point scale ranging from *not at all* (1) to *very much* (6).

5.1.4 Designing the Personal Information Section

In line with the arguments presented in Section 2.7.3, all the personal, background questions were placed at the end of the instrument, following the content items. In order to facilitate more honest and less cliché-like responses, we decided to make the questionnaire totally anonymous (Sections 2.1.3 and 3.3.7). Being aware of the potential sensitivity of asking about personal details (such as gender, age, year of study at university, etc.), we

Illustration 5.3 The "Numerical Likert Scale" used in the Questionnaire

In this part, we would like you to tell us how much you agree or disagree with the following statements by simply circling a number from 1 to 6. Please do not leave out any of items.

Strongly disagree	Disagree	Slightly disagree	Slightly agree	Agree	Strongly agree
1	2	3	4	5	6

(Ex.) If you strongly agree with the following statement, write this:						
I like skiing very much.	1	2	3	4	5	⑥

1.	Learning English is important to me because I would like to travel internationally.	1	2	3	4	5	6
2.	My parents encourage me to study English.	1	2	3	4	5	6

targeted only the most important attributes in the personal information section, and we provided ready-made response options for the respondents to tick (Section 2.6.3). However, in the case of the students' university major, because participants were expected to study a diverse range of subject areas, the question was presented as an open-ended item.

We spent quite a bit of time elaborating the final item focusing of the students' self-assessed English proficiency. In the end, we adapted the scales used in one of the major proficiency exams in Japan (STEP, n.d.) since these scales succinctly explained each proficiency level.

5.1.5 Designing Instructions

Once we had decided the type of items to be used in the questionnaire, we were ready to start writing the various instructions (Section 2.2.2). As for the general instruction introducing the questionnaire, the model instruction in Sample 2.1 (see page 19) was modified to suit the current research context (see Illustration 5.4).

Illustration 5.4 The General Instruction Used in the Questionnaire

This survey is conducted by the School of English Studies of the University of Nottingham, UK, to better understand the thoughts and beliefs of learners of English. This questionnaire consists of four sections. Please read each instruction and write your answers accordingly. This is not a test so there are no "right" or "wrong" answers and you do not even have to write your name on it. The results of this survey will be used only for research purpose so please give your answers sincerely. Thank you very much for your help!

After the general instruction, specific instructions and examples of how to provide answers were provided for each type of questionnaire item (see Illustration 5.3 and Appendix B). It was recommended earlier (in Section 2.6.3) that before the final part in which we ask about personal issues, the instruction should contain some sort of a justification and a renewed promise of confidentiality to counter the respondent's typical reluctance to disclose private information. Because in our case we restricted the personal section to a few basic items, we did not think that these required any special introduction. Finally, in addition to the instructions, we need to think of a title of the questionnaire (Section 2.2.1) and of course we must not forget about a final "Thank you" (Section 2.2.5).

5.1.6 Designing the Questionnaire Format

We saw earlier that the overall appearance of the questionnaire has an important impact on respondents and therefore special attention needs to be paid to format design (Sections 2.1.1 and 2.1.2). As argued before, a four-page booklet format is ideal in many respects, and by using the available space well (e.g., small margins; response options next to the items; appropriate balance between content density and an orderly, clearly marked structure) we managed to include 75 items in the instrument (67 content items and 8 personal background questions) (see Appendix B). We should note, however, that for the piloting of the questionnaire we included 15 additional items and therefore the pilot questionnaire was longer than the final one.

5.1.7 Grouping and Organizing Items and Questions

As mentioned earlier, we used two item formats (Section 5.1.2), characteristic statements and questions. However, the former greatly outnumbered the latter—there were 70 statements and 12 questions. We decided to divide the 70 statement-type items into two parts to break up what would be a forbidding list of monotonous statements, and placed the 12 question-type items in between the two parts. This made the appearance of pages 3-4 of the questionnaire booklet less dense, preventing the respondents from getting overwhelmed.

In light of the significance of mixing up the items belonging to different multi-item scales, we made a special effort to distance the related items from each other as much as possible. Then we selected an appropriate opening item that would give the questionnaire an interesting and non-threatening start (Section 2.7.2)—we opted for an item concerning international travel. Finally, we placed all the questions relating to the respondents' personal background at the end of the questionnaire (Section 2.7.3).

5.2 Translating and Initial Piloting

Having constructed the extended first version of the complete questionnaire, it was time for the fine-tuning of the instrument through extensive piloting. Because piloting needs to be done with respondents who are similar to the target population, at this stage we needed to translate the original English text into Japanese (Section 2.8) so that we could pilot it with native speakers of Japanese. During the translation process, we referred to the Japanese versions of the established questionnaires from which many of the questionnaire items came (Ryan, 2008; Mayumi, in progress), and we also used Internet search engines to check that particular translated words and phrases were sufficiently frequent in Japanese, particularly in questionnaire formats. To ascertain whether the translated questionnaire reflected the contents of the English version, both versions were sent to two Japanese colleagues who were fluent in English and had experience in teaching English to Japanese learners of English. Based on their feedback, the wording of several items was modified.

After we were satisfied with the translation, we used only the Japanese version for the initial piloting phase (Sections 2.8 and 2.10.1). The purpose of this phase was to ask the pilot group (a) whether the Japanese translation was simple and natural, and (b) if they had any comments to make on the format and content of the questionnaire. Ten Japanese people were chosen for this initial piloting exercise: five undergraduate students, four postgraduate students, and one office worker. Their ages ranged between 20 to 32 years old and thus they were reasonably close to the target population in terms of their main attributes. Based on their feedback, the Japanese wording of several items was modified, and these changes were also made in the English version. Illustration 5.5 presents several examples of the original and the modified English expressions.

Illustration 5.5 Original and Modified English Expressions After the Initial Piloting

Original: I can honestly say that I am really doing my best to learn English.
    (*Criterion measures*)
Modified: I think that I am doing my best to learn English.
Original: Learning English is important for me because close friends of mine
    expect me to study it. (*Ought-to L2 self*)
Modified: I study English because close friends of mine think it is important.

> *Original*: I really believe that I will be capable of reading and understanding most texts in English. (*Linguistic self-confidence*)
>
> *Modified*: I believe that I will be capable of reading and understanding most texts in English if I keep studying it.
>
> *Original*: I am confident that the Japanese language and culture will develop steadily. (*Fear of assimilation*)
>
> *Modified*: I think that the Japanese language and culture will develop steadily.

During the initial piloting stage, we have also added two questions to the personal information section in order to be able to interpret the answers better. The first concerned the participants' English teacher (*"Have you ever had or do you have a native English-speaking teacher?"*); the second, their overseas experiences (*"Have you spent a longer period [at least a total of three months] in English-speaking countries [e.g., traveling, studying]?"*).

5.3 Final Piloting and Item Analysis

In order to field-test the instrument and to obtain some data that we could use for item analysis, we carried out the final piloting of the questionnaire (Section 2.10.2). For this purpose we succeeded in recruiting three instructors teaching at the tertiary level in Japan, resulting in a pilot sample of 115 students. Each teacher distributed and collected the questionnaire during their classes. The time the students spent answering the questionnaire was about 15 minutes, which showed that our initial estimates were quite generous. (Of course, we must not forget that the total length of administration is always dependent on the *slowest* respondent in a group, who can take considerably longer than the others.)

The obtained data were submitted to item analysis (Section 2.10.3). We checked the missing responses, the range of the responses, and the internal consistency of the multi-item scales. For this analysis, we used the statistical software SPSS.

5.3.1 Missing Values and the Range of Responses

The ratio of missing data was relatively small (less than 5%) so we judged that there were no systematic missing values. With regard to the range of responses, we were looking out for items which were answered in the same way by almost everyone or by almost no one, because these did not offer enough variation to be usable for most statistical procedures. Our dataset revealed that only one item fell into this danger zone, belonging to the *Travel orientation* scale (*"I think studying English will be useful when I travel overseas."*). It had a mean of 5.74 on the six-point Likert scale and 78.9% of the subjects chose the top score 6. Therefore, this item was removed from the final version of the questionnaire. However, this made the *Travel orientation* scale too short (as only two items remained—this proves that scales must have at least four or five items for piloting!); therefore, an extra item was written and added to the scale. As this item was added after the piloting of the instrument, its adequacy was checked in the final *post hoc* item analysis (see Section 5.4).

5.3.2 The Internal Consistency Reliability of the Initial Scales

In order to examine whether the items within a multi-item scale were internally consistent, we computed Cronbach Alpha reliability coefficients using the "Reliability analysis" function of SPSS (Section 4.3.5). Because our questionnaire was based on a great deal of past experience, and many items have been successfully used in past studies, we expected generally high reliabilities. Indeed, some of the scales displayed such good parameters that they did not need to be touched. For example, the Cronbach Alpha coefficient of the *Ideal L2 self* was 0.88, and the number of items comprising the scale (5) was also appropriate; so this scale was unchanged. However, the majority of the scales underwent some alteration as a result of the item analysis, which underscores the uttermost significance of piloting our instruments.

Within the "Reliability analysis" function, SPSS offers a very useful option: "Cronbach Alpha if Item Deleted." This lists the hypothetical Alpha coefficients that would emerge if each item were deleted. Thus, looking at the results the researcher can immediately see that by deleting a particular item the overall reliability of the scale would increase or decrease. This option can be used for two different functions in questionnaire design:

(a) To improve the overall reliability of a scale by identifying and then deleting items that reduce the scale's Cronbach Alpha. This is a stepwise process—we need to focus on one item at a time—and sometimes it requires several steps (i.e., the deletion of several items) before adequate reliability is achieved (at least 0.70). It can also happen that we reach a point when no further deletion would cause any improvements even though the scale is still not sufficiently reliable—in such cases we either exclude the scale from the analyses or we accept it as a less than perfect solution. When a scale becomes too short as a result of the deletion (i.e., it has only two items), extra items need to be added either by adopting them from previous studies or by writing new ones. Of course, these items have not been through proper item analysis, which is why there is a final *post hoc* item analysis phase after the administration of the final version of the questionnaire.

(b) To reduce the number of items in a long scale with sufficient reliability by deleting those items whose absence will not cause a theoretical gap in the content of the scale and whose deletion will not bring the scale's Cronbach Alpha coefficient below the minimal threshold.

A good example of the first function was provided in our study by the analysis of the *Fear of assimilation* scale (see Table 5.1). The original Cronbach Alpha coefficient of the scale was 0.32, which is far too low. However, SPSS suggested that deleting Item 1 would increase this coefficient to 0.51. This was still too low to be acceptable, but because the scale originally had five constituent items, there was a good chance that deleting a second item might further increase the scale's reliability. This was indeed the case: The deletion of Item 2 resulted in an increased Alpha value of 0.63. At this point we faced an interesting dilemma: Despite the fact that the further deletion of an item (in this case, Item 3) would have increased the Cronbach Alpha coefficient above the 0.70 threshold, this item represented a crucial dimension of the theoretical construct. Therefore, we kept all the three items, and hoped to increase the scale's reliability by adding two new items to it. As can be seen in Table 5.5 (on p. 125), the strategy worked well and the final Cronbach Alpha coefficient of the revised, five-item scale was 0.78.

A good example of the second function of the Reliability analysis procedure in SPSS concerns the *Criterion measures* scale. The Cronbach Alpha coefficient of this scale was 0.88, which is a high figure that would

Table 5.1 Cronbach Alpha coefficients for Fear of assimilation scale

Item	Cronbach Alpha if item deleted		
	Step 1	Step 2	Step 3
1. In spite of the spread of English, I think the Japanese will keep their language and culture.	.51	Deleted	Deleted
2. I think that the Japanese language and culture will develop steadily.	.33	.63	Deleted
3. I think the cultural and artistic values of English are going at the expense of Japanese values.	.25	.50	.72

Item	Cronbach Alpha if item deleted		
	Step 1	Step 2	Step 3
4. I think that there is a danger that Japanese people may forget the importance of Japanese culture, as a result of internationalization.	−.05[a]	.17	.30
5. I think that, as internationalization advances, there is a danger of losing the Japanese identity.	.09	.26	.45

[a] The value is negative due to a negative average covariance among items and this violates reliability model assumptions.

allow us to reduce the number of items in the scale. As shown in Table 5.2, Item 6 was chosen for deletion in the first step because this caused the least drop in the scale's internal consistency reliability, followed by Item 7 in the second round; this deletion still left the reliability at an outstanding 0.86 level.

When we wish to reduce the number of items in a multi-item scale with a high Cronbach Alpha coefficient, we must also take into consideration the content of the items that are considered for deletion. With regard to *Parental encouragement*, for example (see Table 5.3), the Cronbach-Alpha-if-item-deleted statistics provided by SPSS suggested that we delete Item 12. However, in the light of the individual items' contribution to the content area covered by the scale, we decided to discard Item 16 instead.

Table 5.2 Cronbach Alpha coefficients for the Criterion measures scale

Item	Cronbach Alpha if item deleted	
	Step 1	Step 2
6. If I could have access to English-speaking TV stations, I would try to watch them often.	.87	Deleted
7. If English were not taught in school, I think I would try to go to English classes somewhere else.	.85	.86
8. I am working hard at learning English.	.85	.82
9. If an English course was offered at university or somewhere else in the future, I would like to take it.	.85	.85
10. I am prepared to expend a lot of effort in learning English.	.86	.85
11. I think that I am doing my best to learn English.	.86	.84

Table 5.3 Cronbach Alpha coefficients for Parental encouragement scale

Item	Cronbach Alpha if item deleted
12. My parents encourage me to attend extra English classes after class (e.g., at English conversation schools).	.84
13. My parents encourage me to take every opportunity to use my English (e.g., speaking and reading).	.80
14. My parents encourage me to study English in my free time.	.83
15. My parents encourage me to study English.	.81
16. I am often told by my parents that English will be necessary for my future.	.81

Another example of how reliability and content considerations need to go hand in hand is provided by the *Attitudes toward L2 community* scale, which had an initial Cronbach Alpha coefficient of 0.85. As shown in Table 5.4, the reliability analysis results would suggest that Item 17 be deleted. However, this item was linked to Item 19: One asks about attitudes toward Americans and the other toward non-American speakers of English. Therefore, we decided to merge the two items as follows: *"Do you like the people who live in English-speaking countries?"*

Finally, it is always necessary to examine the appropriateness of the item wording of problem items. The Cronbach Alpha coefficient of *Cultural interest* was 0.72, which is high enough to justify keeping the scale as it is. However, we noticed that one of the four items—*"Do you like English TV programs?"*—sounded rather vague in Japanese because it was not clear whether such programs meant ones made in English-speaking countries or TV programs which were broadcast in English, including English TV news made by Japanese TV stations. Therefore, to clarify the meaning of the content, the wording of the item was modified to *"Do you like TV programs made in English-speaking countries?"* This was a successful change, as reflected by the Cronbach Alpha value of 0.75 in the final version of the scale (see Table 5.5).

The only scale that we did not submit to item analysis was *Integrativeness*, even though its reliability coefficient was low (0.54). This scale was taken over from Dörnyei *et al.*'s (2006) instrument used in Hungary, and because part of our study specifically concerned testing the validity of *Integrativeness* in Asian contexts, we had to keep the original item wordings to be able to claim that we had measured exactly the same construct. Fortunately, as shown in Table 5.5, the scale displayed better (though not brilliant) reliability in the main study (Alpha = 0.64).

In sum, during the item analysis we examined all the multi-item scales contained by the questionnaire and made some changes in most of them.

Table 5.4 Cronbach Alpha coefficients for Attitudes toward L2 community scale

Item	Cronbach Alpha if item deleted
17. Do you like the people of the United States?	.86
18. Do you like to travel to English-speaking countries?	.81
19. Do you like the people who live in English-speaking countries (besides the USA)?	.81
20. Do you like meeting people from English-speaking countries?	.81
21. Would you like to know more people from English-speaking countries?	.82

Table 5.5 Summary of the length and reliability of the multi-item scales in the pilot and the final questionnaires

Content area	Number of items with Cronbach Alphas		
	Before item analysis	After item analysis	Final version in main study
Criterion measures	6 (.88)	4 (.86)	4 (.83)
Ideal L2 self	5 (.88)	5 (.88)	5 (.89)
Ought-to L2 self	7 (.80)	4 (.79)	4 (.76)
Parental encouragement	5 (.85)	4 (.81)	4 (.83)
Instrumentality-promotion	4 (.68)	3 (.65)	5 (.82)
Instrumentality-prevention	4 (.68)	3 (.80)	5 (.73)
Linguistic self-confidence	5 (.86)	4 (.84)	4 (.76)
Attitudes toward learning English	10 (.87)	4 (.88)	4 (.90)
Travel orientation	3 (.67)	2 (.80)	3 (.77)
Fear of assimilation	5 (.32)	3 (.63)	5 (.78)
Ethnocentrism	6 (.64)	4 (.61)	5 (.35)
Interest in the English language	5 (.81)	4 (.83)	4 (.80)
English anxiety	5 (.79)	4 (.79)	4 (.81)
Integrativeness	3 (.54)	3 (.54)	3 (.64)
Cultural interest	4 (.72)	3 (.58)	4 (.75)
Attitudes toward L2 community	5 (.85)	3 (.82)	4 (.85)

Table 5.5 presents a summary of the number of items and the Cronbach Alpha coefficients for each scale before and after the items analysis, as well as in the final version of the instrument.

5.3.3 Modification of the Personal Information Items

Based on the results of the piloting, we made two changes in the questions targeting the respondents' personal background characteristics. The first concerned the self-assessment of English language proficiency. In the original question, the scale ranged from "Beginner level" to "Advanced level." However, as it seemed likely that very few respondents would rate themselves as "Advanced," we decided to combine this category with "Upper Intermediate level" under the new label of "Upper Intermediate level and over." The other modification involved adding a question about the respondents' ethnic origin, as we realized that a few non-Japanese learners might also attend the English classes that we would assess. Note that because the purpose of this item was to distinguish non-Japanese from Japanese learners, no specific clarification of their nationality was necessary and so we did not ask for any specific details.

5.4 The Final Version of the Japanese Questionnaire and *Post Hoc* Item Analysis

Based on the item analysis of the pilot questionnaire, we prepared the final version of the instrument. The composition of the multi-item scales is included in Appendix A, and the final instrument (both the English and the Japanese versions) can be found in Appendix B. The questionnaire was then administered in eight Japanese universities to 1,586 students. Table 5.5 presents the Cronbach Alpha coefficients obtained in the main study. As can be seen, the instrument worked well in terms of its internal consistency reliability: Only two of the 16 scales did not reach the 0.70 threshold: *Integrativeness* (which has already been discussed) and *Ethnocentrism*. This latter scale concerns an emotionally loaded issue with a lot of "political correctness" attached to it in Japan (as in many other countries), and we suspect that our failure to produce a satisfactory measure of it was due to a large extent to our inability to combat the *social desirability* bias (Section 1.2.2).

It is recommended in questionnaire surveys to conduct a second round of item analysis—a *"post hoc* analysis" (Section 2.10.3)—using the data of the final survey to check whether the instrument has indeed worked according to expectations, with special attention paid to the items that were added or modified as a result of the pilot study (and which therefore have not been piloted yet). Because of our generally good results, in our specific case this analysis concerned the *Ethnocentrism* scale only. Unfortunately, we did not find any item here whose deletion would have improved the scale sufficiently and, therefore, this variable was excluded from all further analyses.

5.5 Adapting the Questionnaire for Use in China and Iran

After designing the questionnaire for Japanese university students, we had the opportunity to construct and administer two other language versions of the instrument: (a) a Chinese version targeting secondary school pupils, university students, and adult learners of English (principal on-site researcher: Michael Magid); and (b) a Persian version targeting secondary school pupils and university students in Iran (principal on-site researcher: Mostafa Papi).

As a preliminary, it is important to emphasize that motivation questionnaires are unlike tests of cognitive abilities (e.g., language aptitude batteries) that can be transferred from one context to another without any change. As Appendix A shows, even though the two new instruments followed the basic structure of the Japanese questionnaire, many of the items in them were substantially modified or completely rewritten. This partly reflected the different social milieus and target populations in the two learning environments, and partly our evolving understanding of the strengths and the weaknesses of the instrument.

Both new versions were originally constructed in English, so they needed to be translated into Chinese and Persian (Section 2.8) before piloting them. We recruited the help of several local colleagues in this task, and this time the process involved a "back-translation" procedure (Illustration 5.6 presents a sample item with five different back-translations). Special care was taken to avoid complex technical language because both instruments were to be administered to secondary school pupils as well.

Illustration 5.6 An Original English Item from the Iranian Questionnaire with Five Different Back-translations

Original: I consider learning English important because the people I respect think that I should do it.

Back-translation 1: Learning English is important for me because those I hold dear think so.

Back-translation 2: Learning English is important for me because the people I care about and respect think learning English is important.

> *Back-translation 3*: Learning English is important for me, because it is the belief of whom I honor.
>
> *Back-translation 4*: Learning English is important for me because those who I have respect for them think so.
>
> *Back-translation 5*: Learning English is important to me because those who I care more about have such an idea.

The questionnaires were piloted with 152 respondents in China and 100 in Iran. Using the pilot data we conducted a thorough item analysis, and in cases where we had to exclude too many items from a scale, we added extra items taken mainly from established questionnaires. The final Chinese and Iranian instruments contained 67 and 76 content items, respectively, with an additional 8/10 questions asking the respondent's personal background. An interesting variation in the questionnaire format was provided by the Chinese instrument: The questionnaire that was administered here contained both the Chinese and the English texts within the same version, thus extending the length of the instrument to six pages (see Appendix B). This was done partly to make sure that English-speaking respondents understood the meaning of all the items well, and partly for motivational and pedagogical purposes: We believed that the bilingual version would promote positive respondent attitudes and would also encourage participants by boosting their confidence in their English abilities.

The final versions of the instruments were administered to 1,328 participants in China and 2,029 participants in Iran. Table 5.6 lists the Cronbach Alpha coefficients for the multi-item scales. As can be seen, most of the coefficients exceed the 0.70 threshold, which indicates that both versions had adequate internal consistency. Having said that, it is also apparent that the coefficients are somewhat lower than with the Japanese instrument (see Table 5.5). This, we believe, is due to the fact that in designing the Japanese questionnaire we could draw on items used in previous Japanese instruments, whereas the Chinese and the Iranian versions did not have any precursors and everything had to be devised from scratch.

Table 5.6 Summary of the length and reliability of the multi-item scales in the Chinese and Iranian questionnaires

Content area	Number of items with Cronbach Alphas	
	Chinese version	**Iranian version**
Criterion measures	6 (.75)	6 (.80)
Ideal L2 self	5 (.83)	6 (.79)
Ought-to L2 self	7 (.78)	6 (.75)
Family influence	5 (.70)	6 (.70)
Instrumentality-promotion	8 (.78)	6 (.67)
Instrumentality-prevention	5 (.84)	8 (.78)
Travel orientation	3 (.77)	3 (.64)
Fear of assimilation	5 (.78)	5 (.68)
Ethnocentrism	5 (.61)	7 (.76)
Attitudes toward learning English	4 (.81)	6 (.82)
English anxiety	4 (.78)	6 (.74)
Integrativeness	3 (.63)	3 (.56)
Cultural interest	3 (.67)	4 (.76)
Attitudes toward L2 community	4 (.76)	4 (.76)

Conclusion and Checklist

The previous five chapters have provided a summary of questionnaire theory and an illustration of questionnaire development. Hopefully, they have also made a strong case for basing questionnaire design on scientific principles rather than merely on the researcher's common sense. In this concluding section I will draw up a checklist of what I consider the most important points and recommendations for every phase of the questionnaire survey. Good luck with your future questionnaires!

Constructing the Questionnaire
1. Only in exceptional cases should a questionnaire be more than four pages long and take more than 30 minutes to complete; if access to the participants is restricted to a certain amount of time, set the maximum length of the questionnaire with the slowest readers in mind so that everybody can finish within the given period.
2. When deciding on the questionnaire content, start by generating a theoretically driven list of the main areas to be covered.
3. Avoid the use of single-item variables; instead, include a minimum of three or four items addressing every content area.
4. Avoid truly open-ended questions that require lengthy answers.
5. Keep the number of items that are seeking confidential information to the minimum.
6. Be careful about how you formulate sensitive items (for specific guidelines, see Section 2.6.3).
7. Try and make the starter question(s) particularly involving.

8. Make sure that the questionnaire has a clear, logical, and well-marked structure.

9. Personal/factual questions about the respondent should go to the end.

10. Open-ended questions are the least intrusive if they are toward the end.

11. When writing items, observe the following:
    - The best items are often the ones that sound as if they had been said by someone.
    - Short items written in simple and natural language are good items.
    - Avoid ambiguous, loaded, or difficult words; technical terms; negative constructions; and double-barreled questions.
    - Avoid items that are likely to be answered the same way by most people.
    - Include items that concern both positive and negative aspects of the target.
    - For cross-cultural studies, use item wording that is easily translatable (see Section 2.6.2).

12. Strive for an attractive and professional design for the questionnaire; this typically involves:
    - a booklet format;
    - economical use of space with full but not overcrowded pages;
    - an orderly layout that utilizes various typefaces and highlighting options, and appropriate sequence marking (of sections and items);
    - good paper quality.

13. In the initial (general) instructions cover the following points:
    - the topic and importance of the study;
    - the sponsoring organization;
    - point out that there are no right or wrong answers and request honest responses;
    - promise confidentiality;
    - thank the participants.

14. In the specific instructions for the tasks, exemplify (rather than merely explain) how to answer the questions.

15. Thank the participants again at the end of the questionnaire.

16. Allocate sufficient time and attention to the task of translating the questionnaire into the participants' L1.

17. Always pilot your questionnaire (even if most or all the items have been adopted from existing instruments) and submit the items to item analysis (see Section 2.10).

Administering the Questionnaire

18. Make the participant sample as similar to the target population as possible (see Section 3.1.1).
19. Make the sample size large enough to allow for the results to reach statistical significance (see Section 3.1.2).
20. Beware of participant self-selection (see Section 3.1.3).
21. With postal administration:
    - Formulate the cover letter very carefully (for a list of points to be covered, see Section 3.2.1).
    - Print the return address on the questionnaire as well.
    - About two and a half weeks after the original mailing send a follow-up letter, and in another 10 days' time send another one.
    - Apply various strategies to increase the return rate (for a list, see Section 3.2.1).
22. With one-to-one administration, make sure that you brief the questionnaire administrator well and consider giving him/her a cue card with the main points to cover when handing out the questionnaires.
23. With online administration:
    - Advertize the survey through multiple methods such as emails and mailing lists (see Section 3.2.4).
    - Consider using some incentive or some creative technique to stimulate respondents to read your invitation email.
    - For web-based questionnaires, include a progress indicator and pay special attention to designing the first few pages of the questionnaire.
    - Try to reach the respondents several times using multiple methods and, if you can, send at least two reminders.
24. To increase the quality and quantity of offline questionnaire responses in general, apply the following strategies:
    - Provide advance notice.
    - Win the support of the various authority figures.
    - Try to arrange some respectable institutional sponsorship for your survey.
    - The administrator's overall conduct should be friendly and professional, and he/she should exhibit keen involvement and an obvious interest in the project.
    - "Sell" the survey by communicating well its purpose and significance.
    - Emphasize confidentiality.

- Promise feedback on the results for those who are interested (and then remember to provide it . . .).

25. Observe the various ethical principles and regulations very closely (see Section 3.4.1) and obtain the required "human subjects'" approval.

Processing Questionnaire Data

26. As soon as you have received the completed questionnaires, mark each with a unique identification code.

27. Always prepare a backup of the data files. Do it now!

28. Submit your data to "data cleaning procedures" before starting the analyses (see Section 4.3.1).

29. Consider the way you handle missing data very carefully.

30. Reverse the scoring of negatively worded items before starting the analyses (see Section 4.3.2).

31. Consider standardizing the data before starting the analyses (see Section 4.3.2).

32. Start the analyses of your questionnaire data by reducing the number of variables through computing multi-item scales.

33. Compute internal consistency reliability coefficients (Cronbach Alphas) for each multi-item scale.

34. Numerical questionnaire data are typically processed by means of statistical procedures; for most purposes you will need inferential statistics accompanied by indices of statistical significance (see Section 4.3.6).

35. Process open-ended questions by means of some systematic content analysis.

36. Exercise great caution when generalizing your results.

37. Make sure that you include all the necessary technical information about your survey in your research report (for a checklist, see Section 4.6.2).

38. Make use of charts/diagrams, schematic representations, and tables as much as possible when reporting your results.

39. Consider complementing your questionnaire data with information coming from other sources.

40. Enjoy!

References

Aiken, L. (1996). *Rating scales and checklists: Evaluating behavior, personality, and attitudes*. New York: John Wiley.

Aiken, L. (1997). *Questionnaires and inventories: Surveying opinions and assessing personality*. New York: John Wiley.

Akl, E. A., Maroun, N., Klockle, R. A., Montori, V., & Schünemann, H. J. (2005). Electronic mail was not better than postal mail for surveying residents and faculty. *Journal of Clinical Epidemiology, 58*, 425-429.

Al-Shehri, A. S. (2009). Motivation and vision: The relation between the ideal L2 self, imagination and visual style. In Z. Dörnyei & E. Ushioda (Eds.), *Motivation, language identity and the L2 self* (pp. 164-171). Bristol: Multilingual Matters.

Aldridge, A., & Levine, K. (2001). *Surveying the social world: Principles and practice in survey research*. Buckingham: Open University Press.

Anderson, L. W. (1985). Attitudes and their measurement. In T. Husén & T. N. Postlethwaite (Eds.), *The international encyclopedia of education* (Vol. 1, pp. 352-358). Oxford: Pergamon.

Bardovi-Harlig, K. (1999). Researching method. In L. F. Bouton (Ed.), *Pragmatics and language learning* (Vol. 8, pp. 237-264). Urbana-Champaign, IL: University of Illinois, Division of English as an International Language.

Birnbaum, M. H. (2004). Human research and data collection via the Internet. *Annual Review of Psychology, 55*, 803-832.

Brislin, R. W. (1970). Back-translation for cross-cultural research. *Journal of Cross-Cultural Psychology, 1*, 185-216.

Brislin, R. W. (1986). The wording and translation of research instruments. In W. J. Lonner & J. W. Berry (Eds.), *Field methods in cross-cultural research* (pp. 137-164). Newbury Park, CA: Sage.

Brown, H. D. (1994). *Teaching by principles: An interactive approach to language pedagogy*. Englewood Cliffs, NJ: Prentice Hall Regents.

Brown, H. D. (2000). *Principles of language learning and teaching* (4th ed.). New York: Longman.

Brown, H. D. (2002). *Strategies for success: A practical guide to learning English*. New York: Longman.

Brown, J. D. (2001). *Using surveys in language programs*. Cambridge, UK: Cambridge University Press.

Bryman, A. (2008). *Social research methods* (3rd ed.). Oxford: Oxford University Press.

Burstall, C., Jamieson, M., Cohen, S., & Hargreaves, M. (1974). *Primary French in the balance*. Windsor: NFER.

Chamot, A. U., Barnhardt, S., El-Dinary, P. B., & Robbins, J. (1999). *The learning strategies handbook*. New York: Longman.

Chen, C., Lee, S.-Y., Stevenson, H. W. (1995). Response style and cross-cultural comparisons of rating scales among East Asian and North American students. *Psychological Science, 6*, 170-175.

Cheng, H.-F., & Dörnyei, Z. (2007). The use of motivational strategies in language instruction: The case of EFL teaching in Taiwan. *Innovation in Language Learning and Teaching, 1*, 153-174.

Clemans, W. V. (1971). Test administration. In R. L. Thorndike (Ed.), *Educational measurement* (2nd ed., pp. 188-201). Washington, DC: American Council on Education.

Clément, R. (1986). Second language proficiency and acculturation: An investigation of the effects of language status and individual characteristics. *Journal of Language and Social Psychology, 5*, 271-290.

Clément, R., & Baker, S. C. (2001). *Measuring social aspects of L2 acquisition and use: Scale characteristics and administration*. Technical Report. Ottawa: School of Psychology, University of Ottawa.

Clément, R., & Kruidenier, B. G. (1983). Orientations on second language acquisition: 1. The effects of ethnicity, milieu and their target language on their emergence. *Language Learning, 33*, 273-291.

Clément, R., & Kruidenier, B. G. (1985). Aptitude, attitude and motivation in second language proficiency: A test of Clément's model. *Journal of Language and Social Psychology, 4*, 21-37.

Clément, R., & Noels, K. A. (1992). Towards a situated approach to ethnolinguistic identity: The effects of status on individuals and groups. *Journal of Language and Social Psychology, 11*, 203-232.

Clément, R., Dörnyei, Z., & Noels, K. A. (1994). Motivation, self-confidence and group cohesion in the foreign language classroom. *Language Learning, 44*, 417-448.

Cochran, W. G. (1977). *Sampling techniques* (3rd ed.). New York: Wiley.

Cohen, A. D. (1987). Students processing feedback on their compositions. In A. Wenden & J. Rubin (Eds.), *Learner strategies in language learning* (pp. 57-69). Hemel Hempstead, UK: Prentice Hall.

Cohen, A. D. (1991). Feedback on writing: The use of verbal report. *Studies in Second Language Acquisition, 13*, 133-159.

Cohen, A. D., & Chi, J. C. (2001). *Language Strategy Use Survey*. http://carla.acad.umn.edu/ profiles/Cohen-profile.html.

Cohen, A. D., & Dörnyei, Z. (2001). *Taking My Motivational Temperature on a Language Task*. http://carla.acad.umn.edu/profiles/Cohen-profile.html.

Cohen, A. D., & Oxford, R. L. (2001a). *Learning Styles Survey for Young Learners*. http:// carla.acad.umn.edu/profiles/Cohen-profile.html.

Cohen, A. D., & Oxford, R. L. (2001b). *Young Learners' Language Strategy Use Survey*. http:// carla.acad.umn.edu/profiles/Cohen-profile.html.

Cohen, A. D., Oxford, R. L., & Chi, J. C. (2001). *Learning Style Survey*. http://carla.acad.umn.edu/profiles/Cohen-profile.html.

Coleman, J. A. (1996). *Studying languages: A survey of British and European students*. London: CILT.

Converse, J. M., & Presser, S. (1986). *Survey questions: Handcrafting the standardized questionnaire*. Newbury Park, CA: Sage.

Couper, M. P., Traugott, M. W., & Lamias, M. J. (2001). Web survey design and administration. *Public Opinion Quarterly, 65*, 230-253.

Creswell, J. W., & Plano Clark, V. L. (2007). *Designing and conducting mixed methods research*. Thousand Oaks, CA: Sage.

Creswell, J. W., Plano Clark, V. L., Gutmann, M. L., & Hanson, W. E. (2003). Advanced mixed methods research designs. In A. Tashakkori & C. Teddlie (Eds.), *Handbook of mixed methods in social and behavioral research* (pp. 209-240). Thousand Oaks, CA: Sage.

Csizér, K., & Kormos, J. (2009). Learning experiences, selves and motivated learning behavior: A comparative analysis of structural models for Hungarian secondary and university learners of English. In Z. Dörnyei & E. Ushioda (Eds.), *Motivation, language identity and the L2 self* (pp. 98-119). Bristol: Multilingual Matters.

Cumming, A. (1991). *Identification of current needs and issues related to the delivery of adult ESL instruction in British Columbia*. Richmond, B. C.: Open Learning Agency. ERIC ED 353 855.

Davidson, F. (1996). *Principles of statistical data handling*. Thousand Oaks, CA: Sage.

DeVellis, R. F. (2003). *Scale development: Theory and applications* (2nd ed.). Thousand Oaks, CA: Sage.

Dewaele, J.-M., Petrides, K. V., & Furnham, A. (2008). Effects of trait emotional intelligence and sociobiographical variables on communicative anxiety and foreign language anxiety among adult multilinguals: A review and empirical investigation. *Language Learning, 58*, 911-960.

Dommeyer, C. J., & Moriarty, E. (1999/2000) Comparing two forms of an e-mail survey: Embedded vs. attached. *Journal of the Market Research Society, 42*, 39-50.

Dörnyei, Z. (1990). Conceptualizing motivation in foreign language learning. *Language Learning, 40*, 46-78.

Dörnyei, Z. (2001). *Teaching and researching motivation*. Harlow, UK: Longman.

Dörnyei, Z. (2005). *The psychology of the language learner: Individual differences in second language acquisition*. Mahwah, NJ: Lawrence Erlbaum.

Dörnyei, Z. (2007). *Research methods in applied linguistics: Quantitative, qualitative, and mixed methodologies*. Oxford: Oxford University Press.

Dörnyei, Z., & Clément, R. (2001). Motivational characteristics of learning different target languages: Results of a nationwide survey. In Z. Dörnyei & R. Schmidt (Eds.), *Motivation and second language acquisition* (pp. 399-432). Honolulu, HI: University of Hawaii Press.

Dörnyei, Z., Csizér, K., & Németh, N. (2006). *Motivation, language attitudes, and globalization: A Hungarian perspective*. Clevedon: Multilingual Matters.

Duff, P. (2008). *Case study research in applied linguistics*. Mahwah, NJ: Lawrence Erlbaum.

Ehrman, M. E. (1996a). *Understanding second language learning difficulties*. Thousand Oaks, CA: Sage.

Ehrman, M. E. (1996b). An exploration of adult language learning motivation, self-efficacy and anxiety. In R. L. Oxford (Ed.), *Language learning motivation: Pathways to the new century* (pp. 103-131). Honolulu, HI: University of Hawaii Press.

Ehrman, M. E., & Dörnyei, Z. (1998). *Interpersonal dynamics in second language education: The visible and invisible classroom*. Thousand Oaks, CA: Sage.

Eignor, D., Taylor, C., Kirsch, I., & Jamieson, J. (1998). *Development of a scale for assessing the level of computer familiarity of TOEFL examinees*. TOEFL Research Report No. 60. Princeton, NJ: Educational Testing Service.

Ellard, J. H., & Rogers, T. B. (1993). Teaching questionnaire construction effectively: The Ten Commandments of question writing. *Contemporary Social Psychology, 17*, 17-20.

Ely, C. M. (1986a). An analysis of discomfort, risktaking, sociability, and motivation in the L2 classroom. *Language Learning, 36*, 1-25.

Ely, C. M. (1986b). Language learning motivation: A descriptive causal analysis. *Modern Language Journal, 70*, 28-35.

Ely, C. M. (1989). Tolerance of ambiguity and use of second language strategies. *Foreign Language Annals, 22*, 437-445.

Fabrigar, L. R., Krosnick, J. A., & MacDougall, B. L. (2005). Attitudes measurement. In T. C. Brock & M. C. Green (Eds.), *Persuasion: Psychological insights and perspectives* (2nd ed., pp. 17-40). Thousand Oaks, CA: Sage.

Fink, A. (1995). *How to report on surveys (The Survey Kit 9)*. Thousand Oaks, CA: Sage.

Fowler, F. J. (2002). *Survey research methods* (3rd ed.). Thousand Oaks, CA: Sage.

Fox, J., Murray, C., & Warm, A. (2003). Conducting research using web-based questionnaires: Practical, methodological, and ethical considerations. *International Journal of Social Research Methodology, 6*(2), 167-180.

Galt, K. A. (2008). Media review: SPSS text analysis for Surveys 2.1. *Journal of Mixed Methods Research, 2*, 284-286.

Gan, Z. (2009). "Asian learners" re-examined: An empirical study of language learning attitudes, strategies and motivation among mainland Chinese and Hong Kong students. *Journal of Multilingual and Multicultural Development, 30*, 41-58.

Ganassali, S. (2008). The influence of the design of web survey questionnaires on the quality of responses. *Survey Research Methods, 2*, 21-32.

Gardner, R. C. (1985). *Social psychology and second language learning: The role of attitudes and motivation*. London: Edward Arnold.

Gardner, R. C., & Smythe, P. C. (1981). On the development of the Attitude/Motivation Test Battery. *Canadian Modern Language Review, 37*, 510-525.

Gardner, R. C., Tremblay, P. F., & Masgoret, A.-M. (1997). Toward a full model of second language learning: An empirical investigation. *Modern Language Journal, 81*, 344-362.

Gass, S. M., & Mackey, A. (2000). *Stimulated recall methodology in second language research*. Mahwah, NJ: Lawrence Erlbaum.

Gillham, B. (2008). *Developing a questionnaire* (2nd ed.). London: Continuum.

Gliksman, L., Gardner, R. C., & Smythe, P. C. (1982). The role of the integrative motive on students' participation in the French classroom. *Canadian Modern Language Review, 38*, 625-647.

Green, C. F. (1999). Categorizing motivational drives in second language acquisition. *Language, Culture and Curriculum, 12*, 265-279.

Hair, J. F., Black, W. C., Babin, B. J., Anderson, R. E., & Tatham, R. L. (2006). *Multivariate data analysis*. Upper Saddle River, NJ: Prentice Hall.

Harkness, J. A. (2008a). Comparative survey research: Goals and challenges. In E. D. De Leeuw, J. J. Hox, & D. A. Dillman (Eds.), *International handbook of survey methodology* (pp. 56-77). New York, NY: Lawrence Erlbaum.

Harkness, J. A. (2008b). *Round 4 ESS Translation Strategies and Procedures*. Retrieved January 27, 2009, from http://www.europeansocialsurvey.org/index.php?option= com_docman&task=doc_download&gid=351&itemid=80.

Hart, D., & Cumming, A. (1997). A follow-up study of people in Ontario completing level 3 of the Language Instruction for Newcomers to Canada (LINC) program. Toronto: Ontario Institute for Studies in Education of the University of Toronto. ERIC ED 409 745.

Hatch, E., & Lazaraton, A. (1991). *The research manual: Design and statistics for applied linguistics*. New York: Newbury House.

Hopkins, K. D., Stanley, J. C., & Hopkins, B. R. (1990). *Educational and psychological measurement and evaluation* (7th ed.). Englewood Cliffs, NJ: Prentice Hall.

Horwitz, E. K. (1985). Using student beliefs about language learning and teaching in the foreign language methods course. *Foreign Language Annals, 18*, 333-340.

Horwitz, E. K. (1988). The beliefs about language learning of beginning university foreign language students. *Modern Language Journal, 72,* 283-294.

Horwitz, E. K. (1996). Even teachers get the blues: Recognizing and alleviating non-native teachers' feelings of foreign language anxiety. *Foreign Language Annals, 29,* 365-372.

Horwitz, E. K., Horwitz, M. B., & Cope, J. (1986). Foreign language classroom anxiety. *Modern Language Journal, 70,* 125-132.

John, O. P., & Benet-Martínez, V. (2000). Measurement: Reliability, construct validation, and scale construction. In H. T. Reis & C. M. Judd (Eds.), *Handbook of research methods in social and personality psychology* (pp. 339-369). Cambridge, UK: Cambridge University Press.

Johnston, B., Kasper, G., & Ross, S. (1998). Effect of rejoinders in production questionnaires. *Applied Linguistics, 19,* 157-182.

Kasper, G. (1998). Analyzing verbal protocols. *TESOL Quarterly, 32,* 358-362.

Kassabgy, O., Boraie, D., & Schmidt, R. (2001). Values, rewards, and job satisfaction in ESL/EFL. In Z. Dörnyei & R. Schmidt (Eds.), *Motivation and second language acquisition* (pp. 213-237). Honolulu, HI: University of Hawaii Press.

Kearney, K. A., Hopkins, R. H., Mauss, A. L., & Weisheit, R. A. (1984). Self-generated identification codes for anonymous collection of longitudinal questionnaire data. *Public Opinion Quarterly, 48,* 370-378.

Kondo-Brown, K. (2001). Bilingual heritage students' language contact and motivation. In Z. Dörnyei & R. Schmidt (Eds.), *Motivation and second language acquisition* (pp. 433-459). Honolulu, HI: University of Hawaii Press.

Kormos, J. (1998). Verbal reports in L2 speech production research. *TESOL Quarterly, 32,* 353-358.

Krosnick, J. A. (1999). Survey research. *Annual Review of Psychology, 50,* 537-567.

Krosnick, J. A., Judd, C. M., & Wittenbrink, B. (2005). The measurement of attitudes. In D. Albarracin, B. T. Johnson, & M. P. Zanna (Eds.), *The Handbook of Attitudes* (pp. 21-76). Mahwah, NJ: Lawrence Erlbaum.

Labrie, N., & Clément, R. (1986). Ethnolinguistic vitality, self-confidence and second language proficiency: An investigation. *Journal of Multilingual and Multicultural Development, 7,* 269-282.

Lazaraton, A. (2005). Quantitative research methods. In E. Hinkel (Ed.), *Handbook of research in second language teaching and learning* (pp. 209-224). Mahwah, NJ: Lawrence Erlbaum.

Lepetit, D., & Cichocki, W. (2002). Teaching languages to future health professionals: A needs assessment study. *Modern Language Journal, 86,* 384-396.

Levine, G. S. (2003). Student and instructor beliefs and attitudes about target language use, first language use, and anxiety: Report of a questionnaire study. *Modern Language Journal, 87,* 343-364.

Levy, P. S., & Lemeshow, S. (1999). *Sampling of populations: Methods and applications* (3rd ed.). New York: John Wiley & Sons.

Lightbown, P. M., & Spada, N. (1999). *How languages are learned* (rev. ed.). Oxford: Oxford University Press.

Loewen, S., Li, S., Fei, F., Thompson, A., Nakatsukawa, K., Ahn, S., & Chen, X. (2009). Second language learners' beliefs about grammar instruction and error correction. *Modern Language Journal, 93,* 91-104.

Low, G. (1999). What respondents do with questionnaires: Accounting for incongruity and fluidity. *Applied Linguistics, 20,* 503-533.

McDonald, H., & Adam, S. (2003). A comparison of online and postal data collection methods in marketing research. *Marketing Intelligence & Planning, 21,* 85-95.

Macer, T. (April, 1999). Designing the survey of the future. *Research Magazine, 395.* Also: http://www.meaning.uk.com/arts/28.html.

MacIntyre, P. D., Clément, R., Baker, S. C., & Conrad, S. (2001). Willingness to communicate, social support and language learning orientations of immersion students. *Studies in Second Language Acquisition, 23,* 369-388.

MacIntyre, P. D., & Gardner, R. C. (1991). Language anxiety: Its relation to other anxieties and to processing in native and second languages. *Language Learning, 41,* 513-534.

MacIntyre, P. D., & Gardner, R. C. (1994). The subtle effects of language anxiety on cognitive processing in the second language. *Language Learning, 44,* 283-305.

MacIntyre, P. D., MacKinnon, S. P., & Clément, R. (2009). Toward the development of a scale to assess possible selves as a source of language learning motivation. In Z. Dörnyei & E. Ushioda (Eds.), *Motivation, language identity and the L2 self* (pp. 193-214). Bristol: Multilingual Matters.

Mackey, A., & Gass, S. M. (2005). *Second language research: Methodology and design.* Mahwah, NJ: Lawrence Erlbaum.

Mayumi, K. (in progress). Temporal changes in language learner motivation in Japan. Ph.D. thesis, University of Nottingham.

Michaelidou, N., & Dibb, S. (2006). Using email questionnaires for research: Good practice in tackling non-response. *Journal of Targeting, Measurement and Analysis for Marketing, 14,* 289-296.

Mori, Y. (1999). Epistemological beliefs and language learning beliefs: What do language learners believe about their learning? *Language Learning, 49*(3), 377-415.

Moser, C. A., & Kalton, G. (1971). *Survey methods in social investigation.* London: Heinemann.

Murphey, T. (1996). Changing language learning beliefs: "Appresiating" mistakes. *Asian Journal of English Language Teaching, 6,* 77-84.

Nakatani, Y. (2006). Developing an oral communication strategy inventory. *Modern Language Journal, 90,* 151-168.

Newell, R. (1993). Questionnaires. In N. Gilbert (Ed.), *Researching social life* (pp. 94-115). London: Sage.

Noels, K. A., Clément., R., & Pelletier, L. G. (1999). Perceptions of teachers' communicative styles and students' intrinsic and extrinsic motivation. *Modern Language Journal, 83,* 23-34.

Noels, K. A., Pelletier, L. G., Clément., R., & Vallerand, R. J. (2000). Why are you learning a second language? Motivational orientations and self-determination theory. *Language Learning, 50,* 57-85.

Nunan, D. (1988). *The learner-centred curriculum.* Cambridge: Cambridge University Press.

Nunan, D., & Lamb, C. (1996). *The self-directed teacher: Managing the learning process.* Cambridge: Cambridge University Press.

Nunnally, J. C. (1978). *Psychometric theory.* New York: McGraw-Hill.

Oppenheim, A. N. (1992). *Questionnaire design, interviewing and attitude measurement* (new ed.). London: Pinter.

Ortega, L. (2005). Methodology, epistemology, and ethics in instructed SLA research: An introduction. *Modern Language Journal, 89,* 317-327.

Oxford, R. L. (1990). *Language learning strategies: What every teacher should know.* Boston, MA: Heinle & Heinle.

Oxford, R. L. (1995). Style Analysis Survey (SAS): Assessing your own learning and working styles. In J. M. Reid (Ed.), *Learning styles in the ESL/EFL classroom* (pp. 208-215). Boston, MA: Heinle & Heinle.

Pallant, J. (2007). *SPSS survival manual: A step by step guide to data analysis using SPSS for Windows (Version 15)* (3rd ed.). Maidenhead: Open University Press & McGraw-Hill Education.

Phakiti, A. (2003). A closer look at gender and strategy use in L2 reading. *Language Learning, 53*, 649-702.

Popham, W. J., & Sirotnik, K. A. (1973). *Educational statistics* (2nd ed.). New York: Harper and Row.

Porter, S. R., & Whitcomb, M. E. (2007). Mixed-mode contacts in web surveys: Paper is not necessarily better. *Public Opinion Quarterly, 71*, 635-648.

Potaka, L. (2008). Comparability and usability: Key issues in the design of internet forms for New Zealand's 2006 Census of Populations and Dwellings. *Survey Research Methods, 2*, 1-10.

Reid, J. M. (1995). *Learning styles in the ESL/EFL classroom.* Boston, MA: Heinle & Heinle.

Richterich, R. (1980). *Identifying the needs of adults learning a foreign language.* Oxford: Pergamon (for the Council of Europe).

Robinson, J. P., Shaver, P. R., & Wrightsman, L. S. (1991). Criteria for scale selection and evaluation. In J. P. Robinson, P. R. Shaver & L. S. Wrightsman (Eds.), *Measures of personality and social psychological attitudes* (pp. 1-16). San Diego, CA: Academic Press.

Robson, C. (2002). *Real world research: A resource for social scientists and practitioner-researchers* (2nd ed.). Oxford: Blackwell.

Ryan, S. (2008). The Ideal L2 Selves of Japanese learners of English. Unpublished Ph.D. thesis. University of Nottingham. Also http://etheses3.nottingham.ac.uk/550/1/ryan-2008.pdf.

Ryan, S. (2009). Self and identity in L2 motivation in Japan: The ideal L2 self and Japanese learners of English. In Z. Dörnyei & E. Ushioda (Eds.), *Motivation, language identity and the L2 self* (pp. 120-143). Bristol: Multilingual Matters.

Sanchez, M. E. (1992). Effects of questionnaire design on the quality of survey data. *Public Opinion Quarterly, 56*, 216-217.

Schmidt, R., Boraie, D., & Kassabgy, O. (1996). Foreign language motivation: Internal structure and external connections. In R. Oxford (Ed.), *Language learning motivation: Pathways to the new century* (pp. 9-70). Honolulu, HI: University of Hawaii Press.

Schmidt, R., & Watanabe, Y. (2001). Motivation, strategy use, and pedagogical preferences in foreign language learning. In Z. Dörnyei & R. Schmidt (Eds.), *Motivation and second language acquisition* (pp. 313-359). Honolulu, HI: University of Hawaii Press.

Shaaban, K. A., & Ghaith, G. (2000). Student motivation to learn English as a foreign language. *Foreign Language Annals, 33*, 632-644.

Shih, T.-H., & Fan, X. (2008). Comparing response rates from Web and mail surveys: A meta-analysis. *Field Methods, 20*, 249-271.

Skehan, P. (1989). *Individual differences in second-language learning.* London: Edward Arnold.

Spada, N., Barkaoui, K., Peters, C., So, M., & Valeo, A. (2009). Developing a questionnaire to investigate second language learners' preferences for two types of form-focused instruction. *System, 37*, 70-81.

STEP. (n.d.). *Evaluation standards.* Retrieved April 11, 2006, from http://www.eiken.or.jp/english/evaluate/index.html.

Strange, V., Forest, S., Oakley, A., & The Ripple Study Team (2003). Using research questionnaires with young people in schools: The influence of the social context. *International Journal of Social Research Methodology, 6*, 337-346.

Sudman, S., & Bradburn, N. M. (1983). *Asking questions.* San Francisco, CA: Jossey-Bass.

Taguchi, T., Magid, M., & Papi, M. (2009). The L2 motivational self system among

Japanese, Chinese, and Iranian learners of English: A comparative study. In Z. Dörnyei & E. Ushioda (Eds.), *Motivation, language identity and the L2 self* (pp. 66-97). Bristol: Multilingual Matters.

Takahashi, S. (2005). Pragmalinguistic awareness: Is it related to motivation and proficiency? *Applied Linguistics, 26,* 90-120.

Teddlie, C., & Tashakkori, A. (2009). *Foundations of mixed methods research: Integrating quantitative and qualitative approaches in the social and behavioral sciences.* Thousand Oaks, CA: Sage.

Tourangeau, R. (2004). Survey research and societal change. *Annual Review of Psychology, 55,* 775-801.

Tseng, W.-T., Dörnyei, Z., & Schmitt, N. (2006). A new approach to assessing the strategic learning: The case of self-regulation in vocabulary acquisition. *Applied Linguistics, 27,* 78-102.

Umbach, P. D. (2004). Web surveys: Best practices. *New Directions for Institutional Research, 121,* 23-38.

Ushioda, E. (2001). Language learning at university: Exploring the role of motivational thinking. In Z. Dörnyei & R. Schmidt (Eds.), *Motivation and second language acquisition* (pp. 99-125). Honolulu, HI: University of Hawaii Press.

Vandergrift, L., Goh, C. C. M., Mareschal, C. J., & Tafaghodtari, M. H. (2006). The metacognitive awareness listening questionnaire: Development and validation. *Language Learning, 56,* 431-462.

van Selm, M., & Jankowski, N. W. (2006). Conducting online surveys. *Quality & Quantity, 40,* 435-456.

Warden, C. A., & Lin, H. J. (2000). Existence of integrative motivation in an Asian EFL setting. *Foreign Language Annals, 33,* 535-547.

Wenden, A. (1991). *Learner strategies for learner autonomy.* Hemel Hempstead, UK: Prentice Hall.

Wilkinson, L., & TFSI. (1999). Statistical methods in psychology journals: Guidelines and explanations. *American Psychologist, 54,* 594-604.

Wilson, N., & McClean, S. (1994). *Questionnaire design.* Newtownabbey, Northern Ireland: University of Ulster.

Wintergerst, A. C., DeCapua, A., & Itzen, R. C. (2001). The construct validity of one learning styles instrument. *System, 29,* 385-403.

Wright, K. B. (2005). Researching Internet-based populations: Advantages and disadvantages of online survey research, online questionnaire authoring software packages, and web survey services [Electronic Version]. *Journal of Computer-Mediated Communication, 10.* Retrieved December 16, 2008, from http://jcmc.indiana.edu/vol10/issue3/ wright.html.

Yashima, T. (2002). Willingness to communicate in a second language: The Japanese EFL context. *Modern Language Journal, 86,* 54-66.

Yashima, T. (2009). International posture and ideal L2 self in the Japanese EFL context. In Z. Dörnyei & E. Ushioda (Eds.), *Motivation, language identity and the L2 self* (pp. 144-163). Bristol: Multilingual Matters.

Yashima, T., Zenuk-Nishide, L., & Shimizu, K. (2004). The influence of attitudes and affect on willingness to communicate and second language communication. *Language Learning, 54,* 119-152.

Yihong, G., Yuan, Z., Ying, C., & Yan, Z. (2007). Relationship between English learning motivation types and self-identity changes among Chinese students. *TESOL Quarterly, 41,* 133-155.

Young, D. J. (Ed.). (1999). *Affect in foreign language and second language learning.* Boston, MA: McGraw-Hill.

Appendix A
Combined List of the Items Included in the Questionnaires Discussed in Chapter 5

Scales for statement-type items:

1 (Strongly disagree)   2 (Disagree)   3 (Slightly disagree)

4 (Slightly agree)   5 (Agree)   6 (Strongly agree)

Scales for question-type items:

1 (Not at all)   2 (Not so much)   3 (So-so)

4 (A little)   5 (Quite a lot)   6 (Very much)

Note: The tick in the following table indicates the item used in the instrument (**J** = Japanese version, **C** = Chinese version, **I** = Iranian version). (R) indicates a reversed item score (Section 4.3.2).

Criterion Measures

Item	J	C	I
• If an English course was offered at university or somewhere else in the future, I would like to take it.	☑		
• If an English course was offered in the future, I would like to take it.		☑	☑
• If my teacher would give the class an optional assignment, I would certainly volunteer to do it.			☑
• I would like to study English even if I were not required to do so.			☑
• I would like to spend lots of time studying English.		☑	☑
• I would like to concentrate on studying English more than any other topic.		☑	☑
• I am prepared to expend a lot of effort in learning English.	☑	☑	☑
• I am working hard at learning English.	☑		

(to be continued)

(continued)

Item	J	C	I
• I think that I am doing my best to learn English.	☑	☑	
• Compared to my classmates, I think I study English relatively hard.		☑	

Ideal L2 Self

Item	J	C	I
• I can imagine myself living abroad and having a discussion in English.	☑	☑	
• I can imagine myself studying in a university where all my courses are taught in English.			☑
• Whenever I think of my future career, I imagine myself using English.	☑	☑	☑
• I can imagine a situation where I am speaking English with foreigners.	☑		
• I can imagine myself speaking English with international friends or colleagues.		☑	☑
• I can imagine myself living abroad and using English effectively for communicating with the locals.			☑
• I can imagine myself speaking English as if I were a native speaker of English.		☑	☑
• I imagine myself as someone who is able to speak English.	☑	☑	
• I can imagine myself writing English e-mails/letters fluently.			☑
• The things I want to do in the future require me to use English.	☑		

Ought-To L2 Self

Item	J	C	I
• I study English because close friends of mine think it is important.	☑	☑	☑
• Learning English is necessary because people surrounding me expect me to do so.	☑	☑	☑
• I consider learning English important because the people I respect think that I should do it.		☑	☑
• If I fail to learn English I'll be letting other people down.			☑
• Studying English is important to me in order to gain the approval of my peers/teachers/family/boss.		☑	☑
• I have to study English, because, if I do not study it, I think my parents will be disappointed with me.	☑		
• My parents believe that I must study English to be an educated person.	☑		
• Studying English is important to me because an educated person is supposed to be able to speak English.		☑	

(to be continued)

(continued)

Item	J	C	I
• Studying English is important to me because other people will respect me more if I have a knowledge of English.		☑	☑
• It will have a negative impact on my life if I don't learn English.		☑	

Parental Encouragement/Family Influence

Item	J	C	I
• My parents encourage me to study English.	☑		
• My parents encourage me to study English in my free time.	☑		
• My parents encourage me to take every opportunity to use my English (e.g., speaking and reading).	☑		
• My parents encourage me to practise my English as much as possible.			☑
• My parents encourage me to attend extra English classes after class (e.g., at English conversation schools).	☑		
• My family put a lot of pressure on me to study English.		☑	☑
• My parents/family believe(s) that I must study English to be an educated person.		☑	☑
• Studying English is important to me in order to bring honour to my family.		☑	☑
• Being successful in English is important to me so that I can please my parents/relatives.		☑	☑
• I must study English to avoid being punished by my parents/relatives.		☑	
• I have to study English, because, if I don't do it, my parents will be disappointed with me.			☑

Instrumentality—Promotion

Item	J	C	I
• Studying English can be important to me because I think it will someday be useful in getting a good job.	☑	☑	
• Studying English is important to me because English proficiency is necessary for promotion in the future.	☑	☑	☑
• Studying English is important to me because with English I can work globally.	☑		
• Studying English can be important to me because I think it will someday be useful in getting a good job and/or making money.			☑
• Studying English is important because with a high level of English proficiency I will be able to make a lot of money.		☑	
• Studying English can be important for me because I think I'll need it for further studies on my major.	☑		

(to be continued)

(continued)

Item	J	C	I
• Studying English can be important to me because I think I'll need it for further studies.		☑	☑
• Studying English is important to me because I would like to spend a longer period living abroad (e.g., studying and working).	☑		
• Studying English is important to me because I am planning to study abroad.			☑
• I study English in order to keep updated and informed of recent news of the world.			☑
• Studying English is important to me in order to achieve a special goal (e.g., to get a degree or scholarship).		☑	☑
• Studying English is important to me in order to attain a higher social respect.		☑	
• Studying English is important to me because it offers a new challenge in my life.		☑	
• The things I want to do in the future require me to use English.		☑	

Instrumentality—Prevention

Item	J	C	I
• I have to learn English because without passing the English course I cannot graduate.	☑		
• I have to learn English because without passing the English course I cannot get my degree.			☑
• I have to learn English because I don't want to fail the English course.		☑	☑
• I have to study English because I don't want to get bad marks in it at university.	☑		
• I have to study English because I don't want to get bad marks in it.		☑	☑
• Studying English is necessary for me because I don't want to get a poor score or a fail mark in English proficiency tests.	☑	☑	
• Studying English is necessary for me because I don't want to get a poor score or a fail mark in English proficiency tests (TOEFL, IELTS, ...).			☑
• I have to study English; otherwise, I think I cannot be successful in my future career.	☑		☑
• Studying English is important to me, because I would feel ashamed if I got bad grades in English.		☑	☑
• Studying English is important to me because, if I don't have knowledge of English, I'll be considered a weak learner.	☑	☑	☑
• Studying English is important to me because I don't like to be considered a poorly educated person.			☑

(to be continued)

(continued)

Linguistic Self-confidence

Item	J	C	I
• If I make more effort, I am sure I will be able to master English.	☑		
• I believe that I will be capable of reading and understanding most texts in English if I keep studying it.	☑		
• I am sure I will be able to write in English comfortably if I continue studying.	☑		
• I am sure I have a good ability to learn English.	☑		

Attitudes Toward Learning English

Item	J	C	I
• I like the atmosphere of my English classes.	☑		
• Do you like the atmosphere of your English classes?		☑	☑
• I always look forward to English classes.	☑		
• Do you always look forward to English classes?		☑	☑
• I find learning English really interesting.	☑		
• Do you find learning English really interesting?		☑	☑
• I really enjoy learning English.	☑		
• Do you really enjoy learning English?		☑	☑
• Do you think time passes faster while studying English?			☑
• Would you like to have more English lessons at school?			☑

Travel Orientation

Item	J	C	I
• Learning English is important to me because I would like to travel internationally.	☑	☑	☑
• Studying English is important to me because without English I won't be able to travel a lot.	☑	☑	☑
• I study English because with English I can enjoy traveling abroad.	☑	☑	☑

Fear of Assimilation

Item	J	C	I
• I think that there is a danger that Japanese people may forget the importance of Japanese culture, as a result of internationalization.	☑		

(to be continued)

(continued)

Item	J	C	I
• I think that there is a danger that Chinese people may forget the importance of Chinese culture, as a result of internationalization.		☑	
• I think that there is a danger that Iranian people may forget the importance of Iranian culture, as a result of internationalization.			☑
• Because of the influence of the English language, I think the Japanese language is becoming corrupt.	☑		
• Because of the influence of the English language, I think the Chinese language is becoming corrupt.		☑	
• Because of the influence of the English language, I think the Persian language is becoming corrupt.			☑
• Because of the influence of the English-speaking countries, I think the morals of Japanese people are becoming worse.	☑		
• Because of the influence of the English-speaking countries, I think the morals of Chinese people are becoming worse.		☑	
• Because of the influence of the English-speaking countries, I think the morals of Iranian people are becoming worse.			☑
• I think the cultural and artistic values of English are going at the expense of Japanese values.	☑		
• I think the cultural and artistic values of English are going at the expense of Chinese values.		☑	
• I think the cultural and artistic values of English are going at the expense of Iranian values.			☑
• I think that, as internationalization advances, there is a danger of losing the Japanese identity.	☑		
• I think that, as internationalization advances, there is a danger of losing the Chinese identity.		☑	
• I think that, as internationalization advances, there is a danger of losing the Iranian identity.			☑

Ethnocentrism

Item	J	C	I
• I am very interested in the values and customs of other cultures. (R)	☑		
• I respect the values and customs of other cultures. (R)	☑		
• I find it difficult to work together with people who have different customs and values.		☑	
• It is hard to bear the behavior of people from other cultures.			☑
• I think I would be happy if other cultures were more similar to Japanese.	☑		
• I would be happy if other cultures were more similar to Chinese.		☑	
• I would be happy if other cultures were more similar to Iranian.			☑

(to be continued)

(continued)

Item	J	C	I
• It would be a better world if everybody lived like the Japanese.	☑		
• It would be a better world if everybody lived like the Chinese.		☑	
• It would be a better world if everybody lived like the Iranians.			☑
• Other cultures should learn more from my culture.		☑	
• Most other cultures are backward compared to my Chinese culture.		☑	
• Most other cultures are backward compared to my Iranian culture.			☑
• I am proud to be Japanese.	☑		
• I hope that people from other religions would accept Islam as their best way to salvation.			☑
• I think that when people from other cultures are in Iran, they should follow our Islamic rules (e.g., in dressing style and their relationship with the opposite sex).			☑
• I think, compared to what is said in the Universal Declaration of Human Rights and other religions, Islam is more concerned about human rights.			☑

Interest in the English Language

Item	J	C	I
• I feel excited when hearing English spoken.	☑		
• I am interested in the way English is used in conversation.	☑		
• I find the difference between Japanese vocabulary and English vocabulary interesting.	☑		
• I like the rhythm of English.	☑		

English Anxiety

Item	J	C	I
• I get nervous and confused when I am speaking in my English class.	☑		
• How nervous and confused do you get when you are speaking in your English class?		☑	☑
• How afraid are you that other students will laugh at you when you speak English?			☑
• I would feel uneasy speaking English with a native speaker.	☑		
• How uneasy would you feel speaking English with a native speaker?		☑	☑
• If I met an English native speaker, I would feel nervous.	☑		
• I would get tense if a foreigner asked me for directions in English.	☑		
• How tense would you get if a foreigner asked you for directions in English?		☑	☑

(to be continued)

(continued)

Item	J	C	I
• How afraid are you of sounding stupid in English because of the mistakes you make?		☑	☑
• How worried are you that other speakers of English would find your English strange?			☑

Integrativeness

Item	J	C	I
• How important do you think learning English is in order to learn more about the culture and art of its speakers?	☑	☑	☑
• How much would you like to become similar to the people who speak English?	☑	☑	☑
• How much do you like English?	☑	☑	☑

Cultural Interest

Item	J	C	I
• Do you like the music of English-speaking countries (e.g., pop music)?	☑	☑	☑
• Do you like English films?	☑	☑	☑
• Do you like English magazines, newspapers, or books?	☑		☑
• Do you like TV programmes made in English-speaking countries?	☑	☑	☑

Attitudes Toward L2 Community

Item	J	C	I
• Do you like to travel to English-speaking countries?	☑	☑	☑
• Do you like the people who live in English-speaking countries?	☑	☑	☑
• Do you like meeting people from English-speaking countries?	☑	☑	☑
• Would you like to know more about people from English-speaking countries?	☑	☑	☑

Appendix B
The Final Version of the Questionnaires
Used in Japan and China*

---

* 原问卷包含波斯语版本，此处略。

English Learner Questionnaire

This survey is conducted by the School of English Studies of the University of Nottingham, UK, to better understand the thoughts and beliefs of learners of English. This questionnaire consists of four sections. Please read each instruction and write your answers. This is not a test so there are no "right" or "wrong" answers and you do not even have to write your name on it. The results of this survey will be used only for research purpose so please give your answers sincerely. Thank you very much for your help!

Part I

In this part, we would like you to tell us how much you agree or disagree with the following statements by simply circling a number from 1 to 6. Please do not leave out any of items.

Strongly disagree	Disagree	Slightly disagree	Slightly agree	Agree	Strongly agree
1	2	3	4	5	6

(Ex.) If you strongly agree with the following statement, write this:

I like skiing very much.		1 2 3 4 5 ⑥

1.	Learning English is important to me because I would like to travel internationally.	1 2 3 4 5 6
2.	My parents encourage me to study English.	1 2 3 4 5 6
3.	I feel excited when hearing English spoken.	1 2 3 4 5 6
4.	I am very interested in the values and customs of other cultures.	1 2 3 4 5 6
5.	If an English course was offered at university or somewhere else in the future, I would like to take it.	1 2 3 4 5 6
6.	Studying English can be important to me because I think it will someday be useful in getting a good job.	1 2 3 4 5 6
7.	If I make more effort, I am sure I will be able to master English.	1 2 3 4 5 6
8.	I can imagine myself living abroad and having a discussion in English.	1 2 3 4 5 6
9.	I think that there is a danger that Japanese people may forget the importance of Japanese culture, as a result of internationalisation.	1 2 3 4 5 6
10.	I have to learn English because without passing the English course I cannot graduate.	1 2 3 4 5 6
11.	I would feel uneasy speaking English with a native speaker.	1 2 3 4 5 6
12.	I like the atmosphere of my English classes.	1 2 3 4 5 6
13.	I study English because close friends of mine think it is important.	1 2 3 4 5 6
14.	My parents encourage me to take every opportunity to use my English (e.g., speaking and reading).	1 2 3 4 5 6
15.	I am interested in the way English is used in conversation.	1 2 3 4 5 6
16.	I think I would be happy if other cultures were more similar to Japanese.	1 2 3 4 5 6
17.	I am working hard at learning English.	1 2 3 4 5 6

1

	Strongly disagree	Disagree	Slightly disagree	Slightly agree	Agree		Strongly agree
	1	2	3	4	5		6

18.	Studying English is important to me because English proficiency is necessary for promotion in the future.	1	2	3	4	5	6
19.	I believe that I will be capable of reading and understanding most texts in English if I keep studying it.	1	2	3	4	5	6
20.	I can imagine a situation where I am speaking English with foreigners.	1	2	3	4	5	6
21.	Because of the influence of the English language, I think the Japanese language is corrupt.	1	2	3	4	5	6
22.	I get nervous and confused when I am speaking in my English class.	1	2	3	4	5	6
23.	I have to study English because I don't want to get bad marks in it at university.	1	2	3	4	5	6
24.	I find learning English really interesting.	1	2	3	4	5	6
25.	I have to study English, because, if I do not study it, I think my parents will be disappointed with me.	1	2	3	4	5	6
26.	Studying English is important to me because without English I won't be able to travel a lot.	1	2	3	4	5	6
27.	I find the difference between Japanese vocabulary and English vocabulary interesting.	1	2	3	4	5	6
28.	I am prepared to expend a lot of effort in learning English.	1	2	3	4	5	6
29.	My parents encourage me to study English in my free time.	1	2	3	4	5	6
30.	I respect the values and customs of other cultures.	1	2	3	4	5	6
31.	Studying English is important to me because I would like to spend a longer period living abroad (e.g., studying and working).	1	2	3	4	5	6
32.	I am sure I will be able to write in English comfortably if I continue studying.	1	2	3	4	5	6
33.	I imagine myself as someone who is able to speak English.	1	2	3	4	5	6
34.	Because of the influence of the English-speaking countries, I think the moral of Japanese people are becoming worse.	1	2	3	4	5	6
35.	If I met an English native speaker, I would feel nervous.	1	2	3	4	5	6
36.	I have to study English, otherwise, I think I cannot be successful in my future career.	1	2	3	4	5	6
37.	I always look forward to English classes.	1	2	3	4	5	6
38.	Learning English is necessary because people surrounding me expect me to do so.	1	2	3	4	5	6
39.	I study English because with English I can enjoy travelling abroad.	1	2	3	4	5	6
40.	My parents encourage me to attend extra English classes after class (e.g., at English conversation schools).	1	2	3	4	5	6
41.	I think that I am doing my best to learn English.	1	2	3	4	5	6
42.	I like the rhythm of English.	1	2	3	4	5	6

2

Part II

These are new questions but please answer them the same way as you did before.

Not at all	Not so much	So-so	A little	Quite a lot	Very much
1	2	3	4	5	6

(Ex.) If you like "curry" very much, write this:						
Do you like curry?	1	2	3	4	5	6

43.	Do you like the music of English-speaking countries (e.g., pop music)?	1	2	3	4	5	6
44.	Do you like to travel to English-speaking countries?	1	2	3	4	5	6
45.	How important do you think learning English is in order to learn more about the culture and art of its speakers?	1	2	3	4	5	6
46.	Do you like English films?	1	2	3	4	5	6
47.	Do you like the people who live in English-speaking countries?	1	2	3	4	5	6
48.	How much would you like to become similar to the people who speak English?	1	2	3	4	5	6
49.	Do you like English magazines, newspapers, or books?	1	2	3	4	5	6
50.	Do you like meeting people from English-speaking countries?	1	2	3	4	5	6
51.	How much do you like English?	1	2	3	4	5	6
52.	Do you like TV programmes made in English-speaking countries?	1	2	3	4	5	6
53.	Would you like to know more about people from English-speaking countries?	1	2	3	4	5	6

Part III

The following items are similar to the ones in Part 1.

Strongly disagree	Disagree	Slightly disagree	Slightly agree	Agree	Strongly agree
1	2	3	4	5	6

54.	It would be a better world if everybody lived like the Japanese.	1	2	3	4	5	6
55.	Studying English can be important for me because I think I'll need it for further studies on my major.	1	2	3	4	5	6
56.	I think the cultural and artistic values of English are going at the expense of Japanese values.	1	2	3	4	5	6
57.	I am sure I have a good ability to learn English.	1	2	3	4	5	6
58.	Whenever I think of my future career, I imagine myself using English.	1	2	3	4	5	6
59.	I would get tense if a foreigner asked me for directions in English.	1	2	3	4	5	6
60.	Studying English is necessary for me because I don't want to get a poor score or a fail mark in English proficiency tests.	1	2	3	4	5	6

3   *Overleaf*

Strongly disagree	Disagree	Slightly disagree	Slightly agree	Agree	Strongly agree
1	2	3	4	5	6

		Scale
61.	I really enjoy learning English.	1 2 3 4 5 6
62.	My parents believe that I must study English to be an educated person.	1 2 3 4 5 6
63.	I think that, as internationalisation advances, there is a danger of losing the Japanese identity.	1 2 3 4 5 6
64.	Studying English is important to me because with English I can work globally.	1 2 3 4 5 6
65.	I am proud to be Japanese.	1 2 3 4 5 6
66.	The things I want to do in the future require me to use English.	1 2 3 4 5 6
67.	Studying English is important to me because, if I don't have knowledge of English, I'll be considered a weak student.	1 2 3 4 5 6

Part IV

Please provide the following information by ticking (✓) in the box or writing your response in the space.

Gender: ❑ Male   ❑ Female

Nationality: ❑ Japanese   ❑ Non-Japanese

Age: ❑ 18 ❑ 19 ❑ 20 ❑ 21 ❑ 22 ❑ 23 ❑ 24 ❑ other: _____

Year of study: ❑ 1st ❑ 2nd ❑ 3rd ❑ 4th ❑ 5th ❑ other: _____

Major: _____

English teacher   *Have you ever had or do you have a native English-speaking teacher?*

❑ Yes   ❑ No

Overseas experiences: *Have you spent a longer period (at least a total of three months) in English-speaking countries (e.g., travelling, studying)?*

❑ Yes   ❑ No

English ability: *Please rate your current overall proficiency in English by ticking one.*

❑ **Upper Intermediate level and over**— Able to converse about general matters of daily life and topics of one's specialty and grasp the gist of lectures and broadcasts. Able to read high-level materials such as newspapers and write about personal ideas.

❑ **Intermediate level** — Able to converse about general matters of daily life. Able to read general materials related to daily life and write simple passages.

❑ **Lower Intermediate level** — Able to converse about familiar daily topics. Able to read materials about familiar everyday topics and write simple letters.

❑ **Post-Beginner level** — Able to hold a simple conversation such as greeting and introducing someone. Able to read simple materials and write a simple passage in elementary English.

❑ **Beginner level** — Able to give simple greetings using set words and phrases. Able to read simple sentences, grasp the gist of short passages, and to write a simple sentence in basic English.

Thank you for your cooperation!

4

英語学習者に関するアンケート

この調査はイギリスのノッティンガム大学英語学科によって行われるもので、英語学習者の考えや信念をよりよく理解するためのものです。このアンケートは4つのパートから成り立っています。それぞれの指示に従い、回答を記入してください。これはテストではありませんので、「正解」も「不正解」もなく、名前を記入する必要もありません。この調査結果は研究目的のためだけに使われますので、正直にお答えください。よろしくお願いいたします。

パート1

このパートでは、あなたが次の事柄にどの程度共感できるかを、1から6の番号の中からひとつを選んでお答えください。記入漏れのないようにお願いいたします。

全く そう思わない 1	そう思わない 2	あまり そう思わない 3	やや そう思う 4	そう思う 5	非常に そう思う 6

(例) もしあなたの考えが次の内容に非常に共感できる場合、次のように記入します。						
スキーはとても好きだ。	1	2	3	4	5	⑥

1.	海外旅行をしたいので、英語の勉強は大切である。	1	2	3	4	5	6
2.	親が英語の勉強をすすめている。	1	2	3	4	5	6
3.	英語が話されているのを聞くとわくわくする。	1	2	3	4	5	6
4.	異文化の価値観や習慣にとても関心がある。	1	2	3	4	5	6
5.	今後さらに大学やその他の所で英語の授業があれば、受講したい。	1	2	3	4	5	6
6.	英語を勉強しておくといつか良い仕事を得るために役立つと思うので、英語の勉強は大切だ。	1	2	3	4	5	6
7.	もっと努力すれば、英語を確実に身につけられると思う。	1	2	3	4	5	6
8.	外国に住み、英語で討論している自分を想像できる。	1	2	3	4	5	6
9.	国際化によって、日本人が日本文化の重要性を忘れる危険性があると思う。	1	2	3	4	5	6
10.	英語の単位をとらないと卒業ができないので、英語の勉強をしなければならない。	1	2	3	4	5	6
11.	英語でネイティブスピーカーと話をする場合、不安を感じる。	1	2	3	4	5	6
12.	英語の授業の雰囲気が好きだ。	1	2	3	4	5	6
13.	親しい友人が英語の勉強は大切だと思っているので、英語の勉強をする。	1	2	3	4	5	6
14.	親は私に、あらゆる機会を利用して英語を読んだり話したりするなど、英語を使うようにすすめている。	1	2	3	4	5	6
15.	会話の中での英語の使い方に興味がある。	1	2	3	4	5	6
16.	もし他の文化が日本文化にもっと似ていたら楽しいと思う。	1	2	3	4	5	6
17.	英語を一生懸命勉強している。	1	2	3	4	5	6

1

全く そう思わない 1	そう思わない 2	あまり そう思わない 3	やや そう思う 4	そう思う 5	非常に そう思う 6

18.	将来昇進のために英語力は必要となるので英語の勉強は大切だ。	1 2 3 4 5 6
19.	このまま勉強を続ければたいていの英語の文章を読め、理解できるようになると思う。	1 2 3 4 5 6
20.	自分が外国人と英語で話をしている状況を想像できる。	1 2 3 4 5 6
21.	英語の影響で日本語が乱れていると思う。	1 2 3 4 5 6
22.	英語の授業で発言をしているとき、不安になったり戸惑ったりする。	1 2 3 4 5 6
23.	大学の英語で悪い成績を取りたくないので、英語の勉強をしなければならない。	1 2 3 4 5 6
24.	英語を勉強するのはとても面白い。	1 2 3 4 5 6
25.	英語を勉強しないと親が残念に思うので、英語を勉強しなければならない。	1 2 3 4 5 6
26.	英語ができなければ、旅行があまりできなくなるので、英語の勉強は大切だ。	1 2 3 4 5 6
27.	日本語と英語の単語の違いは面白いと思う。	1 2 3 4 5 6
28.	英語の勉強に努力を惜しまない。	1 2 3 4 5 6
29.	時間があるときには英語の勉強をするように、と親はすすめている。	1 2 3 4 5 6
30.	自分は他の文化の価値観や習慣を尊重している。	1 2 3 4 5 6
31.	勉強や仕事等で海外に長期間滞在したいと思っているので、英語を勉強しておくのは大切だ。	1 2 3 4 5 6
32.	このまま勉強を続けたら、将来楽に英語を書けると思う。	1 2 3 4 5 6
33.	英語が話せるようになっている自分を想像する。	1 2 3 4 5 6
34.	英語圏の国々の影響で、日本人のモラルが低下していると思う。	1 2 3 4 5 6
35.	英語のネイティブスピーカーと会うと、不安になる。	1 2 3 4 5 6
36.	英語の勉強をしなければいけない。そうしなければ、将来仕事で成功できないと思う。	1 2 3 4 5 6
37.	英語の授業をいつも楽しみにしている。	1 2 3 4 5 6
38.	私が英語を勉強することを周りの人々が期待しているので、英語の勉強は必要だ。	1 2 3 4 5 6
39.	英語ができれば海外旅行が楽しめるので英語の勉強をする。	1 2 3 4 5 6
40.	親は私に、授業の後さらに英会話学校等で英語を勉強するようにすすめている。	1 2 3 4 5 6
41.	自分は英語の勉強をがんばっていると思う。	1 2 3 4 5 6
42.	英語のリズム感が好きだ。	1 2 3 4 5 6

2

パート2

次のパートは質問形式ですが、パート1と同じ方法で回答してください。

全く そうでない	あまり そうでない	どちらでもない	少し そうである	とても そうである	非常に そうである
1	2	3	4	5	6

(例) もしカレーが非常に好きなら、次のように記入します。						
カレーが好きですか？	1	2	3	4	5	⑥

		1	2	3	4	5	6
43.	ポップミュージックなどの英語圏の音楽は好きですか？	1	2	3	4	5	6
44.	英語圏へ旅行するのは好きですか？	1	2	3	4	5	6
45.	英語圏の人々の文化や芸術をさらに知るためには、どの程度英語学習は大切だと思いますか？	1	2	3	4	5	6
46.	英語の映画は好きですか？	1	2	3	4	5	6
47.	英語圏に住んでいる人々が好きですか？	1	2	3	4	5	6
48.	どの程度英語圏の人々のようになりたいですか？	1	2	3	4	5	6
49.	英語の雑誌や、新聞、あるいは本は好きですか？	1	2	3	4	5	6
50.	英語圏の人々と知り合いになりたいですか？	1	2	3	4	5	6
51.	どの程度英語が好きですか？	1	2	3	4	5	6
52.	英語圏で作られたテレビ番組は好きですか？	1	2	3	4	5	6
53.	英語圏の人々についてもっと知りたいですか？	1	2	3	4	5	6

パート3

パート3はパート1と同じように回答してください。

全く そう思わない	そう思わない	あまり そう思わない	やや そう思う	そう思う	非常に そう思う
1	2	3	4	5	6

		1	2	3	4	5	6
54.	あらゆる人が日本人のような生活を送れば、もっと良い世の中になると思う。	1	2	3	4	5	6
55.	今後さらに自分の専門について勉強をしていくためには英語が必要になると思うので、英語の勉強は大切だ。	1	2	3	4	5	6
56.	英語の文化的、芸術的価値観は日本の価値観をだめにすると思う。	1	2	3	4	5	6
57.	自分には英語学習の才能があると思う。	1	2	3	4	5	6
58.	将来の仕事について考えるときはいつも英語を使っている自分を想像する。	1	2	3	4	5	6
59.	外国人に英語で道を聞かれると緊張する。	1	2	3	4	5	6
60.	英語の資格試験で低い点数を取ったり不合格になりたくないので英語の勉強は必要だ。	1	2	3	4	5	6

3 　　　　　　　　　　　　　　　　　　　裏へ

全く そう思わない 1	そう思わない 2	あまり そう思わない 3	やや そう思う 4	そう思う 5	非常に そう思う 6

61.	英語を学ぶのは本当に楽しい。	1	2	3	4	5	6
62.	英語の勉強をして教養のある人間にならなければいけないと、親は強く思っている。	1	2	3	4	5	6
63.	国際化が進むと日本の独自性が失われる危険性があると思う。	1	2	3	4	5	6
64.	英語ができれば国際的に働くことができるので、英語の勉強は大切だ。	1	2	3	4	5	6
65.	日本人であることを誇りに思っている。	1	2	3	4	5	6
66.	将来自分のしたいことをするためには、英語が必要となる。	1	2	3	4	5	6
67.	英語ができないと、出来の悪い学生と思われるので英語の勉強は大切だ。	1	2	3	4	5	6

パート4

次の項目の□にチェック(✓)を入れるか、空欄に回答を記入してお答えください。

性別：　　　❏ 男性　　　　❏ 女性

国籍：　　　❏ 日本人　　　❏ 外国人

年齢：　　　❏ 18　　❏ 19　　❏ 20　　❏ 21　　❏ 22　　❏ 23　　❏ 24　　❏ その他：＿＿＿＿＿＿＿

学年：　　　❏ 1年生　　❏ 2年生　　❏ 3年生　　❏ 4年生　　❏ 5年生　　❏ その他：＿＿＿＿＿＿＿

専攻：　　　＿＿＿＿＿＿＿＿＿＿＿＿＿＿＿＿＿＿＿＿

英語教員：　英語のネイティブの先生に習ったことがある、あるいは習っていますか？

　　　　　　❏ はい　　　　❏ いいえ

海外経験：　旅行や勉強など、少なくとも計3ヶ月以上英語圏に滞在したことがありますか？

　　　　　　❏ はい　　　　❏ いいえ

英語力：　　あなたの現在の英語力について次の中から一つに印をつけてください。

　　❏中上級レベル以上—日常生活の一般的な事柄や専門的な事柄についての会話ができ、講義や放送
　　　　の大意を理解できる。新聞などの高度な文章が読め、自分の考えを書くことができる。

　　❏中級レベル—日常生活の一般的な事柄に関する会話ができる。日常生活の一般的な事柄に関する
　　　　文章が読め、簡単な文章を書くことができる。

　　❏初中級レベル—日常生活の身近な事柄についての会話ができる。日常生活の身近な事柄について
　　　　の文章が読め、簡単な手紙を書くことができる。

　　❏初級レベル—挨拶や人の紹介などの簡単な会話ができる。簡単な文章が読め、基礎的な英語を用
　　　　いて簡単な文章を書くことができる。

　　❏基礎レベル—決まり文句を用いて簡単な挨拶ができる。簡単な文が読め、短い文章の大意が理解
　　　　でき、基礎的な英語を用いて簡単な一文を書くことができる。

ご協力ありがとうございました！

4

English Learner Questionnaire
英语学习者的问卷调查

We would like to ask you to help us by participating in a survey conducted by the School of English Studies of the University of Nottingham, UK, to better understand the thoughts and beliefs of learners of English in China. This questionnaire is not a test so there are no "right" or "wrong" answers and you do not even have to write your name on it. We are interested in your personal opinion. The results of this survey will be used only for research purpose so please give your answers sincerely to ensure the success of this project. Thank you very much for your help!

我们热诚邀请您参加由英国诺丁汉大学英语系主持的调查。该调查主要是关于中国人学习英语的研究。本调查不是考试，所以没有对错之分。您也不需要署名。我们很想知道您对相关问卷内容的看法。由于本调查的结果主要用于研究，所以请您热心支持。非常感谢您的帮助。

Part I

In this part, we would like you to tell us how much you agree or disagree with the following statements by simply circling a number from 1 to 6. Please do not leave out any items.
请根据以下的问题选择相应的数字代表同意或不同意的程度。

Strongly Disagree	Disagree	Slightly disagree	Slightly agree	Agree	Strongly agree
1	2	3	4	5	6
强烈不同意	不同意	基本不同意	基本同意	同意	强烈同意

(Example) If you strongly agree with the following statement, write this:
比如：要是您强烈同意以下论断，就如以下方式打勾。

I like skiing very much. 我非常喜欢滑雪。   1 2 3 4 5 ⑥

1	Learning English is important to me because I would like to travel internationally. 对我来说学习英语很重要是因为我想去国外旅游。	1 2 3 4 5 6
2	My parents/family believe that I must study English to be an educated person. 我家人认为要成为受教育良好的人，我必须学英语。	1 2 3 4 5 6
3	I think that I am doing my best to learn English. 我觉得自己正尽全力学习英语。	1 2 3 4 5 6
4	Studying English can be important to me because I think it will someday be useful in getting a good job. 对我来说学习英语很重要是因为对**将来找好工作有帮助**。	1 2 3 4 5 6
5	I study English because close friends of mine think it is important. 我学习英语是由于我的好朋友认为英语重要。	1 2 3 4 5 6
6	I can imagine myself living abroad and having a discussion in English. 我可以想象自己在国外生活并用英语和当地人交流。	1 2 3 4 5 6
7	I have to study English because I don't want to get bad marks in it. 我不得不学习英语是因为不想考试分数底。	1 2 3 4 5 6
8	I think that there is a danger that Chinese people may forget the importance of Chinese culture, as a result of internationalisation. 我认为随着中国的国际化，国人可能会忘记中国文化的重要性。	1 2 3 4 5 6
9	I would be happy if other cultures were more similar to Chinese. 要是其他文化更像中华文化就好了。	1 2 3 4 5 6

1

Strongly Disagree	Disagree	Slightly disagree	Slightly agree	Agree	Strongly agree
1	2	3	4	5	6
强烈不同意	不同意	基本不同意	基本同意	同意	强烈同意

10	Studying English is important to me because English proficiency is necessary for promotion in the future. 对我来说学习英语很重要是因为精通英语对我将来的提升是必不可少的。	1 2 3 4 5 6
11	Studying English is important to me in order to bring honours to my family. 学习英语对我来说之所以重要是为了为我们的家庭争光。	1 2 3 4 5 6
12	I consider learning English important because the people I respect think that I should do it. 我认为学习英语重要是由于我所尊敬的人认为我需要做它。	1 2 3 4 5 6
13	I would like to spend lots of time studying English. 我想花大量时间学习英语。	1 2 3 4 5 6
14	I imagine myself as someone who is able to speak English. 我可以想象我能说英语。	1 2 3 4 5 6
15	Most other cultures are backward compared to my Chinese culture. 与中国文化相比，大部分其他文化很落后。	1 2 3 4 5 6
16	Studying English can be important to me because I think I'll need it for further studies. 学习英语很重要是因为我今后的学习将会运用英语。	1 2 3 4 5 6
17	Because of the influence of the English language, I think the Chinese language is becoming corrupt. 由于受英语的影响，我认为中文正在退化。	1 2 3 4 5 6
18	Studying English is important to me because, if I don't have knowledge of English, I'll be considered a weak learner. 学习英语很重要是因为如果我不懂英语，别人会认为我学习很差。	1 2 3 4 5 6
19	Learning English is necessary because people surrounding me expect me to do so. 学习英语之所以必要是由于我周围的人希望我学。	1 2 3 4 5 6
20	Studying English is important to me because without English I won't be able to travel a lot. 学习英语很重要是因为如果不会英语，我将不能经常去国外旅游。	1 2 3 4 5 6
21	I must study English to avoid being punished by my parents/relatives. 我必须学习英语以免被父母或亲人责怪。	1 2 3 4 5 6
22	Studying English is important because with a high level of English proficiency I will be able to make a lot of money. 学习英语之所以重要是因为精通英语可以帮我增加收入。	1 2 3 4 5 6
23	I am prepared to expend a lot of effort in learning English. 我准备努力学习英语。	1 2 3 4 5 6
24	Other cultures should learn more from my culture. 其他文化应该从我们的文化中学到更多。	1 2 3 4 5 6
25	Studying English is necessary for me because I don't want to get a poor score or a fail mark in English proficiency tests. 学习英语之所以必要是因为我不想成绩不好或不及格。	1 2 3 4 5 6
26	Because of the influence of the English-speaking countries, I think the morals of Chinese people are becoming worse. 由于受英语国家的影响，我认为中国人的道德观正日趋恶化。	1 2 3 4 5 6
27	Studying English is important to me in order to gain the approval of my peers/teachers/family/boss. 学习英语很重要完全是为了获得同学、老师、家人和老板对我的认可。	1 2 3 4 5 6
28	The things I want to do in the future require me to use English. 我将来要做的事要求我使用英语。	1 2 3 4 5 6
29	I can imagine myself speaking English as if I were a native speaker of English. 我可以想像我用英语像自己母语一样交流。	1 2 3 4 5 6

2

	Strongly Disagree 1 强烈不同意	Disagree 2 不同意	Slightly disagree 3 基本不同意	Slightly agree 4 基本同意	Agree 5 同意	Strongly agree 6 强烈同意

30	Being successful in English is important to me so that I can please my parents/relatives. 英语学好了我的家人就会高兴。	1 2 3 4 5 6				
31	I would like to concentrate on studying English more than any other topic. 我想花大部分学习时间在英语课程上。	1 2 3 4 5 6				
32	I find it difficult to work together with people who have different customs and values. 与不同的文化背景和价值观的人共事对我来说是困难的。	1 2 3 4 5 6				
33	I have to learn English because I don't want to fail the English course. 我得学习英文是因为我不想英语考试不及格。	1 2 3 4 5 6				
34	I think the cultural and artistic values of English are going at the expense of Chinese values. 我认为英语文化和艺术价值观正削弱我们的价值观。	1 2 3 4 5 6				
35	Studying English is important to me because it offers a new challenge in my life. 学习英语之所以重要是由于它给我的生活带来新的挑战。	1 2 3 4 5 6				
36	It will have a negative impact on my life if I don't learn English. 要是不学英语，我的生活就会受到负面的影响。	1 2 3 4 5 6				
37	Compared to my classmates, I think I study English relatively hard. 与我的同学相比，我认为我学习英语比较努力。	1 2 3 4 5 6				
38	I can imagine myself speaking English with international friends or colleagues. 我可以想象和国外朋友或同事用英语交流。	1 2 3 4 5 6				
39	It would be a better world if everybody lived like the Chinese. 如果每个人都能像中国人那样生活世界会变得更好。	1 2 3 4 5 6				
40	My family put a lot of pressure on me to study English. 我的家人在学习英语上给我很多压力。	1 2 3 4 5 6				
41	Studying English is important to me in order to achieve a special goal (e.g., to get a degree or scholarship). 学习英语的重要性在于它能助我达到一个既定目标，比如获得文凭或奖学金。	1 2 3 4 5 6				
42	Studying English is important to me because an educated person is supposed to be able to speak English. 学习英语的重要性在于它是受过良好教育的标志。	1 2 3 4 5 6				
43	Studying English is important to me, because I would feel ashamed if I got bad grades in English. 学习英语对我来说重要是因为考的分数太低，我会感到没面子。	1 2 3 4 5 6				
44	I think that, as internationalisation advances, there is a danger of losing the Chinese identity. 我想随着中国日趋国际化，中国将面临消失自我的危险。	1 2 3 4 5 6				
45	If an English course was offered in the future, I would like to take it. 要是以后开设英语课，我会学习该课程。	1 2 3 4 5 6				
46	Whenever I think of my future career, I imagine myself using English. 无论将来的职业是什么，我可以想象用英语交流。	1 2 3 4 5 6				
47	I study English because with English I can enjoy travelling abroad. 我学习英语是因为我可以享受国外旅行。	1 2 3 4 5 6				
48	Studying English is important to me in order to attain a higher social respect. 学习英语重要是因为我可以获得社会的尊敬。	1 2 3 4 5 6				
49	Studying English is important to me because other people will respect me more if I have a knowledge of English. 学习英语的重要性在于要是我懂英语，其他人就会更加尊敬我。	1 2 3 4 5 6				

3

162

Part II

These are new questions but please answer them the same way as you did before.
请按照以上方法完成下列问卷。

Not at all 1 根本不	Not so much 2 不太	So-so 3 一般	A little 4 一点	Quite a lot 5 许多	Very much 6 非常		

(Example) If you like "curry" very much and "green pepper" not very much, write this:
比如：要是您认为您非常喜欢咖喱而不是很喜欢青椒，就入示例打圈。

Do you like curry? 你喜欢咖喱吗?	1	2	3	4	5	⑥

50	Do you like the atmosphere of your English classes? 你喜欢你上英语课时的气氛吗?	1	2	3	4	5	6
51	How tense would you get if a foreigner asked you for directions in English? 要是老外用英语向你问路，你会紧张吗?	1	2	3	4	5	6
52	How much would you like to become similar to the people who speak English? 你有多想成为说英文的人?	1	2	3	4	5	6
53	Do you like the music of English-speaking countries (e.g., pop music)? 你喜欢英语国家的音乐吗？比如流行音乐?	1	2	3	4	5	6
54	Do you like the people who live in English-speaking countries? 你喜欢生活在英语国家的人吗?	1	2	3	4	5	6
55	Do you find learning English really interesting? 您感到学习英语真的有趣吗?	1	2	3	4	5	6
56	How uneasy would you feel speaking English with a native speaker? 与一个老外说英语你会感到有多不自在?	1	2	3	4	5	6
57	How important do you think learning English is in order to learn more about the culture and art of its speakers? 你认为学习英文对于了解英语国家的人的文化和艺术重要吗?	1	2	3	4	5	6
58	Do you like English films? 你喜欢英语电影吗?	1	2	3	4	5	6
59	Do you like meeting people from English-speaking countries? 你喜欢和英语国家的人打交道吗?	1	2	3	4	5	6
60	Do you always look forward to English classes? 你总是想喜欢英语课吗?	1	2	3	4	5	6
61	How nervous and confused do you get when you are speaking in your English class? 你在英语课上说英语感到紧张和不知所措吗?	1	2	3	4	5	6
62	How much do you like English? 你有多喜欢英语?	1	2	3	4	5	6
63	Do you like TV programmes made in English-speaking countries? 你喜欢英语国家拍摄的电视节目吗?	1	2	3	4	5	6
64	Do you like to travel to English-speaking countries? 你愿意到英语国家旅游吗?	1	2	3	4	5	6
65	Do you really enjoy learning English? 你真的喜欢学习英语吗?	1	2	3	4	5	6
66	How afraid are you of sounding stupid in English because of the mistakes you make? 说错英语的时候你会害怕出洋相吗?	1	2	3	4	5	6
67	Would you like to know more about people from English-speaking countries? 你想更多地了解英语国家的人吗?	1	2	3	4	5	6

Part III

Please provide the following information by ticking (✓) in the box or writing your response in the space so that we can interpret your previous answers better.

请就以下问题打勾以便我们更能更好地便用您以上所提供的信息。

- ❑ Male　男　　❑ Female　女
- ❑ Chinese　中国人 ❑ Non-Chinese 非中国人（请注明）(Please specify: _____)
- Your age (in years): _____
  您的年龄（按年计算）：_____

- *Have you ever had or do you have now a native English-speaking teacher?*
  英语外教曾经教过或现在正在教你学习英语吗？

  　　　　❑ Yes 是　　　❑ No 否

- *Have you spent a longer period (at least a total of three months) in English-speaking countries (e.g., travelling, studying)?*
  你曾经在英语国家逗留过吗（至少三个月以上，比如学习或旅游）？

  　　　　❑ Yes 是　　　❑ No 否

- *Where are you studying English at the moment? (Please mark more options if necessary.)*
  你目前在哪里学英语？可以多选：

  　　　　❑ at private language school　私人语言学校　　❑ at secondary school　中学
  　　　　❑ at college / university 大专院校　　　　　　❑ with private tutor　私人老师
  　　　　❑ on my own 自学

- *What is your current employment status?*
  你目前的工作是：

  　　　　❑ Secondary school student
  　　　　中学生

  　　　　❑ College/university student (If you tick here, please answer the question below.)
  　　　　大专院校学生（要是选该项的话，请回答以下问题）

- Are you majoring in English?
  你是英语专业的吗？

  　　　　❑ Yes 是 ❑ No 否

  　　　　❑ Working professional　专业人士

- *Please rate your current overall proficiency in English by ticking one.*
  请根据你的英文熟练程度选择下列选项：

  　　❑ **Upper Intermediate level and over**— Able to converse about general matters of daily life and topics of one's specialty and grasp the gist of lectures and broadcasts. Able to read high-level materials such as newspapers and write about personal ideas.
  　　中上到高级——能够进行日常一般生活对话，而且和他人进行主题对话，并能全面领会广播和演讲的主题，能够阅读复杂的材料例如报纸，并记下个人的想法。

5

❏ **Intermediate level** — Able to converse about general matters of daily life. Able to read general materials related to daily life and write simple passages.

中等程度——能够进行日常一般生活对话，能阅读一般的和日常生活相关的材料，并可以记下简单的段落。

❏ **Lower Intermediate level** — Able to converse about familiar daily topics. Able to read materials about familiar everyday topics and write simple letters.

中下程度——能对日常熟悉的话题进行交流，能阅读日常读熟悉的话题，并写简单的信。

❏ **Post-Beginner level** — Able to hold a simple conversation such as greeting and introducing someone. Able to read simple materials and write a simple passage in elementary English.

初上级程度——能进行简单的会话，比如介绍自己或别人以及问候。能阅读非常简单的英文材料，用简单的英文写作。

❏ **Beginner level** — Able to give simple greetings using set words and phrases. Able to read simple sentences, grasp the gist of short passages, and to write a simple sentence in basic English.

初级程度——能用英文单词进行简单的问候，能阅读简单的句子，领会短句，能用最简单的英文写很简单的句子。

Thank you for your cooperation!
谢谢合作！

6

Appendix C
Selected List of Published
L2 Questionnaires

Please note that the use of the term "questionnaires" in this book does not include "tests," "production questionnaires" (e.g., DCTs), or classroom observation schemes (see Section 1.1).

I would like to thank all my friends and colleagues who have helped me to compile this list. I am certain that I have unintentionally omitted several valuable published instruments from the list below. I apologize for this.

Attitudes (See Also "Language Learning Motivation")
- Burstall, Jamieson, Cohen, and Hargreaves (1974): Teachers' Attitudes Scale
- Gan (2009)
- Levine (2003)
- Wenden (1991): Attitudes Questionnaire for Self-Access; Principles of a Learner-Centered Approach

Biographic Background
- Ehrman (1996a): Biographic Background Questionnaire

Computer Familiarity
- Eignor, Taylor, Kirsch, and Jamieson (1998): Computer Familiarity of TOEFL Examinees

Feedback
- Cohen (1987): Feedback Questionnaire (concerning the teacher's marking of an essay)
- Cohen (1991): Teachers' choices in feedback on student written work; Students' reactions to teachers' comments on written work

Grammar Instruction
- Spada *et al.* (2009): Student Preference for Grammar Instruction

Group Cohesiveness
- See Clément and Baker (2001) under "Language Learning Motivation" (also reprinted in Dörnyei, 2001)

Immigrant Settlement
- Cumming (1991)
- Hart and Cumming (1997)

Language Anxiety
- Brown (2002)
- See Clément and Baker (2001) under "Language Learning Motivation"
- Ely (1986b): Language Class Discomfort
- Gardner (1985): French Class Anxiety
- Horwitz, Horwitz, and Cope (1986): Foreign Language Classroom Anxiety Scale (reprinted in Young, 1999)
- MacIntyre and Gardner (1991): The Axometer
- MacIntyre and Gardner (1994): Input, Processing, and Output (IPO) scale
- Young (1999): The appendices of this edited volume contain several anxiety scales by Daly and Miller (Writing Apprehension), Gardner and MacIntyre, Horwitz *et al.* (see above), McCroskey (PRCA—to measure communication apprehension), and Sarason and Ganzern (Test Anxiety Scale).

Language Contact (Quality and Quantity)
- See Clément and Baker (2001) under "Language Learning Motivation"

Language Course Evaluation
- Brown (2001): Language Testing Course; Reading Course
- See Clément and Baker (2001) under "Language Learning Motivation"
- Gardner (1985)

Language Learner Beliefs

- Horwitz (1988): Beliefs About Language Learning Inventory (BALLI) (reprinted in Young, 1999)
- Levine (2003)
- Lightbown and Spada (1999)
- Loewen, Li, Fei, Thompson, Nakatsukawa, Ahn, and Chen (2009)
- Mori (1999): Epistemological Belief Questionnaire
- Murphey (1996)
- Wenden (1991): How I Think I Learn Best

Language Learning Motivation

- Al-Shehri (2009)
- Brown (2002)
- Burstall *et al.* (1974): Pupils' Attitudes Towards Learning French
- Cheng and Dörnyei (2007): Teachers' Use of Motivational Strategies in Language Instructions
- Clément and Baker (2001) contains the complete, multi-dimensional questionnaires used by Clément and Kruidenier (1985), Labrie and Clément (1986), Clément (1986), Clément and Noels (1992), Clément, Dörnyei and Noels (1994)
- Clément and Kruidenier (1983): Language Learning Orientations
- Cohen and Dörnyei (2001): Taking My Motivational Temperature on a Language Task
- Coleman (1996)
- Csizér and Kormos (2009)
- Dörnyei (1990, 2001)
- Dörnyei and Clément (2001): Language Orientation Questionnaire
- Dörnyei, Csizér, and Németh (2006)
- Ehrman (1996a): Motivation and Strategies Questionnaire
- Ehrman (1996b)
- Ely (1986a)
- Gan (2009)
- Gardner (1985): Attitude/Motivation Test Battery (AMTB)
- Gardner, Tremblay, and Masgoret (1997): Version of the AMTB used in the study
- Green (1999)
- MacIntyre, MacKinnon, and Clément (2009)

- Noels, Clément, and Pelletier (1999)
- Noels *et al.* (2000): Language Learning Orientation Scale—Intrinsic Motivation, Extrinsic Motivation, and Amotivation (LLOS-IEA)
- Ryan (2009): Motivational Factors Questionnaire (MQF) (also see Ryan, 2008, for English and Japanese versions)
- Schmidt, Boraie, and Kassabgy (1996) (also contains an Arabic version)
- Schmidt and Watanabe (2001)
- Shaaban and Ghaith (2000)
- Taguchi *et al.* (2009)
- Takahashi (2005)
- Warden and Lin (2000)
- Yihong, Yuan, Ying, and Yan (2007)

Language Learning Strategies

- Brown (2002)
- Chamot, Barnhardt, El-Dinary, and Robbins (1999)
- Cohen and Chi (2001): Language Strategy Use Survey
- Cohen and Oxford (2001a): Young Learners' Language Strategy Use Survey
- Ehrman (1996a): Motivation and Strategies Questionnaire
- Gan (2009)
- Nakatani (2006): Oral Communication Strategy Inventory (OCSI)
- Oxford (1990): Strategy Inventory for Language Learning (SILL)
- Phakiti (2003): Cognitive and Metacognitive Questionnaire
- Schmidt *et al.* (1996) (also contains an Arabic version)
- Schmidt and Watanabe (2001)
- Tseng *et al.* (2006): Self-Regulating Capacity in Vocabulary Learning Scale (SRCvoc)
- Vandergrift, Goh, Mareschal, and Tafaghodtari (2006): Metacognitive Awareness Listening Questionnaire (MALQ)

Language Learning Styles

- See Al-Shehri (2009) under "Language Learning Motivation"
- Brown (1994): Extroversion/Introversion Test
- Brown (2000): Learning Styles Checklist
- Brown (2002)

- Cohen and Oxford (2001b): Learning Styles Survey for Young Learners
- Cohen, Oxford, and Chi (2001): Learning Style Survey
- Ely (1989): Tolerance of Ambiguity Scale
- Ely (1986b): Language Class Risktaking; Language Class Sociability
- Oxford (1995): Style Analysis Survey (SAS)
- Reid (1995): Perceptual Learning Style Preference Questionnaire
- Wintergerst, DeCapua, and Itzen (2001): Learning Style Indicator

Linguistic Self-confidence
- See Clément and Baker (2001) under "Language Learning Motivation"

Needs Analysis
- Lepetit and Cichocki (2002)
- Nunan (1988)
- Nunan and Lamb (1996)
- Richterich (1980)

Preferences for Instructional Activities
- Brown (2000)
- Schmidt *et al.* (1996) (also contains an Arabic version)
- Schmidt and Watanabe (2001)

Self-evaluation
- Brown (2002)
- See Clément and Baker (2001) under "Language Learning Motivation"
- Ehrman and Dörnyei (1998): Sarah Thurrell's "Self-Assessment Sheet for a Writing Course"
- Kondo-Brown (2001): Language Survey of Second Generation Japanese Americans
- Nunan and Lamb (1996)
- Wenden (1991): Evaluation Guide for Notetaking; Questionnaire for a Good Language Learner

Self-identity Change
- Yihong *et al.* (2007)

Teacher Anxiety
- Horwitz (1996): Teacher Anxiety Scale

Teacher Beliefs
- Horwitz (1985): Teacher Belief Scale

Teacher Evaluation
- See Clément and Baker (2001) under "Language Learning Motivation" (also reprinted in Dörnyei, 2001)
- Gardner (1985)

Teacher Motivation
- Kassabgy, Boraie, and Schmidt (2001): The Teacher's World Survey

Teacher self-evaluation
- Nunan and Lamb (1996)

Willingness to Communicate
- MacIntyre, Clément, Baker, and Conrad (2001)
- Yashima (2002, 2009)
- Yashima, Zenuk-Nishide, and Shimizu (2004)

研究案例：

中国大学本科生英语学习动机类型＊1

高一虹、赵媛、程英、周燕

摘要：本文采取问卷的方法考察了中国大学本科生英语学习的动机类型。受试为全国30所大学的2,278名本科生。问卷包括30个有关为什么学习英语的问题，主要根据在多个省区采集的开放式反馈编制而成。我们用SPSS统计软件对数据进行了因子分析和多元方差分析，以探索动机的类型以及个人因素对动机类型的影响。因子分析得出七种动机类型，分别是：内在兴趣动机、成绩动机、出国动机、学习情境动机、社会责任动机、个人发展动机和信息媒介动机。多元方差分析表明，专业和英语水平对学习动机有显著影响。此外，专业与英语水平、年级与英语水平有交互作用。

关键词：英语学习、动机、中国大学生、本科生

[中图分类号] H195 [文献标识码] A [文章编号] 1003-6105（2003）01-0028-11

1. 引言

1.1 研究背景

经典的语言学习社会心理研究（Gardner & Lambert, 1972; Gardner, 1985）十分关注作为学习者特征的学习"动机"或"取向"。Gardner 和 Lambert（1972）认为学习动机或取向主要有两大类：一是"工具型"，即用语言做工具达到某个实际目的，如找一份薪水高的工作；二是"融合型"，即了解和融入目的语文化。动机取向与智力因素一起影响学习的结果。另一较为经典的维度是"内在动机"和"外在动机"（Atkinson, McClelland, Clark & Lowell, 1953）：前者是为了从语言学习活动本身获得愉快与满足，而后者则将此作为途径达到某一目标。这两个维度一般被认为是对应的，即融合性动机是内在动机，工具性动机是外在动机（Chambers, 1999: 52）。

20 世纪 90 年代以来，一些学者提出需要更广泛地借鉴心理学理论

＊ 本文转载自《现代外语》，2003, 26（1）：28-38。

1 本研究得到了北京外国语大学中国外语教育研究中心的资助。作者感谢北京大学社会学系博士生姚立、硕士研究生张磊以及郭志刚教授、南京大学文秋芳教授在统计技术上给予的指点，感谢各院校老师在问卷实施中给予的帮助。

（如马斯洛的需要层次论、管理心理学有关工作满足状况的研究成果），来扩展 Gardner（1985）的经典动机模式（Oxford & Shearin, 1994）。目前不同版本的扩展模式包括了"学习情境"（Dörnyei, 1994）、"自信"（Clément, Dörnyei & Noels, 1994）、"目标显著性"、"效价"、"自我效能"（Tremblay & Gardner, 1995）等新的因素。有关语言学习动机的研究都将关注点集中于语言学习结果（具体化为学习成绩），即什么样的动机导致更好的学习成绩；动机与其他学习者因素——学能、焦虑、学习策略、认知风格、自我评价、对环境的态度等，如何整体地影响学习成绩，各影响因素之间又是什么关系（Gardner, Day & MacIntyre, 1992; Gardner, Tremblay & Masgoret, 1997）。同时，由于在英语教学过程中学习者的因素越来越引起人们的重视，有关语言学习的研究也越来越关注学习者的个人特征差异（年龄、性别、学习策略等），认为语言教学应为不同个人特征的学习者"量体裁衣"（Nunan, 2001: 10; Cohen & Dörnyei, 2002）。

我国有关外语学习动机的实证研究，也大多循着经典及扩展模式的路子，探索动机对学习成绩的促进作用，以及动机与其他影响成绩的学习者因素之间的关系（石永珍，2000；王慧莉，2000；王湘玲等，2002；文秋芳等，1996；文秋芳，2001；吴一安等，1993；杨国俊，2002；张文鹏，1998）。比较有影响的研究大多着眼于关系模式的建立，以现有的动机理论为框架编制测试工具，或者根据实践经验包括尽可能多的因素，动机是许多因素中的一个。这样的研究有利于建立各种因素在何种程度上以及通过什么途径影响学习成绩的整体模式，把握学生学习的宏观规律。但同时包括许多学习者因素的研究也有局限，即每个因素所占测试题项有限，很难对"动机"类别做集中、深入的探索。由于关注焦点是学习成绩，"动机"在一些研究中侧重的是"努力程度"这一行为层面（如吴一安等，1993；刘润清、吴一安，2000）。近来还出现了聚焦于动机内部结构的研究（秦晓晴、文秋芳，2002），探索学习成绩、结果归因、学习兴趣、自我效能、目标定向等因素之间的复杂关系。

综上所述，有关中国学生英语学习动机的研究多采用经典及扩展模式的理论框架。虽然有人认为其中一些因素（如"融合型动机"）不大符合我国的情况，也有人提出"证书型动机"是中国学生的主要动机（华惠芳，1998；石永珍，2000），但还缺少系统的、大范围的实证材料支持。对中国学生的英语学习动机类别（原因或动力来源）尚没有自下而上的、穷尽性的归纳。事实上，除了西方经典理论以及教学经验提供给我们的知识以外，有关中国学生的英语学习动机到底有哪些类型，以及个人特征不同的学生有何学习动机差异，我们的基础实证信息还很缺乏。寻找这些问题的答案，将为宏观英语教学实践以及针对不同学习者群体的"量体裁衣"式教学提供依据。

1.2 研究问题

本研究是国家社科基金项目"英语学习动机与自我认同变化"的一部分，试图通过对大样本的系统调查分析，自下而上地归纳我国大学本科生英语学习动机类型；其主要目的是找出共有的动机类型，其次是考察个人因素对动机类型的影响。具体研究问题如下：1) 中国大学生英语学习的动机有哪些？2) 性别、专业、英语水平、年级、始学年龄等方面不同的学习者，在动机类别上是否存在差异？

2 研究方法

2.1 抽样

本研究采用了分层抽样的方法，抽取了除港、澳、台以及青海、西藏以外的 29 个省、自治区、直辖市 30 所高校的本科生。样本学校包括综合类 4 所、外语类 1 所、师范类 5 所、理工医类 13 所、农林类 2 所、财经/政法/民族/艺术类 5 所。抽样分层依据的是国家教育部 2002 年

表 1 抽样分层

	本科类学校数及占全国本科学校总数的%	样本学校数及占样本学校总数的%	本科类学生人数及占全国本科学生总数的%	样本学生数及占样本学生总数的%	具体抽样方法	抽样专业及学生总数（文/社，理/工，英语）
综合大学	81 (13.57%)	4 (13.33%)	1,123,038 (21.55%)	540 (21.77%)	45人 x3（专业）x 4（学校）	文 180、理 180、英语 180
外语院校	11 (1.84%)	1 (3.33%)	52,479 (1%)	40 (1.61%)		英语 40
师范院校	109 (18.26%)	5 (16.67%)	950,309 (18.23%)	450 (18.15%)	30人 x3（专业）x 5（学校）	文 150、理 150、英语 150
理工医院校	255 (42.71%)	13 (43.33%)	2,235,511 (42.89%)	1040 (41.94%)	80人 x 13（学校）	理 1,040
农林院校	41 (6.87%)	2 (6.67%)	357,541 (6.86%)	160 (6.45%)	80人 x 2（学校）	理 160
财经/政法/民族/艺术院校	100 (16.75%)	5 (16.67%)	493,128 (9.46%)	250 (10.08%)	50人 x 5（学校）	文 250
总计	597	30	5,212,006	2,480		理 1,530 文 580 英语 370

春公布的有关本科学校类型及学生比例的数字。样本学校类别的比例大致相应于总体学校类别的比例；样本学生类别的比例大致相应于总体学生类别的比例（表1）。受试个人因素分布情况见表2、表3。施测时实际发放问卷 2,473 份，回收有效问卷 2,278 份，有效率 92.1%。

表 2 受试者年龄、性别、年级、专业分布

	年龄				性别		年级				专业		
	17岁以下	18-22岁	23-29岁	30岁以上	男	女	大一	大二	大三	大四	理科	文科	英语
人数	6	2060	208	1	1100	1163	830	745	513	185	1,247	565	404
%	0.3	90.5	9.1	0	48.6	51.4	36.5	32.8	22.6	8.1	56.3	25.5	18.2

（注：已剔除各观测值的缺失项，下表同）

表 3 受试者家庭背景、始学年龄、英语水平分布

	家庭背景			开始学习英语的年龄				目前英语水平			
	农村	中小城镇	大城市	8岁以下	9-12岁	13-15岁	16岁以上	四级以下	四级	六级/专四	专八
人数	833	921	484	80	705	1425	54	1410	428	399	19
%	37.2	41.2	21.6	3.5	31.1	62.9	2.4	62.5	19.0	17.7	0.8

2.2 测量工具

本研究的工具是自编问卷，采用了从"很不同意"到"很同意"的李克特五级量表形式（见附录）。问卷主体包括三部分：动机类型、动机强度、自我认同变化。本文涉及的是动机类型部分。这一部分（前30题）的问题编制是探索式的。我们就"你为什么学习英语"征求了南京、湖南、北京和陕西几所高校学生的意见，以数百份学生的开放性书面反馈为基础，归纳出了一批选项。此外我们还根据以往文献加入了少量问题。问题的编制力求穷尽各种可能的学习动因，在对数据进行处理之前，没有明确的分类。

我们先后在北京的三所学校进行了 5 次问卷预测，在分析结果和学生反馈的基础上对问题做了部分删除和调整。最终预测的问卷整体信度（Cronbach α）达到 0.84，三部分的信度均达到 0.65 以上。实测中的问卷整体信度为 0.84，动机类型部分的信度为 0.77。

2.3 数据分析

我们用 SPSS 统计软件对数据进行了因子分析和多元方差分析，目的是探索动机的类型以及个人背景因素对动机类型的影响。

3．研究结果与讨论

3.1 动机类型的因子分析

对问卷前 30 题的分析显示，数据适宜进行因子分析（KMO = 0.86；Bartlett's 球型检定结果显著）。采用斜交旋转（Direct Oblimin）自然归类得出八个因子，累积解释总变差的 57.9%（表 4）；正交旋转（Varimax）的累积解释百分比完全相同。其中第八个因子包括问卷的第 2、3 题，当规定因子个数为七个时，这两个题项与第 4、6、11 合并为一个因子（表 5）。我们认为这五个题项所反映的内容大致相同，即满足（外部所规定的）成绩需要。总体来看，七个因子相对于八个因子的概括力更强，且总变差解释比例达到 54.54%，损失的信息不多。因此，我们认为抽取七个因子较为恰当。各题在因子上的负载量及因子命名见表 5。

表 4 因子特征值及方差百分比

因子	特征值	方差百分比	累积百分比
1	5.76	19.20	19.20
2	3.10	10.34	29.54
3	2.35	7.83	37.37
4	1.54	5.14	42.51
5	1.30	4.34	46.85
6	1.22	4.05	50.90
7	1.09	3.64	54.54
8	1.01	3.36	57.90

表 5　因子结构及负荷[2]

因子 负荷 原始题	因子 1 内在兴趣	因子 2 成绩	因子 3 学习情境	因子 4 出国	因子 5 社会责任	因子 6 个人发展	因子 7 信息媒介
Q21 喜欢语言本身	.81 (.80)						
Q19 对学语言有爱好	.79 (.78)						
Q1 对英语一见钟情	.73 (.73)						
Q20 喜欢英语歌/电影	.58 (.58)						
Q23 喜欢英语文学	.56 (.57)						
Q18 喜欢英语文化	.47 (.56)						
Q4 学习成绩（入学前）		.70 (.64)					
Q6 学习成绩（入学后）		.59 (.56)					
Q3 为升学考试		.58 (.61)					
Q11 获取毕业证书		.54 (.58)					
Q2 父母/学校要我学		.41 (.45)					
Q8 英语课的质量			.78 (.75)				
Q9 英语教材			.73 (.71)				
Q10 英语班			.69 (.68)				
Q7 英语老师（入学后）			.66 (.70)				
Q5 英语老师（入学前）			.42 (.50)				
Q26 出国寻找教育和工作机会				-.78 (.76)			
Q28 移民国外				-.77 (.75)			
Q27 出国体验文化				-.73 (.73)			
Q24 为中国富强尽力					.64 (.66)		
Q25 不辜负父母期望					.56 (.55)		
Q22 让世界了解中国					.51 (.54)		
Q29 人生路上敲门砖						-.69 (.70)	
Q30 教育/修养的象征						-.62 (.64)	
Q16 找一份好工作						-.56 (.60)	
Q13 有用的交流工具						-.53 (.56)	
Q14 获得成就感						-.51 (.54)	
Q15 学好其他专业							-.72 (.69)
Q17 了解世界经济、科技发展情况							-.68 (.68)

　　因子 1 的前三项是对语言的爱好，包括特定目的语和更一般的"语言学习"。后三项是对目的语文化的喜爱，包括歌曲和电影、文学、人

2　表中左列为斜交旋转结果，右列括号内为正交旋转结果。斜交旋转允许因子之间有相关，正交旋转得出的因子相互独立。在本研究中两种结果的差别不大。表中略去了 0.4 以下的负荷。

和文化。总体而言它们都表达了对（目的）语言、文化的兴趣。这种兴趣是内在的，"说不出有什么特别的原因"。因此，它具有明显的"内在动机"特征，又与 Gardner 和 Lambert 经典模式中的"融合性动机"相近，但未必要融入目的语的文化，可能是单纯的欣赏、喜爱。我们将它命名为"内在兴趣动机"。

因子 2 包括五个题项，其中前四个与学习成绩直接有关，最后一项"父母/学校要我学"也与学习成绩间接有关。学习成绩可能意味着"升学"、"毕业"的资格，是目的，也可能是激励自己继续努力的动力。我们将它命名为"成绩动机"。这一因子与以往对苏州（华惠芳，1998）、西安（石永珍，2000）等地调查得出的"证书型动机"以及台湾的"外部要求动机"（required motivation）（Warden & Lin, 2000）类似，与应试相联系。

因子 3 包含了与课程、教材、班级和老师有关的项目，都属于学习情境的影响，可称为"学习情境动机"。它与 Dörnyei（1994）扩展模式中的"学习情境层面"相吻合。

因子 4 的三项都与出国有关，尽管出国的目的有所不同，可能是融合性的"体验文化"、"移民"，也可能是工具性的"寻找更好的教育和工作机会"。我们将它命名为"出国动机"。

因子 5 包含两个有关国家（母语文化）的题项"为中国的富强尽力"、"让世界了解中国"，和一个有关父母的题项"不辜负父母的期望"。国家的强盛与父母的期望归在一起，体现出一种社会责任感，由此可称为"社会责任动机"。这一动机在以往研究中未曾见过。

因子 6 包含的内容较多，有直接、实用意义上的"工具性"动机，如"人生路上敲门砖"、"找工作"、"交流工具"，也包括抽象的、心理层面的"投资"或"文化资本"（Norton, 1995），如"教育、修养的象征"、"获得成就感"。总体来说，它们都与提高个人竞争力和社会地位有关，与未来发展前途有关。我们将它命名为"个人发展动机"。

因子 7 只包含两项内容，但各自的负荷都较高。无论是"学好其他专业"还是"了解世界经济、科技发展情况"，都是以英语作为媒介，获取有关信息。除了以上两项之外，在因子 6 中以较高负荷出现的 Q13"非常有用的交流工具"，在此因子中也有 .46 的负荷（正、斜交负荷值相等，符号相反）。因子 7 可命名为"信息媒介动机"。

第 12 题（在出国或国内升学、求职考试中取得好成绩）在因子 2（成绩）、因子 4（出国）、因子 6（个人发展）各有 0.3 以上、0.4 以下的负荷。该题涉及内容似过多，难以归到一个因子中去，但它并不影响各因子本身的解释力。

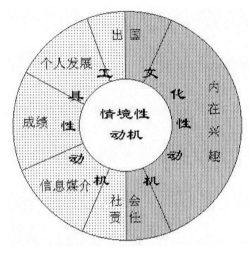

图 1 动机的概念分类[3]

七种动机类型还可在概念上做进一步概括。借鉴经典及扩展模式的理论框架，它们可根据内容划分为工具性、文化性、和情境性三大动机类型（图 1）。"工具性动机"是指用目的语做工具达到特定目的，成绩、信息媒介、个人发展都属于这个范畴，其差异在于工具所服务的目的。"文化性动机"涉及对文化的兴趣和关注，其中内在兴趣指向目的语文化，社会责任指向母语文化。它与 Gardner 等经典模式中的"融合性动机"有相似之处，不同之处在于，"融合性动机"的目的侧重于"融入"目的语文化群体，与母语文化没有直接联系。而本研究中的外语学习者对目的语文化"内在兴趣"认知成份较多，用"融合"或"融入"来概括似乎还不够准确。而且，除了对目的语文化的兴趣之外，受访者还表达了他们对运用目的语实现母语文化与世界沟通的关注。因此社会责任动机中既是工具性的，也是文化性的，因为它是以外语作为工具，来达到传播母语文化的目的。同样，"出国动机"中既有工具性的成份（寻找教育和工作机会），也有文化性的成份（体验文化、移民）。情境性动机独立于以上二者，体现了微观学习情境对学习者的影响。

3.2 各动机类型上的组间差异

我们以性别、年级、专业和目前英语水平为自变量，英语学习动机

---

3 该图仅示意三大类基本独立的动机及其所含内容。情境性动机所处位置并不表示它是其它动机的核心。

类型（斜交旋转因子分析得出的因子值）为因变量，对不同组别的学习动机类型进行了多元方差分析[4]，以考察个人变量对动机类型的影响。

分析结果显示，专业（F[14，3690] = 2.57，p = .001）、英语水平（F[21，5298] = 2.59，p = .000）对动机类型有着显著的主效应；年级与英语水平（F[84，11308] = 2.15，p = .000）、专业和英语水平（F[42，8657] = 1.78，p = .001）有显著的交互作用。性别对动机类型没有显著影响。由于篇幅所限，本文只报告显著的主效应。

3.2.1 不同专业学生的英语动机差异

各专业学生在各动机类型上的得分如图 2 所示。

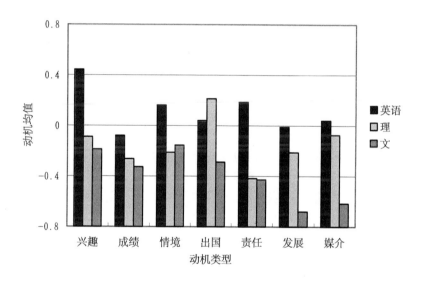

图 2 专业与英语学习动机

其中内在兴趣（F[2，1851] = 4.75）、社会责任（F[2，1851] = 4.84）、个人发展（F[2，1851] = 3.65）和信息媒介（F[2，1851] = 3.76）动机上的专业差异达到了显著水平（p < .05）。总体而言，动机类型的差别主要体现在英语专业与非英语专业之间。英语专业学生在文化性动机和某些工具性动机方面都高于非英专学生。调整后的关联强度指数显

4　SPSS 软件在做多元方差分析时，一次最多只接受 4 个自变量。在综合实践意义以及几次统计尝试结果的基础上，我们选择了性别、专业、年级和英语水平作为动机类型的自变量。没有被选择的变量包括年龄、家庭背景、学校类型、开始学英语的年龄。

示，在七种动机中，内在兴趣与影响因素之间达到了中度相关（9.6%），其余类型为弱相关（6% 以下）。

在内在兴趣动机上，英专学生的得分显著高于人文社会科学（MD = .630, p = .025）和自然科学（MD = .531, p = .028）的学生。他们当初选择英语作为专业，对英语的兴趣可能就是重要原因。在大学里他们比非英专业的学生有更多的机会在较深层次接触英语语言和文化，这反过来也会进一步加强他们对英语的内在兴趣。文、理科学生在内在兴趣动机上没有显著差异。

在社会责任动机上，英专学生的得分也分别高于文（MD = .611, p = .044）、理科生（MD = .604, p = .015）。这可能是因为他们较多接触英语文化，在经历了一定的文化碰撞之后，能够更加深切地感受到中国文化的魅力，以及中国与英美等发达国家的差距，因而更希望用己所学为国家尽力。

反转负向的斜交旋转因子值后，英专学生的个人发展动机高于文（MD = .668, p = .022）、理科生，其中与文科组的差异达到了显著水平。对于英专学生来说，由于其英语能力更直接地与谋求职业联系在一起，也直接关系到学习者未来事业的发展、成就及社会地位，因此他们在英语学习上有比较明确的要求和更大的动力。同样，反转负向的因子值后，英专学生的信息媒介动机也要高于其他专业，其中与文科生的差异（MD = .658, p = .025）达到了显著水平。可见英专学生不满足仅仅掌握语言技能本身，还希望英语成为其获取更多知识和信息的工具。英语对于他们有着更强的工具价值。

3.2.2 不同英语水平的学生在动机类型上的差异

不同英语水平的学生在内在兴趣（F[3, 1851] = 7.32, p = .000）和成绩动机（F = 5.39, p = .001）方面存在显著差异（图 3）。由于样本中已经达到八级的人数很少（此项的有效人数 14 人，占总人数的比例 0.6%），不足以进行概括性的讨论，因此以下讨论集中于另外三个水平组。

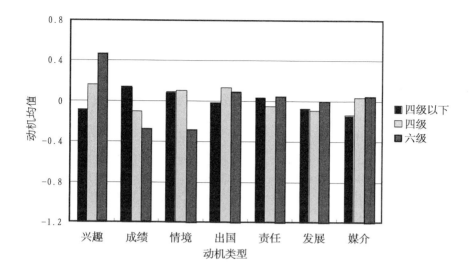

图 3 目前英语水平与学习动机

四级以下学生的内在兴趣动机分别低于已过四级（MD = -.248, *p* = .030）和六级（MD = -.539, *p* = .000）的学生，而成绩动机高于其他学生，其中与六级学生的差异达到了显著水平（MD = .412, *p* = .012）。在很多学校，通过四级考试是能否获得学位证书的标准之一，未过四级的学生忙于为考试和成绩而奔命，内在兴趣难以激发。相比之下，经过了四级尤其是过了六级的同学有条件摆脱考试的压力，从自己的兴趣出发学习英语。"成绩"这一外在动机与内在兴趣动机的此消彼长，与以往的研究结果（如 Brown, 1994）相吻合。

4. 结论

4.1 主要发现

本研究自下而上地归纳了中国大学本科生英语学习动机的类型，主要发现可概括如下。

工具性、文化性、情境性并存。中国大学本科生英语学习动机主要有七种类型——内在兴趣、成绩、情境、出国、社会责任、个人发展和信息媒介。其中情境性动机是独立的一类，印证了经典扩展模式中的"学习情境层面"（Dörnyei, 1994）。个人发展、信息媒介和成绩动机都可说是"工具性动机"（Gardner & Lambert, 1972)，但目的各不相同。

成绩动机可以说较有"应试"语境的特色。虽然"成就动机"普遍存在，但将考试成绩作为决定升学、求职等个人前途机会的主要甚至唯一因素，是包括中国在内的一些亚洲国家和地区教育体制的特色，学习者也因而产生了应付外部要求的动机（Warden & Lin, 2000）。内在兴趣与社会责任动机均以文化为指向，前者与经典模式中的"融合性动机"有相似之处。出国动机、社会责任动机兼容或结合了"工具性"和"文化性"。

外语文化指向与母语文化指向并存。内在兴趣动机以目的语、目的语文化为中心，与"融合性动机"有相似之处，但内在兴趣中有相当多的智力成份（intellectual curiosity），并不一定在情感和身份归属上"融入"目的语文化。与此相对照，社会责任动机是以母语文化为中心的，可能与"齐家治国"的传统理想、一贯的宣传教育有关，也可能与近年来中国国力的强盛、民族意识的兴起，以及英语在国家发展中的特殊地位有关。母语文化中心的学习动机与目的文化中心的学习动机并存，这大概也是较有中国大学本科学生特色的现象。

社会责任与个人发展目标并存。一般来说，外语学习是个人行为，当然会与个人的就业、薪水等联系在一起。不过中国本科生的"个人发展"动机含义较广，不仅包括实际的工具意义（找工作、交流），而且也包括社会地位的象征意义（教育与修养），以及与此相关的心理意义（成就感）。与此同时，还出现了与"个人发展"平行的"社会责任"动机，目标是报效父母和国家。二者并存不仅反映了中国的教育思想传统，而且也反映出当今中国英语教育与整个社会发展的密切联系。

持久性与近因性并存。成绩、情境和出国动机都是对学习者有直接、近距离时空影响的动机，而内在兴趣是有长远影响的动机。典型相关分析结果显示（高一虹等，2002），有必要区分这两类并存而影响范围不同的动机。

专业和英语水平对动机的影响。就专业的影响而言，英专生的文化性动机和某些工具性动机大于非英专生。他们的内在兴趣、社会责任动机高于非英专生，信息媒介、个人发展动机也高于非英专生。就英语水平的影响而言，高水平学生重兴趣，低水平学生重成绩。这也说明从长远来看，培养内在兴趣有利于提高学生的英语水平，而成绩动机不宜过分强化。

4.2 研究局限及未来研究方向

英语学习的动机十分复杂，本研究仅是一个探索性的研究，目的在于归纳英语学习的动机类型，对于不同动机之间的关系并没有深入探寻。由于抽样分层方法及实施的限制，一些个人背景因素的分布不均匀，例如"专业八级"组的人数十分有限，因此结果不足以概括所有英语水平组在动机类型上的差异。对报告的结果如何做出更合理、深入的解释，有待读者提出自己的意见。另外，不同的动机类型是否会同时发生在同一个英语学习者身上，它们之间存在什么关系，以及影响这些变化的因素等，都有赖于今后的研究。

参考文献

Atkinson, J., D. McClelland, C R.A. Lark & E. L. Lowell. 1953. *The Achievement Motive* [M]. New York: Appleton.

Brown, H. D. 1994. *Teaching by Principles: An Interactive Approach to Language Pedagogy* [M]. New Jersey: Prentice Hall.

Chambers, G. N. 1999. *Motivating Language Learners* [M]. Clevedon: Multilingual Matters Ltd.

Clément, R., Z. Dörnyei & K. A. Noels. 1994. Motivation, self-confidence, and group cohesion in the foreign language classroom [J]. *Language Learning* 44: 417-448.

Cohen, A. D. & Z. Dörnyei. 2002. Focus on the language learning: Motivation, styles, and strategies [A]. In N. Schmitt (ed.) *An Introduction to Applied Linguistics*. London: Arnold.

Dörnyei, Z. 1994. Motivation and motivating in the foreign language classroom [J]. *Modern Language Journal* 78: 273-284.

Gardner, R. C. 1985. *Social Psychology and Second Language Learning: The Role of Attitudes and Motivation* [M]. London: Edward Arnold.

Gardner, R. C., J. B. Day & P. D. MacIntyre. 1992. Integrative motivation, induced anxiety, and language learning in a controlled environment [J]. *Studies in Second Language Acquisition* 14: 197-242.

Gardner, R. C., & W. E. Lambert. 1972. *Attitudes and Motivation in Second Language Learning* [M]. Rowley, Mass.: Newbury House.

Gardner, R. C., P. F. Tremblay & A. M. Masgoret. 1997. Towards a full model of second language learning: An empirical investigation [J]. *Modern Language Journal* 81: 344-362.

Oxford, R. & J. Shearin. 1994. Language learning motivation: Expanding the theoretical framework [J]. *Modern Language Journal* 78: 12-28.

Norton Peirce, B. 1995. Social identity, investment and language learning [J]. *TESOL Quarterly* 29: 9-31.

Nunan, D. 2001. *Second Language Teaching and Learning* [M]. Beijing: Foreign Language

Teaching and Research Press.

Tremblay, P. F., & R. C. Gardner. 1995. Expanding the motivation construct in language learning [J]. *Modern Language Journal* 79: 505-520.

Warden, C. A. S., & H. J. Lin. 2000. Existence of integrative motivation in an Asian EFL setting [J]. *Foreign Language Annals* 33: 535-547.

Zhou, Yan. 1996. Social-psychological factors and language learning [A]. In G. Xu (ed.) *ELT in China 1992* [C]. Beijing: Foreign Language Teaching and Research Press, 49-83.

高一虹、赵媛、程英、周燕，2002，大学本科生英语学习动机类型与自我认同变化的关系 [J]。《国外外语教学》（4）：18-24。

华惠芳，2000，试论英语学习动机与策略的研究 [J]。《外语界》（3）：44-47。

刘润清、吴一安，2000，《中国英语教育研究》[M]。北京：外语教学与研究出版社。

秦晓晴、文秋芳，2002，非英语专业大学生学习动机的内在结构 [J]。《外语教学与研究》（1）：51-58。

石永珍，2000，大学生英语学习动机调查报告 [J]。《国外外语教学》（4）：8-11。

王慧莉，2000，一份关于外国学生对英语的教和学的态度的问卷调查报告 [J]。《国外外语教学》（4）：12-15。

王湘玲、刘晓玲，2002，影响理工科学生英语阅读效率的学生因素调查 [J]。《外语教学》（1）：49-54。

文秋芳、王海啸，1996，学习者因素与大学英语四级考试成绩的关系 [J]。《外语教学与研究》（4）：33-39。

文秋芳，2001，英语学习者动机、观念、策略的变化规律与特点 [J]。《外语教学与研究》（2）：105-110。

吴一安、刘润清、Jeffrey 等，1993，中国英语本科学生素质调查报告 [J]。《外语教学与研究》（1）：36-46。

杨国俊，2002，论大学英语学习动机的强化策略 [J]。《外语界》（3）：27-31。

张文鹏，1998，外语学习动力与策略运用之关系 [J]。《外语与外语教学》（3）：25-27。

附录：调查问卷的动机类型[5]

1. 我对英语一见钟情，说不出有什么特别的原因。
2. 我开始学英语是因为父母／学校要我学。
3. 上大学前学习英语，主要是为了升学考试。
4. 上大学前，我学英语的劲头很大程度上取决于我的学习成绩。

5　为了节省篇幅，省略了调查问卷的具体说明，如需了解详情，请与作者联系。

5. 上大学前，我学英语的劲头很大程度上取决于是否喜欢英语老师。

6. 上大学后，我学英语的劲头很大程度上取决于我的学习成绩。

7. 上大学后，我学英语的劲头很大程度上取决于是否喜欢英语老师。

8. 上大学后，我学英语的劲头很大程度上取决于英语课的质量。

9. 上大学后，我学英语的劲头很大程度上取决于所用的教材。

10. 上大学后，我学英语的劲头很大程度上取决于是否喜欢我的英语班。

11. 我学英语的一个重要目的是获取大学毕业证书。

12. 我学英语的直接目的是在出国或国内升学、求职考试中取得好成绩。

13. 学好英语对我很重要，因为它是当今社会非常有用的交流工具。

14. 学好英语能让我获得成就感。

15. 我学习英语，是为了更好地学习其他专业。

16. 学好英语，将来我才可能找到一份好工作。

17. 我学习英语是为了了解世界各国的经济、科技发展情况。

18. 我学习英语是因为对英语国家的人以及他们的文化感兴趣。

19. 我对语言学习有特别的爱好。

20. 对英语歌曲／电影的爱好使我对英语产生了很大兴趣。

21. 我学习英语是因为我喜欢这门语言本身。

22. 我学习英语是为了让世界了解中国。

23. 对英语文学作品的爱好使我对英语产生了很大兴趣。

24. 学好英语，我才能很好地为中国的富强尽力。

25. 学好英语，我才能不辜负父母的期望。

26. 我学习英语是为了出国寻找更好的受教育和工作机会。

27. 我学习英语是为了出国亲身体验英语国家的文化。

28. 我学习英语是为了最终移民外国。

29. 英语是人生前进路上一块重要的敲门砖。

30. 讲一口流利的英语，是教育程度和修养的象征。

通讯地址：(1) 100871 北京大学英语系　高一虹　gaoyihon@public.bta.net.cn
(2) 100871 北京大学英语系　赵　嫒　clarion@water.pku.edu.cn
(3) 100871 北京大学英语系　程　英　cheeringhao@water.pku.edu.cn
(4) 100089 北京外国语大学中国外语教育研究中心　周　燕
zhouyan@public.bta.net.cn

Author Index

Subject Index